Emotions in Finance

Fear and greed are terms that make light of the uncertainty in the finance world. Huge global financial institutions rely on emotional relations of trust and distrust to suppress the uncertainties. Many financial firms develop policies towards risk, rather than accepting the reality of an uncertain future.

Emotions in Finance examines the views of experienced elites in the international financial world. It argues the current financial era is driven by a utopianism – a hope – that the future can be collapsed into the present. It points out policy implications of this short-term view at the unstable peak of global finance.

This book provides a timely account of the influence of emotion and speculation on the world's increasingly volatile financial sector. The author includes absorbing interview material from public and private bankers in the United States, UK and Australia.

Jocelyn Pixley is a senior lecturer in the School of Sociology and Anthropology at the University of New South Wales, Australia. She is the author of *Citizenship and Employment*.

Emotions in Finance

Distrust and Uncertainty in Global Markets

Jocelyn Pixley

CAMBRIDGE
UNIVERSITY PRESS

PUBLISHED BY THE PRESS SYNDICATE OF THE UNIVERSITY OF CAMBRIDGE
The Pitt Building, Trumpington Street, Cambridge, United Kingdom

CAMBRIDGE UNIVERSITY PRESS
The Edinburgh Building, Cambridge, CB2 2RU, UK
40 West 20th Street, New York, NY 10011–4211, USA
477 Williamstown Road, Port Melbourne, VIC 3207, Australia
Ruiz de Alarcón 13, 28014 Madrid, Spain
Dock House, The Waterfront, Cape Town 8001, South Africa

http://www.cambridge.org

First published by Cambridge University Press 2004

Printed in China through Bookbuilders

Typefaces Adobe Garamond 10/12 pt. and Frutiger   *System* LATEX 2ε [TB]

A catalogue record for this book is available from the British Library

National Library of Australia Cataloguing in Publication data

Pixley, Jocelyn F. (Jocelyn Florence), 1947–.
Emotions in finance.
Bibliography.
For tertiary students.
ISBN 0 521 82785 X.
ISBN 0 521 53508 5 (pbk.).
1. Business enterprises – Finance.   2. Risk management.   3. Speculation.   I. Title.
658.155

ISBN 0 521 82785 X hardback
ISBN 0 521 53508 5 paperback

To the memory of my parents, Lorna and Neville Pixley

Contents

Figures

Interviews 2000–2002

FORMER CENTRAL BANKERS

New York – Washington DC, February–March 2002

Alan Blinder: former Vice Chairman of the Board of Governors of the US Federal Reserve System (1994–96); now Professor of Economics, Princeton University, NJ

Lyle Gramley: former Governor of the US Federal Reserve System (1980–85); then at Mortgage Bankers Association of America, Washington DC

UK, March 2002

Sir Alan Budd: former Chief Economist for HM Treasury (1991–97), and former Chief Economist of the Bank of England, also former member Monetary Policy Committee (1997–2000); now Provost, Queen's College, Oxford

The late John Flemming: former Chief Economist (1984–91) and Executive Director (1988–91) of the Bank of England; then Warden of Wadham College, Oxford

Charles Goodhart: former Chief Adviser, Bank of England, former member of the Bank of England's Monetary Policy Committee (1997–2000); now Professor of Banking and Finance at the London School of Economics

Canberra, August 2001

B. W. Fraser: former Governor, Reserve Bank of Australia (1989–96); now board Director, Members Equity and Industry Super. Second interview, 29 June 2002

FINANCIERS AND BANKERS

London

Henry Dale: former banker for fifteen years at Crown Agents, October 2000

Michael Lazar: formerly de Broe, then Schröder's, stockbrokers (1980s); also HM Treasury (to 1994), June 2001. Second Interview, March 2002

Roderick Chamberlain: Coutts Consulting Group; formerly securities broker in the Royal Bank of Canada, Nomura International; Trustee (from 1987) then Chair (1997–2000) of the Institute of Business Ethics, March 2002

Tim Shepheard-Walwyn: formerly Bank of England, then Securities and Investment Board; former Head of Risk Management at SBC (now UBS), also Barclays Bank, March 2002

New York and Pennsylvania 2001–2002

Henry Ouma: former Managing Director of Investments, UN Pension Funds, NYC, May 2001

Henry Kaufman: former Vice-President, Salomon Inc. 'Dr Gloom of Wall Street'. NYC, May 2001. Second Interview, February 2002

Chia Sieu Wong: former investment manager for sixteen years with a large Wall Street investment firm and other investment firms. NYC, May 2001

John Bogle: Founder and former CEO of Vanguard Group of Mutual Funds; Valley Forge, PA, March 2002

Sydney, February 2002

John Edwards: Chief Economist, HSBC, Australia and New Zealand and former Senior Adviser, economic (1991–94) to the Prime Minister of Australia, Paul Keating.

Zürich, Switzerland April 2002

Dr Werner Frey: former CFO and Director Bankleu, and then Credit Suisse; now Management Consultant, Ramistrasse 36, Zürich

Paul Chan: Managing Director, Group Risk Analysis, UBS AG Financial Services Group, Bahnhofstrasse 45, Zürich

Georges Schorderet: CFO Swiss Air; formerly CFO Alusuisse Lonza, Zürich

FINANCE JOURNALISTS

New York City, September 2000

Alan Abelson: Former editor, now lead columnist, *Barrons*, the Dow Jones Business and Financial Weekly. Second interview, May 2001

James Grant: Publisher-editor *Grant's Weekly Interest Rate Observer*; regular finance commentator on CNN and panellist on Wall Street Week

Anya Schiffren: Former reporter for *Dow Jones*; then *Industry Standard*, now at the School of Public Affairs, Columbia University

Brian Hale: Wall Street correspondent, *Sydney Morning Herald* and *The Age* (formerly, later for *The Times*).

Daniel Kadlec: Finance journalist, *Time Magazine*, February 2002

London

Larry Elliott: Economics editor, *The Guardian*, October 2000

Dominic Ziegler: Finance editor, *The Economist*, March 2002

Graham Ingham: formerly with the BBC; now economic journalist, *The Economist*, March 2002

Robert Peston: Former finance editor, the *Financial Times*; now finance columnist, *New Statesman*. Telephone Interview, London March 2002

Sydney, January 2000

Trevor Sykes: Senior journalist, *Australian Financial Review* and 'Pierpont' column.

V. J. Carroll: Former editor, *Australian Financial Review* from 1964; former editor-in-chief, *Sydney Morning Herald* until 1984. Second interview, January 2001.

FINANCIAL PUBLIC RELATIONS

Jonathan Birt: Financial Dynamics Business Communications, Holborn Gate, London. March 2002.

CONFIDENCE SURVEY ANALYSTS

Ken Goldstein: Economist, The Conference Board, 845 Third Avenue. New York, February 2002

Duncan Ironmonger: Professor of Economics, University of Melbourne; Analyst Dun & Bradstreet Expectation Surveys. Sydney, December 2001

Preface

How I created the precise idea of *Emotions in Finance* is the only event I cannot recall. My background in economic sociology led to some useful discoveries about the finance world. My work defending full employment and social policy was a bore to my postmodern colleagues and beneath contempt to neo-classical economists. From 1996, Australia's new right-wing government stifled policy debates: instead of decent employment we were to join a mainly Anglo-American society of shareholder capitalists; our compulsory superannuation must offer 'choice'. Globalisation, by 1997, had become a fashionable term, but I was struck by the IMF's treatment of our neighbour Indonesia: brutal yet totally incompetent. Meantime, I was reading the work of two sociologists, Jack Barbalet's on emotions and Geoff Ingham's on money as a social relation. Both struck a chord just as the dot.com boom was becoming insane. I am old enough to have experienced Australia's ludicrous mining boom. The scrip of Poseidon and Minsec shares bought by my former husband became pretty gift wrapping in 1971, we joked in that carefree time of jobs and freedom. My parents were of the cautious generation. To my mother, a mortgage was OK, better was paying it off. My father was a 'managing director', not a sainted CEO of today. Each had 'blue chip' share portfolios and we lived comfortably.

During the dot.com insanity, modest investors and the millions in investment funds were blamed for their emotions. As part of my world view, I had never been impressed by high finance's mendacity, its promotion of globalisation and its increasing lack of caution. Sociologists seemed captivated either by virtual money or a financial conspiracy, but I took another view, seeing the emotions of uncertainty as the key. Moreover, being on the periphery, Australia is a good vantage point from which to investigate the financial core, since Australia's business sector has copied and amplified its excesses. But we, the people, can temper globablisation, and instead strengthen commitments to international agreements in which economic policy serves social purposes and democratic processes, for which Australia once had some reputation.

Emotions in Finance was the title that attracted my two great publishing editors at Cambridge University Press: Peter Debus who enthusiastically and carefully saw me through, and Phillipa McGuinness who commissioned my idea. When I concluded, I briefly toyed with another title: *High Finance, Deep Uncertainty*. But when I began, my theoretical scepticism required evidence. What were the precise emotions that prevail? I needed 'informed sceptics', so I interviewed a number of influential people in the financial world. They gave me enormous support, arranging for me to interview others, carefully correcting my transcripts and revising their quotes (John Flemming only months before he died) and responding to my further queries generously, Henry Dale in particular. Many whom I lacked space to quote were also enormously helpful. I thank them all: while I am solely responsible for my conclusions, their own wisdom and commonsense shines through.

Jack Barbalet and Geoff Ingham gave sound advice, perfect references to other works and read the crucial chapters. Peter Kriesler has been my closest economic advisor: reading vast chunks of early drafts and tirelessly improving my sociological translation of Keynes. Paul Ormerod supported all my unorthodox endeavours, suggested interview questions on probability, introduced me to Meghnad Desai, Robin Marris and others in London. Both exceptional themselves, Carol Heimer helped me on one path to all the best in Chicago's economic sociology, while June Zaccone sent me to the best New York economists. My other debt is to V. J. Carroll, who inspired me about the urgent need for more sociological than economic analysis in the public domain, and to Mike Lazar, similarly.

There are many others (whole households in other countries) to whom I am grateful. Most and best of all two: my son Sam Dawson became an inadvertent and brilliant research assistant in New York City, Chicago, London and Canberra, at our own expense, and then my main informal editorial advisor. My daughter, Louisa Dawson, formulated ideas for design that ultimately became the cover: artists see while we just write. Both have firmly put up with my obsession involved in writing any book. I had enormous collegial support from my whole School, so while Clive Kessler found my most felicitous phrases and kept me going while Mum was dying, and Paul Jones helped in our shared teaching and was the source of my media understanding, everyone was great. Beyond my School, Michael Johnson saw the whole point of my early idea for the research; Alan Morris and Robert Milliken helped introduce me to financiers and journalists. The Faculty of Arts and Social Sciences at my university have been helpful for years, especially with my Writing Fellowship in 2003; so too the Australian Research Council in grants. Antonny Ivancic provided thoughtful research work, Aileen Woo and Louise Fraser similarly on the manuscript and transcripts, and Harry Blatterer translated, theoretically too, *entscheidungsfreudig*. Venetia Somerset, as the book neared completion, gave scrupulous copy-editing and calm intelligence to see the book out, and while with thanks to so many, any inadvertent errors are mine.

Jocelyn Pixley
August 2004

Abbreviations

AIB	Allied Irish Banks plc
AFR	*Australian Financial Review*
AMP	Australian Mutual Provident Society (Established January 1849; demutualised January 1998)
AOL	America Online
APRA	Australian Prudential Regulation Authority
ATTAC	Association pour une Taxation des Transactions Financières pour l'Aide aux Citoyens
BCCI	Bank of Credit and Commerce International
BoE	Bank of England
BoJ	Bank of Japan
CADs	Current Account Deficits
CB	central bank
EBRD	European Bank of Reconstruction and Development
ECB	European Central Bank
EMH	efficient market hypothesis
FASB	Financial Accounting Standards Board (USA)
FD	financial disclosure
FOMC	Federal Open Market Committee (US Federal Reserve System)
FSA	Financial Services Authority (UK. Established under the Financial Services and Markets Act 2000)
FT	*Financial Times*
GDP	Gross Domestic Product
HSBC	HSBC Bank Australia Limited (founded as the Hongkong and Shanghai Banking Corporation Limited in 1865)
HIH	HIH Insurance Limited (Australian-based)
ICI	Imperial Chemical Industries plc
IMF	International Monetary Fund
ING	ING Group (First titled Internationale Nederlanden Group in 1991)
IPO	Initial Public Offering
IT	information technology

LBO	leveraged buyout
LTCM	Long Term Capital Management (US-based hedge fund)
MAI	Multilateral Agreement on Investment (not ratified)
M&A	Mergers and Acquisitions
MPC	Monetary Policy Committee (Bank of England)
NAB	National Australia Bank
NAIRU	non-accelerating-inflation rate of unemployment
NYSE	New York Stock Exchange
OECD	Organisation for Economic Co-operation and Development
PR	public relations
RBA	Reserve Bank of Australia
REM	rational economic man
S&L	Savings and Loan (known also as thrifts, US mutual savings banks)
S&P	Standard and Poor's (US-based credit-rating agency)
SEC	U.S. Securities and Exchange Commission
SMH	*Sydney Morning Herald*
UBS	Union Bank of Switzerland (UBS AG since 1998)
WTO	World Trade Organization

1

Global Markets or Social Relations of Money

Economic POLICIES AIMING to defend money as a store of value have prevailed for thirty years over postwar attempts at social democracy. It is a complex story of the financial sector regaining some of its former policy control, which had been lost in the national and international initiatives of the 1930s and 1940s, from the New Deal to Bretton Woods, to overcome the Great Depression. Those interventionist policies sought to alleviate economic uncertainty and its attendant shocks; the current anti-inflationary policies attempt to reduce the uncertainty of money's value as a financial asset. But, as this study argues, uncertainty is not only inevitable in economic activity generally but is magnified in finance because money is based on a trust that is inherently problematic.

Uncertainty is unavoidable. Squeezed in one place, it emerges in another. After the postwar welfare state compromises to sustain full employment were disbanded, even Federal Reserve Chairman Greenspan admitted this, behind closed doors in 1996. He said 'product price' inflation can be conquered only at the cost of price–earnings ratios going 'through the roof' (quoted page 111). Recurrent speculative booms and busts bring debt-deflation in their train, historically a common phenomenon. Defenders of economic orthodoxy often argue that asset inflation results from emotional intrusions into a rational world. But emotions are unavoidable. Rational calculations can be based only on the past. Instability continually arises, especially when money is treated as a financial asset. Money entails claims and credits, and so presumes social relations created from prospective and therefore unknowable promises. Secure rational calculation can only be retrospective; it cannot see or reach beyond the horizon separating the future from the present. Yet financial firms, banks and, increasingly, non-financial firms these days trade ever-proliferating claims to future income, creating more debt and more uncertainty. Uncertainty can only be dealt with by emotional projections and, since finance is a vital part of economic activity, the fundamental role of emotions deserves serious analysis.

This book looks at the 'financial heartland', the major institutions where money is controlled and traded as though it were a predictable commodity. It is not. 'The money power', as British Prime Minister Gladstone termed it, is more mundane than its jargon implies. Central banks issue the most trustworthy, most accepted, 'high-powered' money; these monetised debts rely on trust in government debts, as we will see. Yet since the idea of money as 'promise' is counter-intuitive, going against the everyday experience of its tangibility in our hands and wallets, most critics neglect the implied promise that money entails and so leave unexamined the trust on which it rests. Instead they argue that greed drives the City of London or Wall Street. This book, in contrast, argues that finance is inherently emotional, and that *specific emotions in finance* arise from the radical uncertainties of money. Since promises are of uncertain reliability, distrust, sometimes fear, inspires all financial action. This is confirmed by the experience and words of the informed sceptics whose interviews form the basis of this book.

WHY EMOTIONS?

I start from the idea this world is driven by a combination of emotions *and* rationality – not personal or private emotions, and not greed per se. In finance uncertainty is masked (disguised as 'risk', not losses). It cannot be spoken, for it is the unsayable. Since uncertainty about claims is always extreme, decisions rely on future-oriented emotions. Competitive financial firms live and die upon predicting future outcomes which are unknowable, no matter how rational their calculations of past information. Therefore, firms must project emotions and conventions about the unknowable future and, through strategies of a pseudo-rational kind, bring these conjectures back to the present in order to act. The typical emotions are trust and distrust, whereas the typical convention is to assume that the future will resemble the past. These are the inevitably shaky, emotional foundations of finance.

Financial life publicly revels in greed and risk today because these are exciting; inherent unknowability is duller, though fraught. No one knows the future. Each area (from banking to insurance) has its own definitions of risk; however, rarely is the gulf between the future vista (in the jargon, 'expectations') and the inevitable lack of knowledge of the future made explicit. It hides in the 'fine print' or *ceteris paribus* escape clause. As they seek to face uncertainty rationally, huge organisations are driven by trust and distrust. Firms explicitly admit this. Although their in-house jargon is about anonymous markets, the call to 'Trust Us' is implicit in their names. You, sweet investor, are 'made free' by your control over your money.

Yet inside this world, financial firms can barely control all their promises to pay each other. Star CEOs, not just the public, are confused by the latest financial 'product'. Inside this world firms do not know their own (future) interests. They extol competition and insist on complete freedom from government supervision, at the very moment when they are going bankrupt or collapsing from chains of corruption that are often, as we will see, weirdly unintended because unimagined. Both orthodox and Marxian economics assume that rational interests drive the world. Their insistence on this claim reduces all of social life to the economy. But integral to all financial interrelations is a deep uncertainty which unavoidably involves emotions, which are often powerful and usually unperceived.

Central banks try their honest, public service best, but private banks and financial experts demand they be 'credible' in monetising public debt. Governments require them to maintain stability, yet central banks must present government promises as credible to private creditors. What is credibility? No sooner do credibility and trust appear newly stable and deserving of confidence than some new and unforeseen factor intrudes, and genuinely trustworthy reputations are destroyed. As this book shows, these inter-organisational relations of trust and distrust among major institutions involve emotions, which fuel demands for, and even promises of, 'risk-free' money. At each failure, this trust collapses into fear, and mistrust calls forth new futile quests for control over the future. The emotions born not of personal desire but of the unknowability of the future drive economic life as much as does rational calculation.

AMBIGUOUS TRUST IN THE IMPERSONAL MARKET

In the wake of economic crisis and collapse, the losers are so quickly forgotten. To the financial world view, the catastrophic effects on whole countries of speculation on future claims are merely passing tragedies. From a democratic viewpoint, relations of money are in principle important and could be fine in moderation – so long as they are restrained by democratic regulation and oversight. *Caution* is the key emotional term. But the 'money power' has never faced democratic control beyond the flimsy post-1945 controls on capital movements and 'fixed' exchange rates – in contrast to today's uninhibited selling and buying of currencies that float on forex markets – and serious prudential regulations. Yet wild as the numerous financial markets may seem, the Anglo-American financial world is not 'evil personified'. Such talk is extremely dangerous. The racist personifications and scapegoating that were so characteristic of our modern world's murky past were opportunistically resurrected by Malaysia's Dr Mahathir during the Southeast Asian crisis of 1997. As we will see, modern finance is increasingly abstract, impersonal and imprudent. Competitive policies drive cautious and foolish banks to the wall. This is my focus, not any conspiracy in finance nor, in contrast, whether the millions individually involved on the periphery are willing punters or reluctant, fearful investors. Indeed, gambling is far more predictable than financial speculation (since losses are openly inevitable), and billions more people gamble than play the financial markets.

Money continually generates financial crises and when it does it is not 'markets' that are the target of those whose trust has been abused and their savings and houses lost. Rather, the victims correctly specify and loathe commercial (retail) banks or merchant banks, insurance firms or mutual funds across the USA, Europe, the UK, Japan and peripheral countries. Through their public relations efforts these financial institutions are unable honestly to convince people of their probity and innocence. So, as its critics tirelessly recount, 'money power' has far more effective recourse to political lobbying and donations by the peak investment banks, accountancy firms and commercial banks. Though such strategies can backfire, financial power also wields strong if often unseen weapons against those, especially democratically elected legislators, who might aspire to restrain its operations by statutory regulation and oversight. Downgrading of public creditworthiness, hostile mergers and capital 'flights' are rightly feared. These measures may silence democratically elected governments and so demean the political process. While unemployment also results, it is financial losses among middle-income groups of creditors or debtors that often prove a more frightening sword suspended over governments.

The focus of this present analysis is on the forgotten element – the necessity, and the inescapable insecurity, of 'trust' and its emotional consequences – within this mysterious world of the financial heartlands; it is not on whether individuals are willing punters or on the operation of markets per se. Financial organisations are unavoidably involved in *impersonal* relations of trust and distrust. But can routine projections of trust and distrust help to counteract uncertainty, to foster institutional guarantees for the chimera of risk-free money, and to ensure trustworthy reputations? Trust and confidence help to reduce perceptions of uncertainty in financial decisions, but when they foster arrogance, then abuse and collapse, they can easily inspire fear of failure, of financial losses, or of loss of institutional reputation. Trust is an emotion best recognised when it turns into the opposite. In moments of crisis the trust that is intrinsic to financial life may be suddenly transmuted into blame and rage. This book is primarily concerned with the ambiguous nature of this neglected ingredient, trust. In its argument the larger questions about values, democracy and socially beneficial compromises are noted in passing. The practical imperatives of understanding emotions in finance are too important and too misunderstood to be left off the public agenda. Impersonal trust and distrust relations are inherent in modernity, and the trust in money is extraordinarily ambiguous.

Certainty about the economic future is a mirage. To help us cope with its unattainability, to soften the pain born of our ignorance, we put our trust in trust. Yet by doing so, by thrusting trust forward as a bulwark against the unacknowledged implications of uncertainty, we expose and even undermine our trust in trust itself. Our enforced reliance on trust makes trust itself increasingly insecure, fraught and unreliable. We chop off the branch to which we are ever more desperately clinging. So the quest for certainty is futile. And even though recognising its existence, uncertainty must remain unacknowledged by financial organisations, no matter how competent and honest.

John Maynard Keynes makes a major contribution in linking uncertainty to emotions, but his analysis, like many others, started with individual psychological feelings. That is an unhelpful point of analytical departure. To begin with individuals – lone, powerless natural persons who face a world of large organisations in chains of relationships about promises – diverts the analytical focus from those chains of relationships and the institutional world in which they are formed and sustained. And when individuals lose, they are cast as consumers in markets on the 'buyer beware' principle. Many may even experience shame for losing, for having been 'conned', for being stupid. Yet the problem lies not in individual miscalculation or in any personal misplacing of trust; its source lies in those chains of impersonal trust between large financial organisations and in those controlling them. This sense of personal shame, funnily enough, may also apply to those individuals formally enmeshed within this rarefied world of high financial strategising.

BEYOND ORTHODOXY: THE REALITY OF UNCERTAINTY

My book takes existing financial organisations as historically given, questioning only a few key 'events' which shaped or institutionalised specific ways of acting towards the future. It explores how 'social emotions' – those that are inherent within certain institutional complexes – generate expectations in financial decisions and negotiations between these vast organisations of finance. The analysis offered is inspired by sociology, but it draws on the Keynesian tradition in work such as Hyman Minsky's and on perceptive interpreters of Keynes such as G. L. S. Shackle. While it is armed with the Keynesian concept of uncertainty, it offers an explicitly social approach to exploring the ways that trust and distrust are projected, not by the supposedly isolated investors but by organisations, in formulating decisions that may enjoy a semblance of rational conviction.

While this account challenges orthodox economics, its central concern is to investigate trust relationships. It neither debates the abstractions of theoretical economic orthodoxy nor covers the immense detail about institutional structure and evolution that are ably marshalled by political scientists and economic historians such as David Kynaston (1994, 1995) and Glyn Davies (1994) in Britain alone. So too, there are national variations in corporate law and financial regulations. While an enormous specialist literature details every global financial transformation in each country, this study draws on US and UK experiences, with their so-called capital market or 'exit'-type practices (Cerny 1993; Helleiner 1993; Grahl 2001). But no institutional description of 'what is' can ever predict the future, regardless of whether finance is purely 'global markets' or whether national governments and major social groups might resume a democratic role in financial supervision. Since the future is unknowable, and the implications of its unknowability may be terrifying, attention must be paid to the emotions surrounding uncertainty that enable decisions to be made.

When I began this research, many social scientists, not to speak of the public at large, seriously underestimated the extent to which financial organisations rely on impersonal trust and confidence. Keynesian 'uncertainty' was long forgotten. By 1999, the climate of optimism was high, and it was extraordinarily difficult to suggest that stock market excitement for a 'new economy' of internets and e-mails was about impersonal trust. Some perceptive people thought I was onto an unusual and worthwhile idea, but many looked at me in disbelief: they could not imagine that all their money was resting, as usual, on a flimsy edifice of mere emotions. Several years of ensuing scandals brought widespread lack of trust, yet my focus is not so much on the frauds because there are books on every scandal. Rather, I look at the insecurity inherent in the procedures the financial world employs to master the unknowability of the future, and the volatile emotions entailed in its futile quest.

Orthodox economists tend to dismiss sociology for dealing with the 'residue of "irrationality"' or 'tosh' (cited in Ingham 1996b: 224–5). The claims of economic orthodoxy appear to me suspect for a number of reasons. These economists see only risk, not uncertainty; they see money as neutral in the long run; and they regard financial crises as emotional or irrational 'intrusions' into the 'real' goods-and-services economy. Anonymous market actors are said to act rationally in response to purely economic signals and indicators, while remaining detached and abstracted from the influence of social relations, whether with groups or with organisations. This is an unsustainable view also acknowledged in institutional economics which, following Thorstein Veblen as well as Joseph Schumpeter, shows how institutions have developed precisely to deal with uncertainty. The 'rational economic actor' does not exist in the complexity of actual social life. Real, living human beings come first, and the economic actor is a simplified abstraction from what they do. Humans only become human through their relationships. Less orthodox economists are now becoming increasingly sensitive to this fact and its implications, especially through dialogue with other social scientists. They now recognise that their discipline's received wisdom has been as much a source of social problems as any cure for them. Many economists, from recanters to non-believers, now criticise the decades of neo-classical hegemony over public policies, while among academic economists its social irresponsibility and lack of intellectual credibility are exposed. As the supposed ruling monarch of the social sciences, economics has not only been revealed as an emperor with no clothes; its role in keeping clothes from the backs of so many living, real people is also becoming ever clearer.

This book trespasses only lightly on economic turf. Unlike many critiques of economic orthodoxy which rarely move beyond the endless point-scoring that never convinces the faithful, this work neither engages centrally with received economic wisdom nor employs it as a foil for the display of an alternative analysis to that offered by mainstream economics. Rather, it strategically plunders conventional economics in order to raise for public debate issues that lie beyond its own intellectual assumptions and horizon.

MONEY: A SOCIAL RELATION OF DEBTS AND PROMISES

The term 'financial markets' highlights a broad contrast between the present and postwar era, when money and finance played a less prominent role than giant manufacturing corporations, bureaucracies and public institutions. As late as the 1970s, so a consensus across the political spectrum held, a 'central and distinguishing' feature of the modern social world was that it was 'a world of organizations' (Burns 1974: 123). That view was soon sidelined, partly by theoretical criticisms and partly by substantive economic changes. The key term was now 'market', which some saw as synonymous with 'democracy'.

Like those in the area of production, the relationships of money constitute a huge world of organisations. However, financial organisations are very different from the old corporate firms (though they too now invest heavily in financial assets, offer customer credit, and use pension funds). Money is different from commodity and service production, because it magnifies uncertainty. Money is also produced differently. It is debatable whether money is a commodity at all, since it is created from debt relationships. The money in our wallets and purses is part of an abstract chain of social relations of claims and credits, no less organised than plastic card money and bank mortgages. In many ways, money is one of the most enigmatic of social institutions (Wennerlind 2001: 557) because it is 'worthless unless everyone believes in it' (Greider 1987: 226).

The idea of money as an enigmatic social institution and social relation is counter-intuitive – and one that is far less understood today than in earlier eras. Money is highly 'productive'. Differing political views of capitalism, such as those of Keynes and Schumpeter, emphasise the major role money plays in capitalism. Schumpeter argued that money is the *internal engine* driving capitalism (e.g. 1954: 318). Even though orthodoxy uses him to focus narrowly on the heroic entrepreneur, it is finance as the 'gatekeeper of development' that allows Schumpeter's debtor-entrepreneur to act or not (Tobin 1987: 164; Ingham 2004: 201). Georg Simmel's classic text *Philosophy of Money* similarly draws enthusiastic attention to money's enormous 'productive power', not from owning or hoarding money but from 'the money yielded by money' (Simmel 1978: 182). This underestimated but dynamic role explains the instability of money.

All contemporary economists accept that money arises from the debt structure. How? Perhaps because it is counter-intuitive, or even alarming, orthodox economists underestimate the importance of this main premise. They see money as, in the long run, neutral. This view of money as a veil, as mainly barren, underlies all neo-classical views. But this argument is maintained by focusing on one of the functions of money that everyone knows – the one that seems to make sense of our daily experience of exchange. In performing its 'exchange function', money seems easier to use than bartering with a mass of different, cumbersome goods or services. When seen as a handy device, money appears relatively unimportant: as merely a medium, as a passive instrument for simplifying exchange. In this view, if money can be said to do anything at all, then all it does is to send messages about 'real' activities in the 'real' economy, in its price signals. Schumpeter demolished this view long ago: 'you cannot ride on a claim to a horse, but you can pay with a claim to money'; banks are 'merchants of debt' (Schumpeter 1954: 321; Minsky, cited in Ingham 2004: 161).

Money is created from the debt structure and its promise has two dimensions. In one sense, money is a promise or claim of 'payment' in something (Schumpeter's point) – an alienated, exchangeable promise. In its credit dimension, money is a promise to creditors about the borrower's ability to discharge a debt and the issuer's promise to take it back as payment. It is no two-way arrangement like barter exchange, whereby you take my table and in return I get your desk, and the deal is then over. In its 'claim' dimension, money is not simply bipartisan, imprisoned in a single moment in the space between two people. It is a promise into the future, and as token of that promise it can only be created between three parties. No one can believe or trust this token or promissory note unless it includes the 'community that guarantees the money' (Simmel 1978: 177). It is a three-way relation between the credit and debt relations of the economically active groups and the central power that enforces these promises by unifying and issuing a currency and outlawing counterfeiting. Because of its basis in these centrally supported promises of claims *and* credits that create money through chains of public and private debts and government guarantees and safety-nets, money is itself a social relation (Ingham 1996a).

Exchanges that involve no generation of additional debt do not determine the value or 'productive power' of money since they do not create further money. If we pay in full for a car or dress with a cheque or cash, we incur no debt. In contrast, if we issue an I Owe You (IOU) through a hire purchase, a bank loan or a credit card, money is created since we receive the car now 'in exchange for a promise to pay in the future' (Wray 1990: 301). Far from being barren as in the orthodox view, money has 'a value in possession' (Shackle 1972: 13). It gives highly significant economic options. In any private property economy where loans involve interest payments, monetary values are usually accumulated. Those who borrow or issue IOUs face continually growing contractual obligations, whereas those who lend or hold IOUs see their nominal wealth (not inflation-adjusted) expanding (Wray 1996: 447).

The private sphere was where the whole modern edifice of money-creation through IOUs gradually emerged (notably in Renaissance Florence, Genoa and Venice, later Amsterdam, then London). Here the bulk of money is created. Trade credit is very old, and these debtor–creditor relations were common several thousand years before the first coins. Even Babylonian clay tablets were the representative acknowledgement of indebtedness – or tokens of indebtedness which the issuer must promise to accept in repayment of a debt owed. Although the story is a complex one of tax debts and so on, our modern story develops when merchant classes made loans to post-feudal governments and there was a general rise in IOUs from the Renaissance onward. Partly due to the old uncertainties of trading with strangers, Renaissance traders created bills of exchange in their merchant networks between Constantinople and Venice, or Genoa and London, which became pure credit (Ingham 2004: 46; 108). This unfamiliarity, as before, fostered the charging of interest. Interest, in turn, tended to 'orient production toward sale on the market' (Wray 1996: 444). Markets therefore grew as feudalism crumbled, because they were the places for 'earning the means for settling debts' (Wray 1990: 8) and for meeting the interest payments on debts. To the present day, repayments on loans can be made by gaining money from wages, or by expanding the values of the IOUs, say by starting businesses and state ventures, or by raising taxes. The likely proceeds are expected to make true the initial promise to the lender that the IOU will prove to be a 'claim to future wealth' from production of goods and services for sale (Wray 1996: 447). Here is the engine of capitalism.

Money is created out of debt. There is more of it when the volume of credit granted by financial intermediaries increases, and less when debts are paid off. It expands and contracts (Smithin 1994: 5). Most people do not perceive money in this way. It seems, in a disturbing sense, to be created out of nothing to finance loans, and disappears when paid back. Money is a promise, even if, more deeply, its value rests on its being a claim on future wealth, on the promised future wealth creation to be undertaken by non-bank borrowers (Parguez & Seccareccia 2000: 105). The lender has a claim on the future wealth yet to be created by the borrower, but the promise is always uncertain. It can never be known in advance whether borrowers will create future wealth, enabling them to pay the interest (which is the price of their promise to pay). These are long-term uncertainties, whereas borrowing for trading financial assets is even more uncertain, because it entails short-term uncertainties which easily mount up. An enormous chain of uncertainties and a wide range of distrust strategies were institutionalised from these relations of promises, as the exploration of 'impersonal trust' in Chapter 2 will show.

Money is unique in contemporary times, not because it seems less solid and is heavily traded, but because financial assets have vastly expanded in number and significance. As we all know, the form may be plastic or electronic but it is still primarily credit, and in this sense all money has long been 'virtual' and often heavily traded. Late 20th-century money became unique with the massive and contradictory expansion in the proportion of share-owners (rentiers) and debtors just when postwar controls unravelled. Only over the last fifty years or so could low-income working-class customers gain credit from banks (Davies 1994: 338). Types of debt expanded in the 1950s, with the growth of home ownership (with mortgages) and consumerism, beginning with consumer hire purchase plans and the lay-by offered by retail firms and now fully developed in plastic credit cards. Many employees have become shareholders by purchasing private sector financial products. In contrast to the Great Depression, when almost entire working populations were plunged into unemployment by the loss in value of the shares that were then owned by a mere 3 per cent of the people, more than half the English-speaking populations own shares today.

The relation between money and credit is basic to economic thought. However, this point has profound social implications which sociological work highlights but which orthodox economics denies (money is neutral in the long run). The main money creators are usually both Treasury departments and central banks, and private banks. Treasuries and central banks create (high-powered) state money and private banks 'manufacture' credit money from promises of future wealth-creation.

Private banks create money according to conventional rules and practices. Starting with an original deposit of some other people's money, a bank will loan most of it out. The new deposits from the proceeds of the loan can be used to make payments; it too can 'be used as money' (Galbraith 1975: 19). In lending money, a bank may profitably use most of its deposits to loan out perhaps five or eight times over, and some of the money lent will be deposited in its own or other banks. In this sense, banks do appear to create money out of nothing, to manufacture it. However, there is not an infinite growth of money by the merchants of debt. The increase in money stems from a collective sense among all banks that 'loans create deposits' (Schumpeter 1954: 320; Davies 1994: 420). Banks find ways to employ most of the sums created. However worrying this sounds, private banks are not to be confused with central banks.

INSTITUTIONALISING MONEY

Today, private banknotes are mainly backed by government through access to its central bank, which usually holds private bank reserves or deposits, sets the interest rate it charges banks, and lends in emergencies. In many countries banks must retain a reserve or capital requirement, regulated by law and usually lodged in the central bank. In contrast to private bank money, high-powered money is 'the monetary debt of the government and its central bank, currency and central bank deposits', sometimes referred to as the base money. It represents a claim the private sector has on a government: high-powered money is the most exchangeable, the most marketable monetary liability. 'Low-powered' money consists of the private deposit obligations of banks and depository institutions (Tobin 1987: 159). Some private credit instruments have limited transferability by being *potential claims* (unlike high-powered money) and when this 'near money' expands, it is a key source of instability (Ingham 2004: 140–1).

These complex debt relations developed when governments borrowed from private merchants or banks (e.g. Spain from Renaissance Genoa) because near-modern states were weak and often bankrupt from wars and exploration, and many had little capacity to tax (Ingham 1984: 47; Arrighi 1994: 100–30). Tidy sums were made privately from financial deals with financially pressed states. But over time there has been an interesting evolution in the relations between the private banks, the central banks and the state structures that create and stand behind the central banks. The question of who is dependent on whom in these evolving relationships is not always transparent, or as things would outwardly seem. The first combination of public debt and private debt was forged in Britain. J. K. Galbraith explains the loan from wealthy creditors of the new Bank of England by noting that 'the government's promise to pay would be the security for a note issue of the same amount' to private borrowers (1975: 31). William III's Charter (1697) gave the then private Bank of England a privileged monopoly position over all other private banks. National debt had to be serviced by future taxes, and private debt was given legitimacy by a central bank purchasing private bills of exchange at a discount before maturity. The Charter explains the birth of high-powered money, in which the most trustworthy money became government debt, a claim by the private sector. Thus were the two old sources of credit money fused, in a way, into one 'sovereign monetary space': the public debt of state bonds, and the private debt of bills of exchange (Ingham 2004: 128–9). In Gladstone's view, William III had put the state in 'a position of subserviency . . . to induce monied men to be lenders', describing the imbalance as 'the money power supreme and unquestioned' (cited

Kynaston 1995: 19). Similarly, in the USA Thomas Jefferson thought 'the banking establishment more to be feared than standing armies (Galbraith 1975: 28–9).

Treasuries were unable or unwilling to democratise 'the money power'. Britain's measures in this area became a model through global imitation. The Treasury Board's division of the national debt into thousands of separate bonds helped strengthen Treasury's hand against its creditors, since it reduced the 'extortionate interest rates' that could be charged by the sole financier, thereby making Treasury less dependent on the Bank of England and government debt long-term and self-liquidating. Treasury could put new bond issues onto this newly created market in order to repay the previous bonds now due (Braithwaite & Drahos 2000: 144). Government debts gave states little option but to promote and guarantee domestic securities markets and the banks (Cerny 1993: 52). Debts created markets.

Governments constantly tried to check the Bank of England's abuses of government repayments and profiteering from paper money (Kynaston 1995: 20), without great success. Although the Bank Charter Act of 1844 set the Bank of England's management of the national currency on a quasi-public basis, this was defined as an 'automatic, technical' matter rather than a 'public responsibility', giving the central bank distance from Treasury (Bagehot, cited Kynaston 1995: 22).

By this time the entire European credit system depended on the Bank of England for its security. Merchants depended on banks, and banks on the central bank to keep a banking reserve. Central banks became 'trustees for the public' (Bagehot 1962: 17–18) and had quasi-government status by the early 20th century, usually imposed after financial crises. Yet the central banks' far closer connections to private finance than governments is what is important. By the Victorian era, the Bank of England had to gain experience in regulating commercial banks. Prudential regulation arose partly through an institutionalised deal between central banks and private banks, starting in the UK. For simplicity we may recall Mark Twain's umbrella theory of banking: banks tend to lend every umbrella out on sunny days, and recall them all at onset of rain. That is, they lend aggressively with loose credit, creating inflationary finance in an upswing, yet at the onset of panic the surviving banks hoard their reserves and starve firms of liquidity just when it is most needed.

Critics like Walter Bagehot (1962 [1873]) argued that the centralising of trust had to be the Bank of England's responsibility. An overarching, public bank, he said, could prevent bank collapses caused by 'foolish bankers'. A bank run is a collapse of trust not just in foolish banks but in prudent banks alike, in banking itself. Most money is out in overlapping deferrals of a credit pyramid, and only a fraction of deposits is reserved or held back from further lending (less in highly competitive, aggressive lending bouts). No bank can cope if too many depositors withdraw their money at the same time, unless there is a lender of last resort. Some private banks in the 1870s tried to resist the Bank of England's control over their cash reserves and instead arrange the rate of discount themselves. In this debate in the 1870s, the rest of the City of London's bankers recalled the panics and storms of the 1847, 1857 and 1866 when they were rescued by the

Bank of England. Ultimately banks ceded control of short-term interest rates (the charge made by the central bank) in return for the central bank acting as lender of last resort in emergencies (Kynaston 1994: 332). Similarly the Banque de France and Banca d'Italia developed regulations against aggressive lending by commercial banks (Braithwaite & Drahos 2000: 91). The USA, in the last quarter of the 19th century, was equally marked by panics among thousands of decentralised banks. After more serious bank runs and a financial panic in 1907, when the established New York bankers were unable to bail themselves out, the US Federal Reserve System (the Fed) was founded in 1913, directed by US Congress to provide desperately needed financial stability. Even so, the new Fed could do little about 'the hundreds, then thousands' of local banks collapsing each year up to 1933 (Braithwaite & Drahos 2000: 92; see also Macfarlane 1999).

MONEY TODAY: A CENTRAL POWER RELATION

Simmel argues that 'since money is entirely a sociological phenomenon, a form of human interaction', trust and confidence are paramount. But how is trust so important? Through what bonds is trustworthiness established? As relations of promises, we might expect plain speaking and caution from democratic govern-ments. As token of a promise, money cannot be created only between lender and borrower, since a token is not believable without a three-way relation (Simmel 1978: 172) between creditors, debtors and society. These tokens comprise a mass of alienated promises to pay or, in other words, social relationships where money has a double nature, as a public good and a private commodity. When it is more privatised, excessive commodification is often a result. Opposition to central banks from orthodox economics in favour of the market, and from populists in favour of decentred, small-scale local schemes, completely forgets 19th-century bank disas-ters (Henwood 1998: 95). The 'concentration and centralization' of these money relations into central banks (Smithin 1994: 80) became an established means to foster this vaguely specified, highly abstract trust in money as a public good. More precisely, Geoffrey Ingham argues (2004: 141) that monetised debt – a double public/private circuit – is the most trustworthy, most sought-after money, institutionalised in a government's promises to pay from future taxation.

'This is the core of truth in the theory that money is only a claim on society' (Simmel 1978: 177). But in the financial sphere, and with central banks in a little-known deal with the private sector, the state's private creditors can easily disrupt this claim on society. If more credit is created, private banks may expect their central bank to accommodate their aggressive creation of near money. But private creditors may distrust the state's creditworthiness. Higher interest rates appease private creditors but risk debtor default. Domestic credit rationing may hurt local borrowers savagely but not rein in larger enterprises able to borrow offshore (Kriesler & Nevile 2003: 181; Ingham 2004: 144–5).

Money is a central power relation in the development of capitalism, as central as the wage labour–capital relation (Ingham 1984; Minsky 1996). The central banks' relations to the private heartland of commercial banking, simply as supposedly 'neutral' experts, said Bagehot, removed them from public responsibility. Yet, as Ingham argues, there is enormous conflict in money relationships. Neither a central bank nor any other financial organisation can establish or 'produce at will' the standard and 'substantive validity' of money. In his words, money's 'purchasing power can only be established through the struggle between producers and possessors of both money and goods'. This process is always contradictory, for in achieving monetary stability, instability emerges elsewhere (Ingham 1998: 13–14). Uncertainty can be squeezed in one place but will emerge in another. Flights to liquidity are not an option for the whole society, Keynes said, and instability is moved to financial circulation. In his analogy, it is as though a farmer could decide to move the farm (fixed capital) into speculation for a few days, to return to farming at the end of the week. The conflict is between the short and the long term. Although the reason for holding liquidity may not be intentionally speculative, it leads to short-term horizons anyway, of buying cheap and selling dear (Chick 1983: 204–7; Caporaso & Levine 1992: 111–12).

An historical example puts these conflicts in perspective. In the 1920s central bank monetary rates became truly politicised (Kynaston 1995: 27). The price of money, political publics and citizen electors soon recognised, affects unemployment, housing policy and general economic policy. Most strikingly shown by the Depression was how a monetary policy of high interest rates had not prevented the speculative boom of the preceding years. After the 1929 crash's global impact, low interest rates were totally ineffective in reviving economic activity. 'In a metaphor that gained currency at the time', said Galbraith (1975: 213) 'monetary policy was like a string. You could pull it, though with incalculable results. But you couldn't shove it at all'. At the height of the boom, speculators gained far more from asset inflation than any central bank deterrent of higher interest rates, despite its impact on employment, defaults and small business. During a depression, in contrast, a low price of money may still not generate trust, optimism or the necessary entrepreneurial business confidence to borrow, invest or spend – a point Keynes made tirelessly and which this book this book scrutinises.

Depending on the price of money (interest) and the 'real' value of money (whether it is inflating or disinflating), money always involves unequal relations between creditors and debtors. Inflation most hurts consumers with no debts living on fixed savings or unindexed pensions, and so on. Long-term debts (business debts, state debts, or mortgages) and 'real' interest payments are alleviated by rising inflation, whereas a low inflation context aids wealth-holders. The value of their wealth grows subtly, because 'nominal' wealth does not take inflation rates into account compared with 'real' wealth. In today's situation, debts of all kinds may be more or less adequately serviced *as long as* interest rates stay low, employment and businesses flourish, taxes are paid and asset values rise. In the UK, Canada, Japan, the USA and Australia, average household debt levels rose, most markedly in the 1990s, to 120 per cent of annual disposable incomes. The extent varies slightly, but such rises were most common in the Anglo-Saxon countries. Household sector debt is often higher than other sectors, non-financial firms, even financial firms

(Henwood 1998: 59; RBA 1999). That debt subtly grows in low price inflation or stable money, explaining the concern about debt-asset deflation crises. With asset deflation amid mounting debt, firms cannot service debts incurred during a speculative boom and neither can home buyers service mortgages.

Credit is rationed upwards by 'screening' – by bank assessments of credit-worthiness, the wealthy lent vast sums. Pawn shops charge 140 per cent interest and American 'payday' loans can reach 2000 per cent (Henwood 1998: 84); and, of course, credit-card interest rates paid by the relatively desperate are a major source of commercial bank profits. In the case of a famous default by a US hedge fund, Long Term Capital Management (LTCM), in 1998, its huge and complicated debt left the lenders (banks and investment houses) with decreased ability to control its management (Lowenstein 2000: 214). (Mortgage or credit card defaulters have homes repossessed or face prison for failing to pay back debts.) LTCM was bailed out by private lenders, on the principle that if the bank lends me $1000, it's my problem, if $1 billion it's their problem.

One further comment on the deal between the central banks and the private heartland of finance. Only after the Depression was economic policy brought under some government control, and central banks effectively enabled to forestall most bank collapses. Since the development of Euromarkets in the 1970s which began the revival of large-scale financial dealing and excessive commodification of money, central bankers have had great difficulty specifying relationships in setting and maintaining standards of indebtedness. Central banks stand 'somewhere' between government and the private sector, said a Deputy-Governor of the Bank of England (Pennant-Rea 1995: 219), at the same time as the burden of economic management narrowed further to monetary policy. Domestic bank lending is no longer the only source of funds, which reduces reserve ratios and the required pool of funds against which reserves must be held (Schaberg 1998: 209). At the same time, fewer central banks control prudential regulation, as separate supervisory agencies now copy US arrangements. Postwar economic regulation went together with prudential controls, but now larger private enterprises are 'free' to make imprudent decisions. The possibility that monetary authorities may be unable to meet lender of last resort duties cannot be ruled out. As Hugh Stretton argues, 'the world has no precedent or previous working experience of an international system of pure fiat money [government authorised], privately created, publicly guaranteed, and inadequately regulated' (2000: 707, 691).

ASKING THE EXPERTS

Debates on whether governments can regain control over incessant trading in financial assets again proliferate. Inflation-first policies opposed any concern with restoring employment, even measures to support the unemployed with a decent unemployment payment. Financial actors had coveted social and national property, eagerly pursuing the privatisation of utilities and collective savings. Government or non-commercial, mutual insurance and pension funds for wage and salary earners were said to 'crowd out' the private sector. But in fact social property and social *security* undercut the production of private money. Eventually financial speculation took its toll at the dizzy heights as much as for marginalised populations and countries. LTCM collapsed in 1998. Facile 'new economy' explanations – relatives of information society and post-industrial ideas that played down chronic unemployment (Pixley 1993) – tapered off after the April 2000 dot.com crash. Uncertainty seemed obvious, emotions – often bewildered rage – even more so.

From bringing sociology to these debates, the financial world came to seem less a conspiracy than a mundane, highly dangerous game played by people and the institutions of a financial sector that oversimplified and underestimated the reality and character of money as a chain of fragile claims and credits. Breathless talk about rational calculations of risk by a new class of symbolic analysts and knowledge workers was not credible. A proliferation of trust organisations attempting to face the unknowable seemed to explain the situation better (Pixley 1999b, 2002c). The best way to find out was to ask experts in this world, to find some informed sceptics. Much of my evidence is from elite interviews with over forty experienced finance decision-makers, analysts and commentators in major world financial centres. Transcripts of US Federal Reserve meetings are also cited. The focus in these interviews was on exploring ideas about future-oriented emotions, in both seemingly stable and volatile times. Overwhelmingly my data confirm how these emotionally laden and emotion-generating expectations are collectively fostered within and between finance organisations at levels beyond the micro or personal.

Yet these public-spirited people expressed alarm at the present situation. Their concerns about the dot.com boom had often been ignored. Some were not sure about emotions of trust, though by 2002 their thinking had certainly become more focused, as trust was collapsing all round. Many had twenty years' experience and more in finance. These were people who supported capitalism, but many felt that banking was undersupervised, that information was lacking, with modest investors losing dreadfully. Many were most concerned about credit.

THE ARGUMENT

Chapter 2 explains why future-oriented emotions are inescapably and historically entrenched in finance. The counter-intuitive idea of emotions being fostered between corporations, even though only individuals are capable of feeling emotions, is examined. If impersonal trust and distrust drive these organisations (banks must trust to lend; credit raters must distrust the creditworthiness of the entities they assess), then these emotions are standard operating procedures. Shareholder value is historically based on distrust strategies by owners of firms. But owners and corporations are highly impersonal today. Chapter 2 also compares economic views on interest, risk and uncertainty with my views on the essential role emotions play in financial decisions.

All following chapters examine emotions in finance using the interview evidence about the outer to the inner world, and on to interdependencies between financial organisations and their trust in data. Chapter 3 uses evidence from the outer ring of experienced journalists. As this trust position has a vital role in providing information to specific publics, we need to ask how trustworthy are the financial media? What of their sources and their media corporations? Who entices whom?

Chapter 4 considers how professional financiers and central bankers come to decisions. As no one knows the future, we explore how expectations are important. Were there differences in more personal (old school tie) days? Are 'rogue traders' to blame for bank collapses, or are these emotional requirements within firms? As impersonal trust is predominant today and money is again more a fictional commodity – a heavily traded array of promises (treated as if assets) – intuition, judgement and fearlessness are other factors that vary in different contexts.

Trust, fear and anxiety must be felt by individuals, but the finance world consists of interlocking agreements and dependencies. Chapter 5 shows that central bank reputation is 'bestowed' by financial actors whereas formerly central banks controlled the process. If confidence in money is inspired by impression management, when do central bank confidence games appear to be con games? Chapter 6 asks the experts which organisations are the most trustworthy, from central banks to the private sector. Evidence shows anxiety about central bank weaknesses and fairly encompassing distrust towards the private sector – accountancy firms, investment banks, financial press, mutual funds – among informed sceptics.

In attempting to make rational decisions, all finance organisations marshal mountains of data. But, as Chapter 7 shows, the major problem with data is that it can only describe the past; it cannot predict the future: promises may be broken, wealth creation may not eventuate. Reams of numbers and various forms of risk calculations are ultimately matters of judgement and screening, or rather trust and its collapse.

Underlying this whole situation is a cultural and emotional climate of short-term thinking within the financial heartland. Chapter 8 explains it less from libertarian ideological dominance than from a present-oriented utopianism, a necessary, incessant hope that maintains contemporary morale where expectations shatter so regularly. It is a utopianism that worships the god of opportunity.

The implications considered in Chapter 9 are recognising emotions as inevitably involved in attempts to act rationally towards the unknowable future. Emotions cannot be removed from the social relations of money, but the question is which emotions are preferable. Financial organisations are now so oriented to short-term horizons and the insanity of denying uncertainty that a number of otherwise interesting ideas, of imposing more 'market' solutions, or a world trust agency, are pointless from this view. In this extended concluding chapter, I discuss how it is more desirable to reconsider emotions within existing financial institutions, with a revived role for governments through reasoned, democratic debate. That depends on their honestly acknowledging uncertainty, to aim for more cautious, even nervous, long-term horizons within the insitutions on which we all must rely, and to reformulate fiduciary trust in more democratic forms.

2 | Emotion in the Kingdom of Rationality

FINANCIAL ORGANISATIONS AND bureaucracies comprise a vast infrastructure of fragile claims and promises between creditors and debtors. Default is never unthinkable; past trust can shatter. Money is created out of promises between public and private debtors (governments, taxpayers and entrepreneurs, plus us borrowers) and creditors (private global financial institutions, and the public if bondholders and/or savers). Money's vital role in economic activity may often be benign: private creditors finance national debt for sound government activities, allowing more favourably priced credit to foster economic activity which a government can tax to repay its debt. But since the future is unpredictable, these fragile bonds of trust may collapse because 'ventures may fail, taxes cannot be collected, debts cannot be repaid' (Ingham 2004: 132–3). Economic 'decline' can set in ('depression' is an emotional term disliked by today's economic and political leaders). All economic decisions are made in an environment of uncertainty, with profound implications for our understanding of expectations about the future. And this fragile structure is bonded through trust between huge and remote organisations – an unlikely social bond, perhaps, in the hard-headed world of money although *bond markets*, for example, are one expression of this trust with global ramifications.

This chapter shows that trust is a primary emotion for coping with uncertainties about the intentions, honesty, ability and promises of officials managing large organisations in both private and public sectors. Corporate or state policies and lines of responsibility are extremely important in creating reputations for trustworthiness, far more than personal trust. Moreover, however honest and capable, the inevitable lack of prescience among all parties is rarely acknowledged. In the private sector, decisions to lend, borrow and invest rely on trust and distrust towards those with whom they must deal: caution has unfortunately diminished. As the financial field is so large, so interdependent, these primary emotions have become institutionalised, otherwise the system could not operate as it does. Conventions (see page 33 below) and expectations like trust and distrust are the only ways to project financial futures as controllable so that board members can make decisions and corporations can act. Mere individuals, in contrast, have a vague confidence that banks and regulators will keep their trust relationships safe from dangers.

In asking how finance is emotional, I show the financial field as an irreducibly social world of impersonal and unavoidable emotions. I look at the field as a whole, rather than at individuals, mainly to see how emotions in finance were historically shaped and instituted in legal and corporate forms. Impersonal techniques of distrust were consolidated from the uncertainties inherent in dealing with strangers. This chapter briefly shows how personal feelings of distrust recorded by early capitalists and financiers led to the formation of impersonal trust-inducing strategies in surveillance organisations like accountancy firms and credit-rating agencies. The trust so created by the future-oriented financial world is unlike many familiar meanings of the word 'trust' because it underlies dry economic terms such as 'interest', 'rationality' and 'expectation', as we will see. Trust in the future is the basis of these seemingly rational terms. Behavioural finance (psychology) and rational actor models (the 'rational economic man', or REM) rarely emphasise how uncertainty differs from risk and probability, which I briefly compare. My focus is on ordinary actions among finance organisations, because wild moments where panic is obvious are the cumulative outcomes of routine decisions of trust or distrust in boardrooms of banks or central banks. This chapter, therefore, lays the groundwork for exploring interdependent emotions in finance.

EMOTIONS IN THE CORE FINANCIAL STRUCTURES

It is hard to underestimate the difficulties of moving beyond conventional accounts that focus on individual agents, even though the financial field primarily consists of the great banks and other major financial institutions. Orthodox economists see individual investors acting rationally in financial markets, independently calculating their risk preferences; when disaster occurs, it is merely because these masses have allegedly succumbed to fear and greed. But a more adequate theory would show how and why emotions function in the core structures of the financial world. Financial leaders explain booms and busts as due to 'irrational exuberance', implying an emotional crowd psychology. To orthodox economists, emotions are something apart from the 'normal' rational behaviour of economic activity. Emotions are impulsive and unpredictable, and therefore embarrassing for positivist REM models aiming for prediction (as we will see).

Orthodoxy makes light of uncertainty, or of any inherently unpredictable factor, because to do otherwise means admitting that rational interpretation of information is unreliable and emotions like trust are required. What kind of trust, it may be asked. Financial activities are far more future-oriented than most. Consider an orchestra or a construction team: their primary aim is to do the present task as well as possible. In finance the present task, as in all forecasting, is to guess the future 'well', a difficulty, as Keynes said (1937: 214), because compared to the unpredictability of finance, the weather is 'only moderately uncertain'. Future-oriented emotions are intrinsic to economic decisions because organisations must neutralise uncertainty in order to act. The kind of trust or distrust involved is therefore not a personal disposition to be trusting or fearful but is strategic: a watchful suspicion is a standard operating procedure before decisions. It switches between trust and distrust according to evidence which only the future validates or not. Because the future-orientation is so stark in finance, expectations must be formed about an unknown future of potential, if actively chosen, losses or gains. Only trust or distrust can neutralise the lack of future evidence and provide a semblance of rationality to calculations necessarily based on past evidence. Indeed, even in politics, renowned for its mendacity and viciousness, the complete lack of knowledge about future electoral outcomes is openly acknowledged, whereupon the losing leader is often in tears.

Historians show how various emotions have played an important role in the business cycle. Charles Kindleberger, who has tirelessly recorded the thousands of panics and crashes in 300 years of modern financial history, complains how orthodoxy dismisses his work as merely anecdotal (1989: 243). He uses an 'irrational exuberance' thesis, where emotions are absent in stable times. Manias are like a 'virus' infecting a healthy financial world (1989: 248). For Keynes, 'animal spirits' are irrational, but in stressing uncertainty he argues that private investment relies mainly on animal spirits and the convention of extrapolating the past into the future, whether in unstable or apparently calm times.

Walter Bagehot, famous London banker and editor of *The Economist*, saw the entire business cycle in emotional terms. In asking 'Why Lombard Street Is Often Very Dull, and Sometimes Extremely Excited', he said *trust* explained the behaviour on London's money markets (Bagehot 1962 [1873]: 61). Bagehot wanted a stronger central bank as a necessary trust organisation, as we saw in Chapter 1. His reference is not to crowd emotions but to 'foolish banks' and the public responsibility of the Bank of England, because he rightly holds organisations accountable for their decisions. The so-called mass crowds and herd panics, or the 'contagions' of depositors demanding their money, are, rather, the result of mistaken organisational decisions, understandable lack of prescience or lack of caution by banks in facing the unknown. Consider, likewise, this headline in 2003: 'It wasn't our fault: the rating agencies' defence', after Standard & Poor's and Moody's were criticised for 'being asleep on the job' over record global corporate debt defaults, collapsed insurers and 'too late' downgrades (from America's Enron company to Australia's HIH insurance firm). The headline describes a structure of trust in credit ratings (triple A to D for default), an interactive relation of trust between diverse organisations which are remote or socially distant. There are no face-to-face relations involved when organisations trust credit-raters' published grades on the creditworthiness of nation-states or corporations and, more importantly, these grades cannot be prescient. S&P's representative will 'cheerfully' admit (afterwards) that it has no 'crystal ball' (Baker 2003).

'Credibility', a well-used term in finance, is less commonly framed as an individual issue only. Credibility obviously pertains to organisational trustworthiness, future predictability or, literally, believability. All these emotions (trust, distrust, the expectation or anticipation of credibility) give often unnoticed *feelings of control over the future* to decision-makers, and foster an *esprit de corps* when an organisation has reached a decision. Individuals in such situations experience physiological symptoms: when adrenalin makes a fear felt, when shame causes blushing, or when 'oxytocin rushes' are generated by others' show of trust, or *love*. But love or shame are wrongly assumed to be more emotional than trust. Hormone research on oxytocin suggests it produces 'lust and trust' in those on whom either trust or love is bestowed (Grimes 2003). These are relationships driven by obsessively future-oriented expectations about whether promises will be kept ('she loves me, she loves me not') and, in financial decisions, enabling a fraught leap into uncertain circumstances. Dithering or outward anxiety is unforgivable in these environments, as we will see. Finance emotions do not arise from individual feelings. Trust and distrust are social emotions constituted within and between powerful organisations for rationally coping with the unknown in decision processes, later 'felt' as emotions by individuals or groups of them. Futures cannot even be imagined without these neurologically based emotions (Damasio 1994).

Orthodox economics (rationality) or psychology (irrational emotions) only focus on individuals. Behavioural psychology in *finance* argues that emotions lead to mistakes in calculating probability and therefore to irrational judgements. Innate predispositions and emotional tendencies are said to 'reside' in particular or stereo-typical individuals. This is true, but only if one focuses on individuals. Ideas of 'herding' or 'irrational exuberance' are imputations about statistically average individuals in collective or specific groups (often patronising and unproven, such as 'mum and dad' investors). They cannot explain social phenomena like trust-worthiness or credibility. Way beyond individuals are the social relations of a complex field of financial firms, central banks and global pension funds facing the unknown, which they can only manage through specific, requisite emotions which drive their guesswork. Both neo-classical economics and behavioural finance ignore the interactive, socially constituted nature of corporate strategies and how even the best-laid schemes go wrong (Oatley 1992: 162). This, in a financial world seeking unattainable certainty, is what no one wants to hear.

TRUST AND DISTRUST IN THE IMPERSONAL WORLD

As I have argued, the mighty corporation was neglected across the social sciences after the 1970s. The preferred objects of study became markets and an allegedly new 'information society' (a term popularised by Daniel Bell between his 'post-industrial society', Marshall McLuhan's 'Gutenberg Galaxy' and the later 'globalisation'). These once-fashionable terms avoided not only the obvious – governments and corporations – but also the continuous expansion of specifically modern forms of social relationships and integration, as Craig Calhoun rightly argues (1992). Of course, increasingly large-scale markets are another continuity in modernity, but so too are the abstract developments of *indirect* relations between impersonal corporations. These developments are indisputably the defining difference between today's modern social life and early modernity. Indirect, remote relationships of individuals to these vast organisations are nearly always controlled from afar by the corporation or faceless bureaucracy: we are integrated through our plastic cards to a bank; our personal credit or employee details are subject to re-analysis by a central administration against whom we may need an ombudsman to correct the record. These are relationships against which lone individuals may complain or from which they may exit, but often at great cost and always with 'please hold the line'.

This does not mean that any of us are beyond personal, face-to-face relations, simply that modern life is not explained by such direct, two-way relationships. Personal ties are the stuff of everyday life, partly as continuities from pre-modern traditions. Yet today's 'primary', intimate ties are submerged by, and often sentimentalised in defiance of, the corporations and bureaucracies which are overwhelmingly dominant in the world. We seek recognition in our primary and our secondary relations too, say at workplaces or in voluntary associations, but as lone individuals we are acknowledged by organisations only by number, rank or in aggregate, if armed with effective demand like cash. By looking at organisations rather than persons, my analysis moves beyond conventional preoccupations which personalise a firm in its leader and see 'markets' everywhere else. Indeed, the impersonal, indirect relationships between firms and/or bureaucracies is as likely to be symmetrical and certainly as two-way as those very different face-to-face relations between individuals (Pixley 1997, 1999a). Many find this focus difficult, mainly because laws and theories explaining these corporate innovations were based on a time when trust organisations and fiduciary (trust) laws were emerging. Early forms of legal trust were so much part of a 'personal' and face-to-face world that the bourgeois brothers' name was the capitalist firm or bank (Baring Brothers or Salomon Brothers). Today, however, very similar laws and trust entities define indirect relationships among impersonal corporations, family names rarely surviving.

During the 20th century, corporations became oligopolies autocratically managed for growth, their names memorable because of their longevity, not their relatively obscure 'managing director' – another passé term. As well, the era of currency regulation was one where stock exchanges generally focused on domestic firms, built to last and provide steady dividends. And firms were, at least, largely free of the uncertainties from volatile currency movements and so forth. After the 1970s, redefinitions occurred, with oligopolies construed as mere agents to principals: the idea that management is only there to increase shareholder value is almost taken for granted today. This is what the 'financialisation of life' is about. But although firms and banks must aim at stock values alone, the vast bulk of large corporations *remain* oligopolies with no personal owners. Modern corporations have extraordinary legal and informal powers beyond any 'natural person', yet they claim legal 'person' status as well. The asymmetry between actual 'natural persons' and investment banks or corporations is extreme. When control is relatively certain, such asymmetry hardly needs trust.

Why and how is trust involved? Agent–principal relations of trust arose from distrust over a myriad uncertainties facing early capitalist firms. The early modern 'fiduciary' (trustee) was a semi-stranger delegated to manage a firm, entrusted by another stranger, an owner with a face: a network of semi-strangers produced trust out of distrust. Fiduciary laws are modernity's first responses to coping with economic strangers – fleeting but still relatively face-to-face 'secondary' relations.

Modern corporate law defines a firm's existence as a fiduciary one, that is, one based on trust. Corporations do not exist in order to employ people but because 'others entrust it with their money' (Stinchcombe 1990: 201). Fiduciary arrangements in corporate law are moral obligations to other categories – usually creditors first, shareholders second, and excluding employees and historically customers too. The specific 'impersonal' emotion of a fiduciary relationship is trust, as fiduciaries are legally authorised to act on behalf of others, and trusted to safeguard others' interests without benefiting improperly from their duty of care. What all this means needs unravelling.

For a start, what are the uncertainties and insecurities of shareholders that require trust? If we look back briefly, they may seem the same as when owners first delegated management and entrepreneurial investment decisions to strangers. Yet that classic separation of ownership from control is of a completely different order today. These fiduciary relations emerged when capitalist enterprises ceased to be owner-managed. How could an owner delegate to a manager? Today, millions own abstract parcels of rights and stocks far removed from corporate ownership, but originally fiduciary laws were formulated individually.

Owner-managed firms were driven by debt obligations and competition. Capitalist enterprises had to seek new profit-making chances continuously, or 'be doomed to extinction' (Weber 1976: 17). In this way, specific emotions were institutionalised in the owner-person: optimism, envy, fear of bankruptcy, and the aggressive pursuit of profit. But if owners delegate to a mere manager, how can their own firm's survival through relentless pursuit drive such a person? In capitalism's early days, the transition from owner management was bitterly opposed and fraught with trust problems. Delegation to managers involved the creation of impersonal trust organisations, rules and legislation, because owners' trust was inspired by distrust.

In his interpretation of the rise in modern management in early modern Britain, Sidney Pollard (1965) emphasises what became, in effect, impersonal relations of distrust. Lynn Zucker (1986) explores the institutional production of trust in 19th-century America. The result was, for example, credit-raters to assess trustworthiness of borrowers, insurance to spread perceived vulnerability of uncertain, potential losses, and 'anti-trust' legislation to deter collusion among firms.

'Bitter experience' of British entrepreneurs and fashionable economic theories of the 18th century fostered a hard view among owners that 'large-scale management was to be avoided at all costs' (Pollard 1965: 12). However surprising it may seem today, a consensus among owners then was that managers could not be trusted with any delegated responsibility or power. Adam Smith was a firm opponent of joint-stock companies because directors, 'being the managers of other people's money', were likely to be less vigilant; unless a company undertook only simple and routine procedures, 'negligence and profusion' were virtually inevitable (cited Pollard 1965: 12–13). In a similar development of distrust as when banks used (or misused) the money of others, joint-stock companies seemed, overwhelmingly to owners and creditors, to give rise to mismanagement. This included fraud, dishonesty and personal enrichment by managers: 'Fees, Sweetnings' and 'Pickings' by their dependants, wastefulness and a 'tendency to invest in status, power or influence rather than productive equipment' (1965: 13–14).

Pollard's words might be describing yesterday's headlines, but these former direct relations with strangers are now indirect and abstract. 'The wonder was that there should be a body of men willing to invest in [companies] in each new generation, rather than that the public should distrust their managers' (1965: 14). Creditors, of course, fearing defaults, distrusted governments and banks. In Britain, joint-stock scandals as early as 1698 of 'frauds, embezzlements and high-handed disregard of the share-holders' interests' (1965: 19) continued well into the 19th century. Pollard cites abundant examples of 'over-expansion, faulty capitalization', and 'dishonest, absconding or alcoholic managers' (1965: 20–1). These experiences, he says, inspired economic theories that 'self-interest was the only possible driving force'. But we may ask whose interests, vulnerabilities and greed were imputed – those of owners or managers? Such recorded debates about personal distrust led to the theory that joint-stock companies sought profit through monopoly (control over prices), which harms the 'public interest' (consumers), rather than 'efficiency' (economies of scale with competition) – that is, cheap prices and more tacitly, high dividends for owners (rentiers). This legacy fostered theories that indirect administration of large companies invited fraud and laziness, which harms 'owners' (Pollard 1965: 21). Such theories are behind today's neo-classical economics, agency theory in particular, and behind many contemporary national and global policies. Likewise the rise of capital markets such as stock exchanges, according to Benjamin Friedman (1987: 73), is largely because they perform private ownership functions of attempting to assess the future value and to spread the vulnerabilities of stocks and other capital assets.

If distrustful feelings were common among owners, Pollard argues that they were 'a serious libel on the newly rising profession of industrial managers' (1965: 22). Distrust was socially constructed and often inaccurate, yet became institutionalised at the organisational peak. And, just as central banks became the ultimate trustees of banks almost inadvertently after catastrophic bank runs (Chapter 1), accounting procedures to produce trustworthy agent–principal relations were also cobbled together, from old master–steward and merchant laws. Managers – agents of owners – wanted accountants to meet managerial hopes for 'certainty', for powers of control over the whole (unruly) firm and for 'rational' decision-making (Pollard 1965: 209). Owners aimed to control their managers from a distance through accountants.

Merchants depended on agents to be honest and capable, and used double-entry bookkeeping accounts to answer the question 'Am I being cheated?' (Carruthers & Espeland 1991: 43). Intentional lies and fraud were nothing to the uncertainties of later industrial companies. Manufacturers faced acute problems in guessing future income from existing fixed investment, let alone proposed new ventures (Pollard 1965: 220). The Joint Stock Companies Acts (of 1844 and 1868) and the 1900 Companies Act in Britain expanded the audience to the state: 'Accounts were now *legally* required to answer the questions, are investors being cheated? and is capital being maintained?' (Carruthers & Espeland 1991: 47). Mistaken predictions inherent in uncertainty, not always fraud or incompetence by those entrusted, are blurred problems that are my greatest concern.

Impersonal distrust of strangers in the USA also created accountancy firms, government legislation and credit-rating agencies. Many studies focus on fraud rather than uncertainty – understandably, given the robust numbers of what Susan Shapiro calls *Wayward Capitalists* (1984). In comparing Wall Street's rank dishonesty uncovered in 2002, a *Barrons* article cites criticisms of 1870. Owners *and* managers seem to be colluding against wealthy individual shareholders:

> All the worst evils of stock manipulations have their birth and abiding-place in the secret counsels of the Rings and Cliques – of that association of railway, steamship and telegraph directors, presidents and heavy shareholders who find it consonant with their consciences and their purses to water stock, pay dividends out of capital, to invent that anomalous feature in finance known as capitalised earnings, to utter unauthorised new stock; to do everything which will keep them outside of prison bars by means of shrewd lawyers and complaisant judges. (J. K. Medbury, cited in Donlan 2002)

'Watering stock' is recording equity in excess of tangible assets, like today's counting 'goodwill' as equity. 'Uttering unauthorised stock' is now against the law, but resembles current practices of issuing or 'uttering' stock options. This puts off the time when the stock is created but still dilutes the equity of shareholders. Collusion is always tempting since insider trading is past knowledge, not uncertain but a sure thing against others' share values.

During the late 19th century, booms and crashes alternated regularly. After Wall Street's 1929 crash, relations of trust or distrust became far more impersonal. President Roosevelt's 1933 legislation created the Securities and Exchange Commission (SEC) and strengthened systems of impersonal trust, requiring external accountancy firms to assess corporate accounts. Moreover, and following Britain here, US commercial banks could no longer act as investment banks (Glass-Steagall Act). Elements of personal trust remained in Britain, because the City–Bank of England networks, like the European financial networks, remained a prominent source of regulatory inducements to trustworthiness until at least the 1970s (see Chapter 4). But in the USA impersonal trust relations were extensive, including the US Federal Reserve, which gained increased national and postwar international duties of currency supervision and regulating high finance.

THE FLUCTUATING POWER OF SHAREHOLDERS

Large corporations developed, regulated and geared for growth. Their fiduciary responsibility as trustees for shareholders was only one of many other functions. Berle & Means, in *The Modern Corporation and Private Property* (1932), still defended the old principle. They saw grave dangers now that America's corporate system no longer 'rested on the self-interest of the owner' (1932: 8) but on hired managers. Shareholders could not control managerial 'abuse'; corporate powers included the 'power of confiscation' of part of the profit stream (1932: 247), that is, management could restrict dividend payouts to refinance growth. Retained earnings for reinvestment grew, as profits from their larger market share grew, freeing firms from stockholder influence and possibly even dependence on banks. By the 1950s, Berle himself admitted that the state played such a strong role in US corporations – in subsidising research, educating the workforce, and in Keynesian demand management – that private profitability had become 'alien' (Henwood 2003: 4). Whether industrial corporations reduced their dependency on bank and other loans is under dispute (Mizruchi & Stearns 1994: 321).

What is the most adequate way to describe corporations in their 1960s form? Distrust by 'owners' now had a minimal role, later to be resurrected in totally abstract form. At that time, J. K. Galbraith argued that a 'new industrial state' was entrenched, but since corporations were non-democratic 'price-administering oligopolists' (1977: 257), he wanted democratic input in their management. In marked contrast, Milton Friedman insisted that American corporations were not entities but *agents* for owners, and should revert to one sole purpose: to improve profits for shareholders. In between democratic and anti-democratic critics, the conservative sociologist Daniel Bell argued the business corporation was a significant entity in 'service to society' (1976: 292). Bell criticised Friedman because he did not see corporations as legal agents or 'artificial persons' entrusted merely to create stockholder value. In Friedman's neo-classical terms, a corporate executive is 'an employee of the owners of the business'. This employee should again be made directly responsible 'to make as much money as possible' for the owners, aka 'employers' (cited Bell 1976: 292). Bell rejected all this. Corporations were self-financing – to this day few large ones rely significantly on the sale of equity capital to stockholders. Thus firms are mostly self-owning and do not risk stockholders' capital alone. No longer exclusive, share-owners' entitlement was only to 'some fixed share'. Stock ownership is so dispersed in pension and mutual funds that stockholders have 'little continuing interest in the enterprise'. Against Friedman at the time, Bell (1976: 294–5) asserted, 'it is politically and morally unthinkable that [employees'] lives should be at the mercy of a financial speculator'. Yet now they are.

Like Bell, economist Robin Marris in *Managerial Capitalism* (1998 [1964]) defended those former corporate purposes. Major sectors of economic activity in North America, Japan and Western Europe comprised corporations that grew internally and fostered general growth and stability (1998: xiii, xix). Marris rightly argues that corporations cannot revert to classic entities. The problem is defining them. Marris's important argument turns on who owns corporations. Shareholders' property is their shares. But shares are merely a bundle of rights to vote at annual general meetings, to buy and sell 'shares', and proportional rights to dividends or capital distribution. Shareholders are not the legal owners of a corporation's assets (1998: 10; 14–16).

Marris shows that the established 'managerial capitalism' of the 1960s was not subject to shareholder control, but rather to threats of takeover bids. Threats had often improved corporate performance even while directors retained discretion. The 1960s, however, saw the beginning of corporate raiders and mergers. The story is told by a London financier:

> **Lazar:** The excessive financialising of business life was started in this country by a man who ran a company called Sears and he introduced the hostile takeover bid to the UK . . . He took stakes in family companies in which everyone thought that the family still had a majority control, but in fact they didn't, because they'd sold down their shareholdings over the years . . . He went round taking control of these companies and he frightened them into giving him control, and as a consequence he put together a huge conglomerate. This was in the 1950s . . . Of course, with his success lots of people started imitating him. This led to the concentration of power in various sectors of the market in the hands of fewer and fewer men, and the building up of more and more conglomerates. It had all happened in America earlier, but by the 1970s British conglomerates like Hanson, BTR and Goldsmith had become large and aggressive enough to terrify the life out of American industrialists [and] . . . made several successful takeover bids of large companies, stalking people on both sides of the Atlantic. (4 June 2001)

Early raiders justified hostile takeover bids to a deeply suspicious public by alleging that takeovers would remedy shareholders' lack of trust in management. Although claiming to replace managements who do not maximise shareholder wealth by those who would, shareholders in acquiring firms usually lose. According to Marris, broader economic objectives vanished, so too potential independence from bank financing. Strategies of outsourcing, downsizing and share options for CEOs (Marris 1998: 19–20, 112–16, 170) are based on distrust about managerial discretion. Instead, straitjackets on management must be sought to make them act as trustees (agents) of shareholders alone. Distrust threatens to ruin trustees if they fail, however honestly. It works by imputing dishonesty, opportunism and greed onto management in order to foster trust in a supposedly predictable future. However, management, external directors and so on tend to live down to these imputations, unpredictably.

THE CONCEPT OF IMPERSONAL TRUST

How can we define the trust and distrust generated in this novel policy context of inadequate regulation of global investment firms? Trust by owners has become as important as in the days of personal owners, but in the name of shareholder value, today the form of trust is *impersonal*. Who are the owners? Corporations after the 1970s were treated to distrust strategies to restore trust – the fiduciary relation of 200 years. Yet this trust is hardly on the part of millions of shareholders, since they do not 'own' the firm. Corporate relationships are predominant – few sole individuals own corporations. Many argue that pension funds and institutional investors have gained increasing control over companies (e.g. Miller 2002: 166).

They use audits and management consultant firms as strategies to prove that the sole aim of a firm is to increase shareholder value. Aggressive mergers and leveraged buyouts (LBOs), as well as demands from pensions funds to lift share prices in a mere six months, have not improved corporate performance (Miller 2002: 168, 174). Cycles of corporate collapses have occurred each decade, but so too among the great old investment firms. Since instability is prevalent, attempts at control are also unstable, and only alike in being based on distrust.

The kind of distrust resembles the early distrust by owners towards managers, but now the relations are remote. The aim of each sector's control strategies is to reduce uncertainties and vulnerabilities. Since uncertainty cannot be overcome, distrust is deployed to generate trust. Among many theories about trust, the most relevant concept of 'impersonal trust' is developed by Susan Shapiro (1984, 1987) and Carol Heimer (1985, 2001). As we shall see, it is not a general trust in static senses of a moral good, or a trusting atmosphere. Rather, legal promises must be trusted, discounted or distrusted by others, the same with conjectured future profits. This kind of trust entails plans and schemes – a strategic concept at the inter-organisational level that is socially distant. These trust relations are about decisions because the illusion of certainty generated by trust provides a pseudo-rationality to decisions.

Strategic trust seems like an 'interest-based' account, but the basic nature of uncertainty means that interests cannot be known into the future. Interests change in unforeseen directions; unimagined vulnerabilities suddenly appear and firms may collapse from not foreseeing long-term interests. Trust is itself asymmetric as it takes time and strict rules to build a trustworthy reputation but an instant to shatter one, and it is nearly impossible to rebuild. Where debates on trust see interest-based trust as one of ascribing trustworthiness or its lack to other organisations, it is also a functional strategy aiming to ensure that promises are kept (Hardin 2001: 7). At heart, the function of trust is to control the future. But it is a vain hope, because the future is uncontrollable and the distrust, institutionalised in organisations so long ago, and revived in impersonal forms in recent times remains just as counter-productive as before.

Acts of entrusting or distrusting can be promises, contracts or inducements for the other to behave in the trusted manner. Exacerbated by the heightened impact of financial expectations on business life today, money as promise is always uncertain. So the impersonal trust, which is so often shattered after honest failures *or* intentional betrayals, raises all the contrary emotions further. In such environments, or, as Barbalet (2002: 146) puts it, in any system framed by competition, trust is an emotional means of control. Decisions to borrow for a future venture cannot be rationally made: the future is unknown, so trust is indispensable. Trust enables decision-makers to renounce any further information since it is all *past*, to assume a 'wary indifference' (Luhmann 1979: 22, 24) and to 'increase the tolerance of uncertainty'. Unlike blind faith, which needs no proof, argues Niklas Luhmann, the absence of contrary evidence is necessary for any trust, but trust extrapolates from or 'overdraws' previous, unreliable information (like an overdrawn bank cheque). Through sheer conviction, trust gives an emotional assurance of success or 'makes good' the complete deficiency of knowledge of the future. Trust is a 'springboard for the leap into uncertainty' (Luhmann 1979: 33). Economist Victoria Chick argues that speculators do not ignore uncertainty but act on their 'best guess, *as if* certain even though not' (1983: 211; her emphasis). Once contrary evidence arrives, trust is shattered. Mistrust, anger, public outrage and confusion are outcomes rarely noticed in the trust literature. Corporations make 'honest' mistakes from failed schemes or mistaken interests, and can destroy their carefully built reputations.

'Impersonal trust' is conceptually different from 'social capital' and general trust (Fukuyama 1995; Misztal 1996; Seligman 1997). In some accounts, trust is often just a 'good thing' and intrinsic to personal and symmetrical relations. The term is often used in the sense of a disposition to trust or lack of trust which has little orientation to the future. Dispositional and non-strategic trust is often loyalty or familiarity, irrelevant in the highly strategic, future-oriented financial world. Comparative work by Inglehart on whether highly democratised political cultures foster 'general trust' shows national variations (see Inglehart et al. 1998: 23), but strategic trust for 'control' is different from general trust, which is held in common, expecially among populations with genuinely democratic institutions. In contrast to these concepts, impersonal trust among corporate entities is about calculations and choices in the expectation of future gain: choices that can end in loss. Many accounts neglect to say that trust entails potential abuses such as exit, betrayal and defection according to Russell Hardin (2001: 5); even fewer consider that unintended failures of trust arise from fundamental uncertainty. Financial decisions involve both formal contractual trust *and* impersonal trust in claimed future profits, because it is difficult to distinguish between intended abuse and unintended, unimagined failures. Trust begins where past knowledge ends.

Other strategic accounts of trust accounts assume that the future is a manageable one of mere risk, which is calculable (e.g. Hardin 2001). They take their cue from orthodox economics, which see the future in terms of measurable risk distributions. With so little uncertainty, trust in the future is hardly necessary. This book's position is that there is no knowledge of the future, therefore trust strategies provide an illusion of control.

For orthodox economists, trust acts as a lubricant in the monetary and financial system – it can help oil things along. Oliver Williamson (1993), for example, sees trust as providing a vaguely beneficial cultural atmosphere for business relations, but not as a strategy for facing uncertainty; the future is a potentially knowable one of calculable risks. This is the prevailing but unsustainable orthodox view, as we will see. Few economists analyse trust (Smithin 1994; Perelman 1998), certainly not as an emotion, nor do they go beyond its vital role in markets. No market exchange – except in a spot market – is possible without trust due to inevitable delays between payment and delivery of goods or services.

Trust is different at primary and secondary levels (face-to-face, personal), and at indirect, impersonal and mediated levels. Many relationships, of course, do not involve trust. In a completely asymmetrical relation, expected social control over the weak party is so certain that the stronger party hardly needs trust. Trust is required in situations of choice, vulnerability and uncertainty about others' future behaviour. These generate trust problems (Heimer 2001: 54–9) because only with vulnerable interactions (winners and losers, rewards and costs) does uncertainty matter about unpredictable outsider intentions and actions. Trust, unlike confidence, arises from choice in acknowledged uncertainty (Hardin 2001: 5). Uncertainty of potential future losses is chosen in a decision to trust 'the future'. If it does result in loss instead of gain, blame falls on the decision-makers. Confidence is about qualities of perceived uncertainty and is a matter of lack of choice (Sztompka 1999), not an actively chosen vulnerability. If misfortune occurs, blame is cast elsewhere.

Corporations and government bureaucracies are the other side of an asymmetrical gulf from natural persons. 'Persons' are vulnerable in their relations to all corporate forms, where neither trust nor impersonal distrust is possible (Heimer 2001: 73) and where loyalty, faith or confidence, cynicism, fear or fatalism are more likely. Asymmetrical relations between the 'natural person' and organisations inspire theories of surveillance. No one disputes that the capacities of organisations far outweigh those of lone individuals, who must create other organisations such as a consumer association or a trade union for any defence. Consider the dreadful abuse meted out to a whistleblower or a subordinate merely voicing concerns. Moreover, the power balance and two-way communication channels *among* organisations is of another order, because symmetry is possible, and so too the forms of trust at this level are impersonal ones. These shade into secondary face-to-face relations wherever office-bearers meet, but only as representatives of the organisation that prescribes their duties of negotiating deals and presenting a credible face of the firm. Policies outweigh personal trust and friendships, after retirement, are organisationally irrelevant. In Shapiro's account (1987: 625), impersonal trust is a 'kind of social organisation' where 'principals' invest resources or property to another 'agent' to act on their behalf for uncertain future return. Guardians of trust simulate personal trust either through fiduciary norms or structural constraints on trustee roles that 'imitate contract', or through regulatory watchdogs that 'mimic personal social control' (1987: 636). Shapiro shows how impersonal trust mechanisms paradoxically create a spiral of trust problems between organisations.

Impersonal trust is the emotional serpent in the Eden of assumed rationality. In constant conditions of uncertainty, corporate 'rational choice' is about forced options, endless decisions about the unknown which are not possible without trust. The problem is more systemic today: corporations will not openly admit to uncertainty. For Shapiro, impersonal trust is 'truly the foundation of capitalism' (1984: 2). She is rightly concerned with crime where, in the arena of financial securities, trust is both intrinsic and 'a superb setting for larceny' because futures transactions provide 'ample time to expropriate or exploit the front money' – to manipulate trust, to 'commit fraud through misrepresentation' and to 'abuse insider fiduciary positions though misappropriation and self-dealing' (1984: 9).

Even so, in the highly future-oriented world of finance, inherent, 'radical' uncertainty is as important as intentional corporate crimes. There are many grey areas. Genuine mistakes are not negligence; intentional fraud is different from lack of caution and foolishness; lenders trust their loans will be paid back but perhaps the long-run failure to generate wealth was not 'intentional'. For Shapiro, a 'functional substitute for trust' can only be with strategies that remove agency, choice and uncertainty: 'All efforts to reduce uncertainty – whether through familiarity, reciprocity, threats of sanction, procedural rules, policing, compensatory side bets, or whatever – seek to induce trust. I do not consider personalized control to be all that different from the other measures' (Shapiro 1987: 636). Institutional mechanisms produce trust, Shapiro argues. They can also lose it, but without agency, choice and uncertainty, the vast financial sector of stock exchanges and financial firms could not exist.

EXPECTATIONS AND INTEREST: RATIONAL, EMOTIONAL OR BOTH?

Corporate emotions are not as divorced from orthodox analyses as they seem, but orthodoxy excludes *future-oriented* emotions, those most relevant to finance. Typically the social sciences keep rationality and emotions poles apart. Orthodox economics irrationally insists on knowable futures while imputing emotion categories (e.g. implicit greed, not fragile trust), categories they use to construct models of an allegedly predictable future.

Max Weber is prominent in insisting that modern calculation and means–end rational action drove out irrationality, displacing spontaneous emotions (Weber 1978: 28–9). In this instrumental action, the end is adjusted if costs or consequences appear too great. Rational action oriented to an ultimate value is also irrational from the perspective of means–end rationality, because the value is supreme and hence there is indifference about the costs of defending it. Contemporary emotion research does not see emotions as irrational but accepts that rational means–end action is highly cost-conscious and consistent, whereas rational value-oriented action is indifferent to costs. Both are highly predictable. The investor *will* count the costs and the captain *will* go down selflessly with the ship (but equally, the alcoholic *will* inevitably drink). Emotional action is, in this view, completely unpredictable and, like value action, indifferent, or more precisely, 'oblivious', to the costs (Flam 1990: 42–3). Such a view applies to emotions fuelled by the past, so that anger or hate are oblivious to consequences when directed to past shames and betrayals. But *the future is itself unpredictable*, and all future-oriented emotions are obsessed with imagining consequences and costs, whether successfully or otherwise. Trust and distrust are strategic but fraught; so too is early love.

Orthodox economic rationality is a means–end procedure which involves optimising or maximising expected benefits, whether utility or profits. Emotions are held to play no role in rational choice, because they introduce irrationality. Keynes did not introduce his dubious concept of 'animal spirits' because he considered emotions to be rational: most economists agree with Weber. Keynes's triumph was to introduce the future-orientation and problem of anticipations, whereas I argue that rationality about the unknown requires emotions. Interest, on the other hand, is a core orthodox concept, allegedly free of emotion (or values). It is based on assumptions that individuals are universally self-seeking and opportunistic. This self-interest is at the heart of theories of rational choice. Let us see.

INTEREST, A HYBRID OF AVARICE AND REASON

According to Jon Elster, a well-known proponent of rational choice, such choice involves three optimising operations (Elster 1999: 284). The first is choosing an optimal action, depending on one's 'desires and beliefs'; the second is optimising beliefs (expectations), depending on available information; and the third is spending only 'optimal resources' on acquiring information. Rationality fails either from 'indeterminacy' or irrationality, in other words, passions (1999: 285). Emotions subvert rational choice from a 'lack of regard for consequences – including the lack of regard for more information' or from social norms and values fostering shame, 'visceral anger' or guilt (1999: 287). But information, as we saw, cannot predict consequences, and shame is not necessarily 'irrational'.

Elster, however, says economists should not ignore emotions because they interfere with rational interested action, which is 'dispassionate'. Passions, he argues, undermine 'reason' and 'interest' (Elster 1999: 334–7, 355–6). Interest is a motive common to a social group 'that aims at improving the situation of [a subgroup] in some respect such as pleasure, wealth, fame, status, or power' (1999: 340). Such a formula is awkward and implausible. If his mildly framed 'improving' aim of interest were a 'relentless pursuit' of wealth or power, it would be remarkably like a passion.

Albert Hirschman's *The Passions and the Interests: Political Arguments for Capitalism before Its Triumph* (1997) shows how the meaning of passion for money – the traditional sin of avarice – gradually became 'innocuous' interest. Renaissance thinkers debated how passions could tame each other, and how greed eventually seemed more 'prudent' and reasonable than 'wild' passions for power and sex (Hirschman 1997: 31–5).

'Interest' as a hybrid of a passion (avarice) and reason (Hirschman 1997: 45–6) is a major imputation of revived orthodoxy. A cause of celebration in popular culture and above all in finance – 'Greed is Good' – it is studiously ignored in the social sciences. Orthodoxy is most culpable for redefining greed as rational self-interest. Greed is unseemly and reduces human motivation to one mean-spirited drive. A large literature insists that altruism is as much a major motive as avarice. 'Wets' in the economics profession defend altruism (value-oriented rational action) against passion-less, 'dry' self-interest. Economist Bob Rowthorn criticises neo-classical economists' 'jaundiced' view of interest, which implies opportunism, cheating and dishonesty. Interest is unconstrained by 'moral considerations' (1996: 20, 30). Selfishness is not humanity's sole motivation. Moreover, the greed behind imputations of economic interest ironically creates further uncertainty, greater distrust.

It is ironic because greed/interest is a conceptual relative of 'expectations': Hirschman adds a crucial comment, nearly an aside on Machiavelli's pessimistic diagnosis of the ruthless if brilliant Florence of his day. The Prince can safely assume that humans are invariably 'ungrateful, voluble, false, hypocritical, cowardly, greedy'. Hirschman remarks how useful this upgraded view of an 'interest-governed world' has been to economics. The use, he says, lies in the 'predictability and constancy' thought to reside in subsequent allegations that 'Interest Will Not Lie' (cited Hirschman 1997: 49).

EXPECTATIONS

Emotions are (allegedly) unpredictable, whereas rational means–end action driven by interest is predictable. This idea was a bedrock for 19th-century economists, whose predictive models are very attractive to entrepreneurs, bankers and investors seeking knowledge about future profitability. How convenient to use models for decision-making, and to forget that the imputation of interest might generate greed – an unpredictable emotion, as seen in CEO incentive structures like Enron's and so on. These models that impute greed and opportunism are at the heart of distrust strategies. But even in finance, where self-interested greed seems so obvious, amassing ever more is often driven by fear of the future: millions are needed to manage unpredictable losses. A more modest claim about interest is in simple survival – which shows plausible regularities or *relative predictability*. As an Australian Prime Minister, Ben Chifley, apparently once said, 'at least you know interest is trying'. Where politicians, as I said earlier, at least admit to complete lack of knowledge about electoral outcomes, orthodox models of rational choice are untroubled about the unknowable future.

Contemporary economics is deeply divided about uncertainty. G. L. S. Shackle, a postwar interpreter of Keynes, shows how classical economists banished future-time from their labour market models, by assuming hand-to-mouth economies. In a labour market of paupers, an expected, 'hoped for' price and the actual, recorded price seem alike. Whenever poverty and urgency require exchanges made at speed, the time-gap between 'hoped for' expectation and eventual result is drastically limited: market prices appear timeless. This is not scientifically predictable; it only describes those paupers or peasants who cannot afford to wait for a better price for their labour or goods, who usually draw on the convention of hitting on yesterday's price (Shackle 1972: 157).

Other theories attempted to predict the behaviour of firms and banks (booms and busts) but by the 20th century quite politically diverse positions, those of Keynes and Hayek, insisted on acknowledging uncertainty. Gunnar Myrdal was important for explaining the vast gulf between decisions made at any point in time and their future outcomes (Shackle 1967: 91–2). It may be difficult to gain adequate information about the past and present, especially when one is powerless (though many economists still struggle over 'information asymmetries'). But it is impossible to gain any information about the future.

Ignorance and uncertainty are magnified by the existence of money, Myrdal argued. Take discretionary income – choices, options. Those with sufficient money beyond immediate, urgent needs can put off decisions. They can toy with whether to invest extra money, whether to use it for consumer purchases, or to speculate, or lend it out at interest – a rainy day – or to stuff it under the bed. Myrdal's point about a decision that can be deferred is that it remains unknown to those deferring the decision, let alone anyone else. Money implies ignorance because these unknown non-decisions recur endlessly. Therefore everyone's ignorance of which preference might be taken, in turn creates an intense future-orientation. Profit calculations and investment decisions for Myrdal are simply 'something in a man's mind' (Shackle 1967: 110), a mere expectation.

Fundamental uncertainty about deferred decisions cannot give models about wealthy individuals, the millions in the 21st century with some discretionary income, or the behaviour of banks, corporations and treasuries. With a 'liquidity preference' as an option, expectations about the future must directly influence all prices (Shackle 1972: 226). These prices when 'revealed' in the financial markets, Keynes argued (1964: 151), govern most investment that keeps an economy in or out of a depression.

What influences the 'mere expectations' that govern a whole economy? Keynes suggested two main influences: convention and emotion. On conventions used by decision-makers to 'save our faces as rational economic men', he says:

(1) We assume that the present is a much more serviceable guide to the future than a candid examination of past experience would show it to have been hitherto. In other words we largely ignore the prospect of future changes about the prospect of which we know nothing.

(2) We assume that the *existing* state of opinion as expressed in prices and the character of existing output is based on a *correct* summing up of future prospects, so that we can accept it as such unless and until something new and relevant comes into the picture.

(3) Knowing that our own individual judgment is worthless, we endeavour to fall back on the judgment of the rest of the world which is perhaps better informed. That is, we endeavour to conform with the behavior of the majority or the average. The psychology of a society of individuals each of whom is endeavoring to copy the others leads to what we may strictly term a *conventional* judgment. (Keynes 1937: 214, his emphasis)

Any fluctuation in the value of assets is, as Shackle (1972: 223–5) puts it, 'the apex of a pyramid of guesses about guesses' about the majority's guesses. The 'majority' are those with more wealth or power. The convention is hard to define because few boundaries exist between 'today's opinion of what will be tomorrow's opinion, and the actual prevailing opinion which has anticipated tomorrow by being generally adopted today' (1972: 225).

Keynes said that 'animal spirits' or business confidence was the other influence on expectations. While admitting he was ignorant about what drove psychological moods like fluctuating 'animal spirits' of investors (Vickrey 1957: 377), this is partly because his individualism ignores organisational trust relations. Keynes imputes group characteristics and motivations to three 'strategic' economic groups of individuals (not organisations): investors, speculators and consumers. The investor is imputed an essential role in determining the rate of investment: investors' expectations are 'potent' but the future is uncertain. As Robert Lekachman puts it:

> In Keynes this uncertainty engenders a convention and explains an emotion. The convention is reliance on the rule that the future will resemble the present. The present is at least solid and this solidity induces an habitual adjustment which itself influences expectations. Uncertainty about the future also explains the grip which emotion in the form of waves of exaltation achieves over the business community, that pervasive optimism often unrelated to economic events which Keynes dubbed 'animal spirits'. It is well-known to the financial community as the 'state of business confidence'. Thus into the last home of rationality in economic affairs, Keynes introduced two interlopers, convention and emotion. (Lekachman 1957: 349)

Uncertainty – the unknown future – simply cannot be calculated or dealt with logically, so habits and emotions are essential. Jack Barbalet (1998: 85) argues that the convention that agents are only ever 'secure' about today's facts, which they build into expectations about the future, is paradoxical. Keynes is the major thinker to highlight the emotional anticipations that enable agents to act. What happens, according to Barbalet, is that decision-makers' emotions help them import 'a future' into the present (to inspire them to decide, to act). However, this is through a 'reverse projection, of the present into the future'. In formulating expectations then, a 'pseudo-rationality is created by projection' (Barbalet 1998: 86).

Expectations are formed through a convention and emotions; Shackle (1972) calls them conjectures built on imagination and hope. Rational choice theorists completely oppose these views, saying there is no necessary need for emotions in decision-making. Consulting 'gut feelings' may help, but it suspends rational choice. Elster (1999) takes neuroscientists to task, although they demonstrate that the human brain is unable to imagine any future or to choose, to act decisively, without the physical stimulation of anticipatory emotions (Damasio 1994: 50–8). In neuroscience, rational thought, like maths, is possible without emotions (in specific brain injury cases) but not imagination or creativity; therefore expectations (potential consequences, even 'risks') cannot be imagined without emotions. According to Paul Damasio (1994: 173–5), learned 'somatic markers' from prior emotional events – a personal 'history' – become habitual time-savers, like 'gut feelings' for Elster (1999: 287) yet that common term does no justice to the importance of somatic markers for expert, discretionary judgement (chapter 4). If a firm has barely survived a divisional debt-default, that somatic marker will be institutionalised throughout the organisation. Given fundamental uncertainty, making any choice about the future is impossible without emotions and imagination.

Orthodox economists do not accept fundamental uncertainty. Risk is calculable and 'indeterminacy' only means ignorance about whether the costs of gaining sufficient information exceed the benefits (Elster 1999: 289). Yet *today's* information cannot foretell anything about a later outcome. Elster admits that not every outcome of every possibility can be accounted for, but he has a facile solution: 'a rational person would know that under certain conditions it is better to follow a simple mechanical decision rule than to use more elaborate procedures with higher opportunity costs' (Elster 1999: 290–1).

He suggests tossing a coin or waiting for 'a little click in my mind' (1999: 296), because emotions are merely a 'functional equivalent . . . that reason, if left undisturbed, could have come up with by itself' (1999: 291). This assumes there is reliable information today about the future; it is just too costly and time-consuming to get it. If 'reason' waits, the future will indeed unfold, but reason per se neither acts nor knows the future. Elster's hunch is that successful stock market investors are those who deploy this click in their minds of 'vastly more complex mental calibrations, not because they consult their emotions' (1999: 296). But in face of the unknown, any decision must require an emotional preparedness to launch it. Thus one might hope, trust or even pray that the cool mechanical rule, the calibrations or mind-clicks will work out – in the future. Imaginative projections cannot reduce actual uncertainty: emotions can reduce the debilitating aspects of uncertainty.

UNCERTAINTY OR RISK?

Rational choice theorists do not allow for the unknown, only probabilistic risk. Although all economists use the term 'expectation' and institutional economics developed theories about debt obligations of firms and unfulfilled expectations, based on work of Veblen and Schumpeter (Spotton & Rowley 1998), other divisions quickly arose to counter these disturbing ideas about expectations. One, from the Keynesian revolution itself, was the idea that if researchers surveyed what people say they 'expect' they will do in the future, the results could be used for macroeconomic forecasts. This is a type of empiricism which investigates structures of expectations and attitudes, in the hope that this aggregated data can predict future behaviour – what people actually do eventually – at a macroeconomic level (Katona 1957: 361). Ironically these early Keynesian research programs failed to deal with time (Lekachman 1957: 343–51). They assumed fixed tastes and preferences and forgot the self-fulfilling and ultimately self-denying tendencies of their predictions. Attitudes are tenuously linked to behaviour. However, this has not stopped the forecasters, nor the policy changes which overturned cautious approaches to finance.

The neo-classical view in the 1970s aimed to demolish Keynes's whole idea that intangible emotions and shifting expectations governed economic decisions. In particular, it resurrected debunked ideas about the neutrality of money and also cast uncertainty in terms of risk. Here, expectations do not face uncertainty but a future world of measurable risks. Risks can be calculated with probability distributions which can describe future outcomes. Expectations are rationally formed through calculations and 'calibrations'. Beyond the semantic complexity of risk (see Chapter 6), a major problem is that risk has to comprise a set of known chances to be measurable – anything that is unmeasurable is a true uncertainty (Knight [1921] 1964: 231), as we will see.

Sliding from uncertainty to a less frightening risk gave birth to a theory called 'rational expectations'. All actors have so much information, so rapidly available, that they can calculate 'future probability functions'. There are no 'crucial' eco-nomic decisions where rational expectation theories would be unable to draw inferences about how 'behaviour would have differed' (Lucas & Sargent, cited Davidson 1990: 69). Actors can incorporate possible changes in expectations into their models. Paul Davidson calls this the 'robot' model of extrapolation from the past, because choice, agency, deferred unknowable decisions – hallmarks of free markets – are ruled out. Inconsistencies did not halt the influence of neo-classical policy triumphs even after their view of money being neutral in both the long-run *and* the short-run (e.g. Lucas above) was confounded by events.

An apparently less determinist approach, called the 'efficient market hypothesis' (EMH) did accept that markets are unpredictable, but only in the sense that markets are unbeatable. It moved debate resolutely into financial markets (ignoring insti-tutionalists' debate on corporate expectations and uncertainty). The 1980s version had armies of traders and investors searching for mispriced securities, futures or currencies the whole time. They arbitrage away the gaps between values and prices (Haugen 1997: 642). The EMH assumes that traders incorporate into prices all the information of what each thinks the fundamental value of the currency or stock will be worth (say in later dividends). As information is so widely available, whenever new (unpredictable) information becomes known, prices can change (Ormerod 1998: 15). Markets are efficient in two senses here: first that prices instantly reflect all or most of the relevant information for future prospects, as adduced by the 'wisdom' of millions of independent investors. Second, they are unpredictable, since no one can beat the market (without illegal inside information). The advice accordingly is that investors should follow the market and not bother listening to stock market analysts (Haugen 1997: 642).

Cracks in the theory appeared in the early 1980s when currency traders argued that the dollar was over-valued. It became a hot story in the financial press, yet those same dealers, so concerned about the high value of the dollar that they talked about it for two years, continued to buy until it crashed in 1985 (Ormerod 1998: 14). Why had they not incorporated their information two years before? Many could demonstrate also that fluctuations in prices vary far more than corporate earnings (e.g. Shiller 1989), in reality a problem of the quality of traders' judgements. A simplistic version (markets *were* 'efficient' as in 'accurate') held sway in the 1990s. So much for the idea that new information will rapidly reflect changes in fundamental value. Keynes took a dim view of the quality of investors' judgements. Moreover, investment banks are frequently under competitive pressures and exposure from debts (therefore traders cannot easily sell even though they know they *should*), which rarely appears in orthodox accounts (Spotton & Rowley 1998: 676).

EMOTIONS AND PROBABILITY

Criticisms even within orthodoxy about how the market did not seem to be so 'rational' (after the 1987 crash) saw developments in chaos theory and the use of mathematical models of ant behaviour to stress economic unpredictability (e.g. Kirman 1993). Economists who stuck to a future of measurable risks until the

2000 crash tended afterwards to welcome cognitive psychologists – even with their evidence about emotions. But despite recent Nobel Prizes, there is a catch. These psychologists argue that rational choice is deficient only because most people tend to be bad at working out probability distributions (Rabin 1998) and they make 'systematic errors': this argument lies behind Greenspan's 'irrational exuberance' thesis (though not until 2003 did the Fed quote behaviourists: 'Fed finds the sweeties' 2003). Even more 'radically', according to one, 'we don't always accurately predict our own future preferences' (Rabin 1998: 12). This hardly seems radical when, for Myrdal long ago, we may choose to defer a decision because we don't know our future preferences, and we intend leaving them unpredictable. Here lies the unmeasurable and unknowable – an horizon way beyond knowable risks. Daniel Kahneman won a Nobel Prize in October 2002 for his work with the late Amos Tversky on how human errors are mainly due to an 'overconfidence' arising from lack of knowledge of how probability works. People mistakenly believe they will win at the next dice throw. Some studies show that esteemed experts are more likely than lay people to be 'susceptible to overconfidence', more so with 'rich models of the system' like an 'economy' or 'stock market' (Rabin 1998: 32).

Cognitive psychological debates about probability are, unfortunately, best applied to gambling (if not perfectly suited to it), not financial decisions. However much prudent investment so easily becomes speculation and thus appears to be a gamble, it is less 'certain' or 'beatable' than a flutter at the races. Shackle's distinction is important; it makes unpretentious sense. Unlike gambling, 'subjective' probabilities, which are the 'risks' of investment decisions, involve imagining a number of rival or quite incompatible hypotheses about the future. In a race, only one horse can win, or two might tie after a gallop around a set circle. Leaving aside that no one can imagine every future and contradictory possibility in economic life (limitless, unknown): an exhaustive search would condemn decision-makers 'to dip endlessly into a bottomless bran-tub' (Shackle 1972: 22). As well, mutually exclusive hypotheses cannot be averaged or weighed, despite the temptation to call 'weights' probabilities. If quite opposite hypotheses are as likely, it is ludicrous to argue that one vista is half or a quarter as likely to happen as others. Shackle suggests decisions are personal judgements based on conjectures (1972: 22).

Statistical or 'objective' probabilities do apply to gambling, because these measure an invariant, existing system with set rules, such as betting with two dice on a table. Unless the dice are loaded (the horse drugged), or the table suspiciously wobbly, a probability distribution can 'predict' the odds, as the chances are known. These statistical probabilities constitute knowledge, whereas with uncertainty, only imagination can conjure up futures (Shackle 1972: 17–22). In the financial world nothing is invariant, predictable, even when situations appear stable because all those promises can easily unravel by fair means or foul. By definition, the future does not exist. The 'moderately uncertain' weather (Keynes 1937: 214) does not 'heed' the forecasters, quite unlike human reflexivity. Decision-making can intentionally change in response to those forecasts, and therefore falsify or trick them (Mieg 2001).

Extrapolating from gambling to business decisions and the share trading that flows from those decisions is a faulty move because the emotions involved are not comparable. It is also patronising to small shareholders who, others freely admit, are bound to be risk-averse if they have little wealth (Kirman 1993: 152). Cognitive psychologists say people are averse to losses, and cannot walk away from the gambling table or the poker machine to cut their losses. However, psychologists argue that people's observed tendency to keep sunk investment costs is similarly 'irrational', as the failed shares should be sold. In gambling odds, 'the past is irrelevant' and the future is your only source of assessing a better prospect ('All too human' 2002; Gittins 2002). This psychology literature positions small investors as error-prone in failing to be perpetual gamblers. The imputation attempts to 'blame' day traders for the recent speculative bubble. It tells them to face a prospect of forever searching the unknowable future as they are mistaken in keeping the dud stocks (using the scrip as wallpaper and getting on with life).

Robert Shiller's *Market Volatility* (1989) and *Irrational Exuberance* (2000) are based on large samples of institutional and individual investors. His surveys show that emotions, even down to physical symptoms like 'sweaty palms, tightness of chest, irritability, or rapid pulse' (1989: 388) play a large role in finance decisions. He assumes that emotions are generated mainly by herd behaviour among 'diffusion' investors – his term for those who are allegedly swayed by emotive influence from the finance media (Shiller 2000: 228–32). 'Smart' investors in the financial heartland are apparently independent of influence.

Failures of the human mind to calculate probability, people's fear of losses, their comfort in herds and their limited capacity to store and process information are not wrong – they are merely inapplicable to financial decisions. Even ideas about how decision-makers make do through 'bounded rationality' or incomplete contracts (Williamson 1991b) imply that information about the future could be possible.

Indeed, what is remarkable in debates about risk is the extent to which this socially conditioned knowledge has enabled so many to reduce their perception of uncertainty by holding to economic theories that do in fact neglect it, as David Dequech rightly suggests (2000: 4). Humans are never independent of influences either: we are constituted by social relations.

Less orthodox economists, such as institutionalists, retain the Keynesian 'large world' of fundamental uncertainty (Dymski 1996: 378), which cannot be dealt with by probability distributions of risk. For others decision-makers mainly oscillate between 'haven't a clue' inactivity or follow 'animal spirits' in a 'damn the torpedoes, full speed ahead' approach, therefore making what Davidson calls 'inconsistent choices' (1991: 130, 1996: 61). Many explanations for stock market volatility (such as De Bondt & Thaler 1985) use behaviourist models of winners and losers, or divide 'value' traders seeking 'fundamental' worth of companies, from 'chartists' or technical analysts following the past movements of prices (Ormerod 1998: 18). Switching from one to another hardly explains why expectations are 'subject to sudden and violent change' (Keynes 1937: 214), as we will see.

In all these years of economic theorising, many have regressed from where Keynes left the issue – at the phenomenon of herding, where individuals are swayed by emotions and conventions. Indeed, Bagehot's description of Lombard Street in the 1870s notably introduced *trust and suspicion* – specific emotions, both rational and irrational, considering his insistence on financial regulation. On the London stock exchange, 'good times' engender frauds and dubious schemes for new companies, followed by collapse when 'the whole structure is delicate' (Bagehot 1962: 78).

> All people are most credulous when they are most happy; and when much money has just been made . . . there is a happy opportunity for ingenious mendacity. Almost everything will be believed for a little while . . . But the harm they have done diffuses harm, for it weakens credit still further.

> Credit – the disposition of one man to trust another – is singularly varying . . . After a great calamity, everybody is suspicious of everybody; as soon as that calamity is forgotten, everybody again confides in everybody. (1962: 64)

As credit weakens – Bagehot was, even then, more concerned about organisations – more harm builds up, in a distressingly familiar manner. Individuals play minor roles in the credit structure of interconnected banks. Similarly, Max Weber argued in 1896 that banks influenced prices far more than individual actors. In futures trading, 'the great host of small speculators, equipped with little more than a good pair of lungs, a notebook and a pencil . . . have no choice but to follow the watchword given "from on high" – in other words, by the big banks.' Weber explains that 'dear bidding' by the banks leaves small speculators no option but 'blind speculative buying'. Even though they all know it will end 'sooner or later', no one knows *when* and everyone hopes 'the losses will hit someone else' first (1978: 375). Weber mentions the game of Black Peter, Keynes, musical chairs: Bagehot simply sees trust and gullibility. But firms and banks dominate.

The rational choice model is so abstract it cannot theorise even the least contentious aspects of organisations or of persons. It assumes relentlessly short-term aims of both, and these *may* seem slightly predictable, sometimes. Predictable aims are one thing, uncertainty of achieving them utterly different. Firms face difficult decisions between short and long-term profits, growth or profit, profit or safety (Stretton 2000: 371) – a balance or 'minimax' to every decision. But these often backfire. Interminable conflicts over profits can undermine the aims of long-term growth, different again from struggles for corporate survival in a competitive capitalist economy. These are all mere hopes. None is analogous to everyday individual economic behaviour. Only under extreme situations – a civil war, an earthquake – is sheer personal survival at that brutal level. Although slippages between organisations as actors and human persons as actors are common, the two are not comparable.

Even a small business, say a little bakery firm, is not motivated by an individual baker's human 'self-love', which conventional economists incorrectly impute to the capitalist enterprise (Korczynski 1996: 16). Enterprises do not *feel* any self-love, but engage in competitive struggles far more brutal and planned than the struggles an individual might have in personal life – sellers against sellers and buyers against buyers. Corporate campaigns are waged in interest conflicts between sellers and buyers to buy cheap and sell dear: many lose, in a climate of bitterness (lawsuits) or disappointment (redundancy). None of this can be reduced to a simple formula of orthodox accounts – such as firms acting opportunistically 'with guile' (Williamson 1991b). Economic liberals like Weber were brutally frank about 19th-century competitive struggles in the financial markets over the value of money: not between individuals, but among industrial firms and banks to secure 'the means to power' (Weber 2000: 369). Weber showed regulatory financial organisations like central banks, government treasuries and private monopolies (Weber 1978: 82–3) trying to defend themselves against global and 'selfish interests of the large banks' (Weber 1976: 375). These creditors engaged in struggles against debtors (entrepreneurs and governments), just as today.

Money was never neutral. Yet Weber argued that rationality displaced emotions because he saw interest conflicts as predictable. Calculations in money terms were based on outcomes of creditor–debtor struggles – one tending to the fragility of inflation, the other potential horrors of deflation (Ingham 2004: 201–4). But long-term and short-term interests prevail at unpredictable times, deferred decisions are unknowable and therefore calculations are based on a pseudo-rationality of projections of trust and distrust. Competition itself stimulates 'thrills and dangers', an imposed *esprit de corps*, while emotions of trust and distrust render uncertainty 'actionable'. Through contracts, businesses form cooperative relationships, but interminably monitor and dissolve them in lawsuits once a trusted reputation vanishes. Humans suffer enormously – if irreparably financially and emotionally – after one analogous face-to-face battle (ask a whistleblower).

The intolerable nature of uncertainty for profit-seeking organisations is a key point for economist Hyman Minsky. His instability hypothesis explores how instability emerges paradoxically from stability (1985: 37–50). In stable times, business units gradually become more confident about taking on higher levels of acceptable debts. They may take increasingly speculative positions until reaching a Ponzi stage of a spiral of debts to pay debts.

How does all this occur? Firms, bureaucracies and banks have extraordinary intelligence-gathering capacities, far beyond persons. Yet they make mistakes, face uncertainties, formulate expectations, make decisions and act. Corporations are of course made up of groups of individuals, but they are all positioned by the structure, policies and ritual procedures of the organisation. Individuals only play a part in writing the corporate book in which they are written (to paraphrase Pascal). Although non-thinking and un-feeling, firms are rational and emotional, and sometimes ethical. Organisations require and elicit specific rational and emotional action from office-bearers and subdivisions of staff, and require standards of ethical behaviour – too often, misguidedly low. Too often, policies impute mean-spirited opportunism in distrust strategies which easily backfire (Pixley 2002a & b). What this all means is that instead of starting from a micro level of individuals and jumping to inscrutable macro levels and models, the framework here explores how the middle or 'meso' level of organisations copes with this contemporary environment.

EVIDENCE FROM THE EXPERTS

My task is to explore the kinds of confidence, trust and suspicion between business units and banks that fuels overconfidence and turns into its opposite. Decisions draw on past data and probability models to minimise uncertainty. But knowledge is of the past, no matter its quantity. The 'information society' concept is already passé – but not its attendant, foolish hope. We have seen how expectations are two-way projections of imagination and hope, a pseudo-rationality of expectations which attempt, as Negri put it, to unite the present and the future (1988: 24). While nothing can guarantee any certainty of future events whatsoever, it seems that corporations act on the expectation or rather the trust and hope of 'certainty of the convention' – that later profits will meet their previous expectations ('validate' is Minsky's term). Where governments used to guarantee the convention with Keynesian demand management, corporations today are enmeshed with financial firms and institutional trust agencies: control may seem beyond emotions. Yet central banks are in a prominent trust role. It is, in my view, at impersonal and increasingly inter-organisational levels that the emotions of mere expectations are entrenched and global government agencies attempt to guarantee financial expectations.

In developing this framework about the social origins of expectations in impersonal trust, I turned to ask experts in the field. Such neglected issues could only be explored with those experienced in high-level finance decision-making, yet sceptical about the contemporary financial heartland. Quantitative survey methods (such as Robert Shiller's) demonstrate that investors do report actual physical symptoms of their emotional states (see Shiller 1989: 389–92). Interviews move beyond that because they cast light on the collective nature of decision-making and how outcomes of decisions in turn affect organisations.

Interviews explored direct questions (Dexter 1970; Smart & Higley 1977) about the ambiguities of trust: How would they compare personal types of trust (old school tie) with impersonal trust? What were typical procedures in reaching a decision? How is data used (Chapter 6)? Two diagrams were considered (Figures 4.1 and 4.2 in Chapter 4), one showing post-Keynesian assumptions about expectations and confidence under uncertainty (Dequech 1999), the other drawn up from my sociological research on emotions and Keynesian views. Trust may imperceptibly lead to excessive trust or negligence, yet decisions are unavoidable. Interviews explore whether finance decisions are possible without trust, and how reputation and credibility are understood. Each sector's assessment of other financial institutions' trustworthiness and reputation was canvassed, sometimes policy implications as well.

My evidence is comparative, cross-country and cross-sector, not a representative sample of populations of investors. Shiller's quantitative survey material (1989) showed that 'gut feeling' is predominant in American stock market decision-making among 'smart' institutional investors (his evidence differs from his conclusions, in my reading). I compared practitioners and commentators, from public institutions, mainly central banks (Washington DC, London and Canberra) and private banks (Wall Street, the City of London, Zürich and Sydney), with historically changing aims, relationships and procedures of public and private organisations. I interviewed forty-two people including finance journalists in these major financial centres and many other experts with indirect associations.

My selection of 'informed sceptics' was based on quality and expertise and not on mere habituation to the worlds of boardrooms and central banks. Many were highly critical if not worried, even when so accustomed to the finance sector's self-proclaimed logic. Some took the Weberian view that emotions are irrational, embarrassing and lead to dysfunctional effects (Gabriel 1998: 309). Those who accepted emotions came from both public and private and with academic and non-academic expertise of senior practitioners. The main division (only among those I interviewed, of course) was national, because Americans and Swiss were more expansive about emotions than British or Australian.

Moving on to Chapter 3, we start by exploring the public's primary impersonal trust agency to the world of money – the financial media. In interviews with journalists and editors, questions focused on the institutional trust role of the media and their views of finance organisations.

3

The Financial Media as Institutional Trust Agencies

Whenever FINANCIAL NEWS turns bleak, investment banks and treasuries issue responses and politicians make pronouncements. The content depends on what kinds of political and economic conflicts are going on, but the message is the same. Politicians either blame their opposition's failures or attempt to deny bad news by citing evidence of 'sound' fundamentals elsewhere in the economy. Occasionally, new incumbents to office may highlight grimness – like President Bush in early 2001, whose negative statements were criticised for creating self-fulfilling prophecies. These edicts show that impressions and the emotions they generate are recognised as having considerable force in finance. Most political and economic leaders urge pundits to 'talk up' the economy. Their oldest and most common refrain is to attack the media: if only the press focused on economic strengths, confidence would be restored. 'Don't let me hear you not singing' was a headline after the Menzies government blamed the Fairfax press for Australia's 1961 recession. Scapegoating is perennial, V. J. Carroll emphasised (18 January 2001). So much for orthodox economists' concepts of 'perfect information' and transparency in free markets. More seriously, the vital role of journalists in informing different publics about our social promises – institutionalised in money – rarely sees the light of day.

Attempts at press censorship also occur during times of financial optimism, but less overtly, since *any* acknowledgement of emotion is too dangerous – 'talking down' a boom will often be blamed for causing a crash. Here the criticism is the opposite, but still, it is the media alone that are deemed to be emotional. Robert Shiller made the charge, just before the Nasdaq (dot.com) inflation declined in early 2000, that the financial media played a significant role in talking up what he called an 'irrational exuberance' into a 'speculative bubble'. In the same vein, his own book could be held responsible for the bubble's later collapse, if that is how emotions in finance do operate. But Shiller is of course no Dr Greenspan, the size of whose briefcase, let alone the inflection in his every pronouncement, was treated as an omen back then. Greenspan only used the term 'irrational exuberance' once, in 1996, creating temporary panic among traders and gaining disfavour from Washington DC politicians (Hartcher 2003). Thereafter, for the duration of the

43

asset inflation he tended to defend the idea of the 'new economy'. By and large, journalists merely followed, or trusted 'Dr G'. There is a hierarchy in the credibility and impact of these statements.

This chapter discusses the role of the financial media. The argument does not turn on whether or not the news media, or more so 'the News' (Keynes's term for all financial information) are to blame for volatility. Rather, the concern is with the financial media's institutional trust role of providing full, fair and accurate financial information to the public, their organisational capacity to fulfil this role, and journalists' tangential position outside the chain of financial organisations. To explore these questions, I draw on my interviews with finance journalists. We discussed their constraints, the role of media ownership, and their main sources for providing trustworthy information to the share-owning or speculative public (institutional and individual) and for giving fair assessments to broader publics: pension fund holders, workers, unemployed populations. Did journalists create the Nasdaq boom, as some argue? Finance news relies on diverse powerful sources, from central banks and government treasuries to publicly listed corporations and their auditors, legal assessors, raters, purveyors of financial assets and PR. The information created daily is voluminous, possibly overwhelming for providing fair and independent, or crucial commentary.

'IN TRUST' TO WHICH PUBLICS?

Depicting the finance media as institutional trust agencies is essential for developing my main argument on the emotional underpinning of financial decision-making. Starting from Keynes's observations about how 'the concealed factors of utter doubt, precariousness, hope and fear' are too often hidden by hypotheses of 'a calculable future' (1937: 222), I argue that all financial decisions face uncertainty – an intolerable situation were it not for the anticipatory emotions of trust, confidence, optimism, and their opposites of distrust and pessimism. These emotions play an important but little understood role in the collective generation of expectations. Without emotions, future possibilities cannot be envisaged, even calculated (see Chapter 2). Emotions easily oscillate from optimism to fear and constant charges about who is to blame. In attributing blame about which organisation can be trusted or no longer trusted, journalists face multiple audiences and rely on numerous sources, from financial organisations in the core, to semi-peripheral and peripheral ones.

What is the position of finance news agencies? Media corporations are not financial 'actors' since they are driven by a different logic from banks, accountancy firms and credit-rating agencies. Even so, media corporations are often owned by, or themselves own, finance and business concerns. While finance news is essential to the financial world, media corporate profits depend on advertisers, ratings and specific audiences, in that order. Journalists depend on finance organisations for their sources, but are in trust–distrust relationships with all financial sectors and populations.

And this is contentious, because whenever the finance media treat finance actors as an aggregate of equals, their trust role with various audiences is already compromised. The most organised *core* segments of finance (Baker 1987) try to maintain the power to define what is money. In contrast, populations of small rentiers are patronised as 'mum and dad' shareholders. These least organised, most peripheral asset-holding populations cannot define money at all, often having precarious opportunities to make money with their life savings.

The consequence of finance journalists' reporting responsibilities is that their audience is no longer the finance sector and a small wealthy elite. Today's finance news agencies are in trust relationships with widely varying audiences. Some of these trust roles are mutually contradictory. Not only has the audience for finance news grown considerably, but so have the potential dangers. High levels of household debt in English-speaking countries go with higher share-owning (half the adult population in the USA, Canada and Australia directly own shares) and heavy involvement in pension funds and property speculation. How the finance media deal with these differences in influence and powerlessness is a crucial question, as is the phenomenal growth in data collection which financial journalists must report.

While I draw on specialist news media literature, my focus is the institutional trust role. Asking the experts – self-styled sceptical journalists – about the potential for professional journalism is a way to explore whether the financial press can be effective in its reporting responsibilities, which involve such different audiences. National variations in journalists' independence and sources of news, as well as reasons for growth in specifically financial PR firms, are set against Shiller's counter-argument in *Irrational Exuberance* (2000) on the major role he ascribes to the finance media in influencing the Nasdaq boom. He is a prime example of the blame-laying approach in the financial arena. His criticisms of the press are clichés about media rhetoric and 'emotionalism'. This contrasts to the ways that sceptical finance journalists see their roles. The contrast enables me to show that the impersonal trust roles of the press are primarily economic relationships – not a temporary intrusion of the irrational into them, as argued by orthodoxy. Keynes, as we will see later, was far more perceptive on the role of 'the News' in speculation.

PROFESSIONAL SCEPTICS IN THE FINANCE PRESS

Between 2000 and 2002 I interviewed experienced practitioners of professional journalism from relatively independent news agencies in the UK, USA and Australia. Television journalists are only excluded because the USA has only one underfunded public television broadcaster (PBS) with highly respected standards of news reporting, so fairness dictated talking only to professional print journalists. Independence for journalists means that corporate conflict of interest and related managerial interference in what professional journalists may write (say, about a company owned by their firm) are limited. Generally, institutional defences of 'fourth estate' independence for professional journalism are not strong when fourth estate and/or democratic ideals of free speech must contend with media corporations that often treat news reporting as just another business. In the case of newspapers, media specialists propose a range of remedies such as a revised code of ethics and/or the incorporation of editorial autonomy into company articles (Jones 2000: 245). Further remedies emerge from my evidence.

The interviews compare independence with typical pressures. All are doubters of various kinds, rather than merely 'bearish' during a bull market. Even in 2000, before the major corporate and finance scandals became public knowledge, most were brutally frank: in most sectors of finance there are lies, cheats, spin doctors and 'quiet corruption'. If journalists are vulnerable to such sources (Tiffen 1989: 197), is it possible for finance news agencies to fulfil their trust role to the public? These informed sceptics expressed concern about the media's roles.

On the question of trust, they are mainly concerned about professional standards in bringing questionable practices and dubious claims to public light, and providing contextual analysis to inform citizens. For a British journalist on *The Economist*, professional, expert explanation is one key role:

Ingham: In the case of markets, explanation is one of the biggest tasks a journalist can perform because very few people understand what markets do . . . and the relationship, if you like, between the individual behaviour of market participants and the cumulative impact of that . . . You look at the financial market and it's peopled largely by men and women under the age of 40, often under the age of 30, and I think that's increasingly true of that area of journalism. You get very few people now who have been through a recession. (15 March 2002)

The ideals of professional journalism are expressed in terms of fiduciary duties to the public, by a finance journalist on the general magazine *Time*:

Kadlec: A journalist's role is not to say what's popular . . . If we're talking up the market because the market's going up, then we're failing in our duty. Throughout the internet boom I think that there was some healthy scepticism. I know that I personally was sceptical . . . There were columnists in *New York Times* and in *Newsweek* who were sceptical. *Barrons* are almost sceptical to a fault. They have decided that they are going to be the voice of sour thinking . . . that's the role they've adopted, and it's not a bad role. (26 February 2002)

A daily newspaper, *The Guardian*, accentuates a very similar account. For the financial editor, Larry Elliott:

Elliott: The press asks the questions that the general public want to have asked, which should be the role of the journalist. We act as an agent of the public and hold up corporations or public institutions to account. We have the access that members of the public don't have, so as a result . . . we are expected to ask searching questions and not just accept whatever they tell us. That . . . [is] the theoretical ideal, although the press doesn't always live up to that, you know, in practice. (5 October 2000)

These ideals of trust are not always met. Although the media are blamed for a bull market, the logic of journalists' news values would suggest that uncovering a scandal is highly newsworthy. Yet sceptics all stressed how their critical commentary is barely heard during a bull market when the agenda – or 'the issue' – overwhelms these news values, and standards generally. It undermines accuracy and, in worst cases, plain honesty. Can this responsibility rest only with reporters?

Starting with honesty, during 2000, two London journalists were fired and some of the aces covering Wall Street were caught for accepting payments for rigging the market. In Sydney, serious payments were paid by Australia's 'big four' commercial banks to two leading radio talkback hosts, to temper their listener-led criticisms of bank policies. But none of this is at all new, as a former editor of the *Australian Financial Review* said:

Carroll: In the 1870s, the *Financial Times* finance editor was accepting money from the promoters of Dunlop, and shares, and pushing the shares. It was the done thing. It only came out in bankruptcy proceedings. (18 January 2001)

Aside from plain ethical standards (also among the bribers), the prevailing issue agenda can easily pre-empt values of newsworthiness. Rodney Tiffen links the prevalence of an issue to an ideological inconstancy in the news media (1989: 196). Switching sides is only tangentially related to journalists' usual or routine conservatism, because of professional news values. In Tiffen's view, the news is normally ideologically conservative because the newsworthy are the influential figures, whether bank CEOs, neo-classical economists or investment analysts. However, journalists must compete for fresh unexpected stories. If scandals are uncovered, the prevailing news-frame can suddenly shift, whereupon many more journalists will uphold professional notions of watchdog and adversarial roles and question received wisdom (1989: 196). In the normal course of things it is difficult to maintain consistent professionalism in the face of this ideological inconstancy, if not promiscuity.

Interviews compared reporting standards, often those of sports reporting with finance news, which are a more relevant and professional analogy than may appear at first sight. These journalists had written sceptically when the bull market was raging. They appear to express a sense of existential isolation. For those reporting Wall Street in 2000 even as the bull market declined, nothing could alter the prevailing news-frame, no matter their high standards of reporting.

Hale: We're not really so much [expressing] words of caution, I wouldn't say wisdom. It's more like we're *standing there* and we're watching the game. And we're saying, but no that team's not winning when everyone else is saying they're winning and I see that team has scored four goals and that team hasn't scored any when that isn't true . . . The reason people say we've got a perspective, and say that we're cautious is because we're not going with this huge flow; it's that we're not being just shills for the system. (13 September 2000)

Hale refers to 'shills', confidence trickster's apprentices. For Anya Schiffrin, with seven years' experience on *Dow Jones* (the subscription 'wire' service for the banks and trading houses), the experience is similar. She seems like a distant spectator of a game of cynical trust:

Schiffrin: The way I feel is that it doesn't matter what the reality is, it's all based on what other people think anyway. So when I used to cover the foreign exchange market, there were very predictable reactions [forex traders' comments are invariably reported]. If there is some problem in Europe, everybody would buy the Swiss franc and everybody always had pat rationalisations, even though they made no sense . . . The whole point was that everybody knew that the market would work in a certain way, and it's interesting how people are so *cynical* about it . . . [However,] it seems just more like a game to them and everybody plays along, and it doesn't matter what the reality is, as long as everybody follows the rules. So in that sense trust is important, but if someone said 'Hang on, this is ridiculous' . . . that would be breaking a rule in a way. (19 September 2000)

Journalists can rarely dispute this game; few have financial expertise. At the height of a boom, reputable newspapers seem to have difficulties in hiring expert financial journalists. Alan Abelson, former editor of *Barrons*, suggests a number of reasons:

Abelson: Even with the expansion of the economy and the markets, it's hard to find people. Journalists are not interested in the economy and finance. They'd much rather do something grander – politics, let's say, drama criticism, foreign-country reporting. Financial journalism seems like pretty grungy kind of work, and it is in some ways. I mean, looking at balance sheets and income statements. It's kind of like the salt mines of journalism. It's hard to get people to begin with. The second thing is that people who are really interested in this stuff – I mean, think of it – why should they, at best, make $50 000 or $60 000 or $100 000 when they can make millions? (21 September 2000)

Journalists with financial expertise, perhaps impressed by status symbols, interview major players on fabulous salaries. There are plenty of openings during a boom, and unless they were sceptical – even 'impelled' by professional journalist ideals – they are unlikely to stay in journalism. The same in Sydney:

Carroll: Towards the top of the boom, journalists get lured away by the temptations of the big rewards to be had from going into merchant banking . . . So, a decline in reporting standards occurs inevitably. I remember in the late 1960s during the nickel boom, the *Financial Review* was heavily criticised because it tried to be sceptical of all the claims . . . And we were criticised for 'missing the boom'. That itself showed the state of mind of the critics; they didn't see that it was our role to be sceptical in the boom. Fortunately, the Australian Stock Exchange had a sceptical chairman, Jim Cooper, who tried to bring some element of commonsense and sanity to the market, but it's hard when the hysteria takes over, as it has in our market now with cyber stocks, for what, six years? (18 January 2001)

Thus far, the evidence does not support the idea the profession creates the issue. They mention leadership elsewhere in the financial world – private and government – with far greater influence in creating the issue and fostering a specific emotional climate. Media corporation policies also have a significant role.

MEDIA CORPORATIONS ARE THE EMPLOYERS

Criticised by Right and Left for having 'power without responsibility' (see Curran & Seaton 1997), many media firms these days are diversified conglomerates. Here I compare the professional independence that the big conglomerates may give to journalists with the explicit and implicit aims of the business of news. Media outlets are segmented towards various publics – to the finance elite themselves (*Financial Times* and *Wall Street Journal*), to 'educated publics', class segments, and age or status groups. Commercial media use many techniques for attracting audiences – generally not the largest but those with the greatest amount of money for spending on consumer goods (Burns 1977: 66). Although audiences rise in booms, financial newspapers now have consumer and lifestyle supplements to broaden circulation for attracting advertising revenue: status envy, greed, laziness and hopes for security are emotional appeals to reap gains from the 'wealth effect'. None of this is connected to professional journalism or public trust, but to news as just another business.

Finance news agencies are politically conservative (mostly) and politically powerful. Their profitability is about market share. Many news corporations have a patchy record for fostering professional journalist ideals of free speech or acceding to journalists' demands about their public responsibilities to inform citizens (Curran & Seaton 1997). In a boom, corporate standards of trustworthiness, reliability and 'sanity' tend to slip – everywhere. Headlines are dramatically emotional, and can be dramatically incorrect. The front page of *Esquire* of October 1998 asked, 'What Did You Do After the Crash, Daddy?' – an ugly broken china head was the accompanying picture – suggesting fear and insecurity. But 1998 turned out to be a financial hiccup. So what is the role of media corporations in the finance world?

The Enron-type scandals of 2002 had been corporate secrets, so any press story would previously have been libellous. These scandals, therefore, could hardly be attributed to the financial media's direct actions or investigative failures but, before then, criticisms tended to support Shiller's position that the media talked up the 'bubble'. Among journalists turning on their profession or their media corporations (more rarely), Howard Kurtz, in *The Fortune Tellers: Inside Wall Street's Game of Money, Media and Manipulation* (2000), attacked 'the media' for 'mindlessly trumpet[ing] each prediction' made by 'aggressive' analysts from investment houses like Merrill Lynch, Morgan Stanley and Goldman Sachs. Whenever a recommendation turns out 'spectacularly wrong', it is suddenly 'old news' with 'zero accountability' (Kurtz 2001; PBS Newshour 2000). Later, when American investors were suing stock analysts for 'systematic fraud . . . on an industry-wide basis', media corporations tried to repair their own damaged reputation of trust. Bullish analysts were derided as 'false prophets' by the very 'media that publicised them' (Jackson 2001). This hypocrisy suggests that the finance media are far from irrelevant to stock price movements and finance generally.

Media corporations, even the most reputable, do not always recognise their longer-term interests in gaining broad access to publicly available information from short-term goals. These might be those of trumping their competitors on the occasions when access is gained to corporations.

Schiffrin: I don't think it ever really, really questions the basic premises. The Securities & Exchange Commission just issued this regulation FD [about financial disclosure]. The rule is that retail investors have to be given the same information as institutional investors. This is really important because favoured analysts have had 'nudge, nudge, wink, wink' roles. So, amazingly, the *Wall Street Journal* wrote letters complaining, because they want the scoops. You'd think that a media organisation would be in favour of open access to information. (19 September 2000)

Notable differences in corporate policies between television and print media, such as the structure of television journalist incentives, are important, as Hale remarks about North America:

Hale: It's hard to guess the ratio of the naive to less naive (i.e. been around/seen it all before etc.) . . . After watching/listening to/reading the US media for years, I'd have to say that the TV is almost entirely uncritical. Even the body language gives it away on the financial TV channels. When the indices are rising strongly they're all smiles and happy; when they're falling they're glum and telling people not to panic (i.e. sell). To be honest I don't know whether this is naivety so much as recognition on their part that their ratings (and their own jobs/salaries etc) hang on rising markets . . . Thus they actually are the ones who are cynical in the true sense of the word.

The print media tends to have a higher ratio of questioning sceptics in places like the *Wall Street Journal* and *Barrons* (sometimes *Business Week*), but they're pretty thin on the ground elsewhere so overall in print maybe it's 20 per cent/80 per cent. (23 November 2000)

Television is not the only uncritical news organ of finance, because magazines started as trade journals are often gossip pages of status envy. Yet whether boosters or sceptics, the influence of media outlets during a bubble is not clear-cut:

Ziegler: The CNBC – these channels were definitely cheerleaders for stocks, even CNN. If the Dow was hitting a high, this would be cheered on by newsreaders. There was corruption there of course with some of the other TV cheerleaders, but whether that was responsible for the mood I don't know. In the financial press there are certain publications like *Forbes* and *Fortune* that are generally pro-business and tend to make heroes and charlatans out of corporate types, [and] personalise rather dull business people. And *The Economist*'s view on the duty of trust? I think it's true that we don't work on the view of increasing shareholder value. Our job is to entertain readers with a degree of integrity that we have because we're editorially independent. Whether we feel we have a greater role than just producing uncorrupted publications, I would be cautious about exaggerating our influence. (14 March 2002)

Even so, most privately owned media corporations rarely offer informed commentary, least of all television:

Abelson: The financial press – unfortunately, its basic problem, with the usual exceptions, is that it's really uninformed. It doesn't come fully equipped to do the job that it should be doing. When we talk about the financial press . . . you have to divide it up these days into various segments. There is television which like all television, it's moronic really, and it tends, if anything, to exacerbate the problems rather than to explain them. The real problem is that you have people who don't know what they're doing, doing it. The *Wall Street Journal* does a very good job, but it's a daily paper, so it has the constraints of time and whatnot. I think that the press *means* to do well, but good intentions are not particularly the same thing as good execution. However, for the most part, I would say it's a lot better than it used to be. (21 September 2000)

For media corporations, advertising revenue is the primary aim, whether by securing a larger or a wealthier audience (Curran & Seaton 1997: 54–7, 85). General television or tabloid outlets have different aims from their specialist counterparts, and greater popular impact than broadsheets and serious weeklies like *Barrons* or *The Economist*. V. J. Carroll explains the logic of the pitch of daily papers and financial television shows:

Carroll: You can't sell newspapers or get viewers on television if you're going to be sceptical, and say, 'Look, don't take any notice of that.' That's not what people want to hear! It's as if the racing pages were to say 'They're all dogs, don't bet on any of them.' To a large extent, the media does become institutionalised in pushing the interests of what they're reporting. (18 January 2001)

The issue agenda on what can be said depends on the market segment. When stocks fall, many popular money and investment magazines lose audiences from negative carping: less wealthy audiences want hope. On *The Economist*, however, financial collapse is detrimental neither for journalist news values nor for readership:

Ingham: The best time to be an acknowledged journalist is when the bottom is falling out. That's when you read most about it . . . What I'm saying is that when things are really bad, that's when economic journalists hit the bar because that's when people are interested. They want to know what's going on and how badly they are going to be hurt. They want to know whether their house is going to be worthless, or their shares, and why. (18 March 2002)

Differences then, depend on types of audience and company policy towards professional independence and investigative journalism. Journalists remain anonymous on *The Economist*, for example, to minimise the cult of personality, according to Ingham. Even so, whereas the high-water mark of investigative news declined after the 1970s, the history of financial reporting is entirely different. Investigation declined elsewhere, according to the former editor of *Barrons*:

Abelson: But not in finance. Because finance has always been the stepchild of journalism, as far as American journalists go, it started out as kind of an adjunct to the advertising department. It was nothing but a promotional area really . . . But it gradually developed and as interest in the economy and in the stock market [grew] . . . so did the coverage. And the coverage is a lot better – for all that it's flawed it's a lot better now than I can ever remember it being. If anything, the problem is that there is a lot of investigative zeal without too much intelligence behind it, so they don't know what they're investigating. (21 September 2000)

Similar stories are recounted about the British counterparts of the prestigious US finance media.

Peston: Forty years ago the *Financial Times* was just an establishment paper. It reported whatever companies said as gospel. Now the *FT* is much more critical and sceptical. Both the *FT* and *Wall Street Journal* are hugely trusted. Very few others are, but maybe if the *FT* became even more investigative it could lose that trust. Before, *FT* journalists trusted companies and slavishly wrote down their press releases. (26 March 2002)

The extent of investigation has grown, and despite or because of its elite financial readership, the *Financial Times* was often responsible for uncovering the British corporate scandals mentioned by Larry Elliott:

Elliott: Most of the papers have a dedicated squad of people who are not tied to a day-to-day routine. They might be given three months. There are people on *The Guardian* and on other papers. We have got about three or four people who dig away . . . The financial press have uncovered some pretty big scandals here over the last ten or fifteen years – the Barlow Cloud scandal, Maxwell, BCCI. (5 October 2000)

Carroll compares those former days of advertisers' influence, when an editor rarely wanted gloomy business news:

Carroll: The Melbourne Herald Group (Keith Murdoch) was very, very suscep-tible to the strength of advertisers . . . Keith Murdoch was a booster. He firmly believed in boosting everything. You could never knock anything, and you couldn't knock retailers. So you had to continually try and make everything as glowing as possible . . . It wasn't vicious or even blatantly outrageous, but you couldn't be negative, you couldn't be negative. To a large extent that occurs in all newspapers. (18 January 2001)

Editors' views about news values highlight editorial independence. Conglomerates of publishing and printing companies acquired assets in industrial and financial firms during the 1970s. Their diversification partly diminished during the 1990s, though still leaving conflicts of interest. When owned by Thomson Organization,

The Times even admitted, when reporting another arm of its own conglomerate, that its coverage 'tends, certainly, to be drily factual' (cited in Curran & Seaton 1997: 82). Although proprietorial intervention in the British press, which remains the best regulated and most professional, is less significant than in the pre-war era of press barons (Curran & Seaton 1997: 82–3), it still varies. In the case of *The Economist*, the experience may be different from many newspapers:

Ingham: The Editor isn't wondering whether this is going to sell papers or not. In deciding what is the best cover story on Monday morning, the Editor is making a judgement about what is of news value. (18 March 2002)

This comment – about a specialist magazine, granted – still lends strength to the lack of evidence of any direct relation between media companies' profit and the content of the news (Tiffen 1989).

INEQUALITIES OF MONEY: TRUSTWORTHY TO THE WEAKEST PUBLICS?

Financial reporting responsibilities were formerly to the finance sector and the well-off; now the audience is much larger. Many media headlines (often reporting rationalisations of financiers) refer to minor investors as 'mum and dad shareholders'. It implies that their ignorance is somehow a factor in rapid stock and other asset movements. But in finance the most organised core segments try to maintain control over the definition of money. There are constant pressures for liquidity and for the newest and most risk-free 'instrument' at each collapse in trust in the previous specific bundle of assets by major players. When journalists treat finance actors as an aggregate, or fail to seek connections between major players or fail to explain how 'mums and dads' suffered losses, their trust role is compromised. In contrast, Alan Abelson remarked about the US bull market, '*Now*, the problem is, it isn't play money. This is retirement money, this is education money. It's really, you know, the guts of their lives tied up in the stock market' (21 September 2000).

News values are selected, argues Tiffen (1989: 53), according to their market demand, not from readers or viewers. The major reference point of news judgement is competition from rival papers or channels and from other journalists. On occasion this may enhance public accountability and professional journalism, but often the media pick up and drop news stories at a whim. The vagaries of newsworthiness means that the media have little pressure to give continuity and consistency (Tiffen 1989: 192). A study of coverage in British tabloid as well as broadsheet newspapers of one day's news event (a cut in interest rates announced in March 1996) concluded that readers were not supplied with contextual information, and the economic terms and relations between the variables mentioned were left unexplained. It seems that 'news context' is less important than 'newspaper context', which aims to persuade readers of the paper's authority, in an entertaining, emotional manner, where self-promotion by the paper overrides provision of context (Goddard 1998: 88).

Graham Ingham related the role of financial regulators to issues of newspaper context: 'Every time there's a bank failure or an investment scandal, the media in particular tends to whip up an hysteria implying that regulators are there to eliminate risk, and they're not.' As he said, often the victims of investment banks' incompetence are the banks themselves, but Maxwell, for example, 'was breaking the law and that's what regulators are there to prevent' (18 March 2002).

Differences in quality among the print media are often significant. Yet the interviews all suggest that only a small proportion of reporters explain the most elementary issues – for instance that the stock market is not 'risk-free' – until after the problem emerges. Both the optimistic and pessimistic news, therefore, enhance self-promotion of papers. Brian Hale, in one contrasting example, linked two issues here that are rarely explained. In the USA, when margin loans amounted to $US234.4 billion at the end of 2000 and as the Nasdaq inflation eased downwards, margins were being called in which benefited 'short sellers'. In an article in the *Sydney Morning Herald* (Hale 2000a), in which he wondered if the US Federal Reserve might have somehow defended margin borrowers to ward off a massive downward spiral, Hale said:

> Selling (shorting) stocks you don't own with the intention of buying them back at a lower price and pocketing the difference has been the best way to make money on Wall Street for two months. At the moment it even seems like a lay-down misère because there's a horde of margin investors who bought on borrowed money and are now forced sellers, depressing share prices further whenever stocks start to tumble.

Consistent and contextual approaches, with good detective work, are unlikely to have impact, on specific occasions, many sceptics argued. Take the 'fever' of Initial Public Offerings (IPOs):

Elliott: I've been writing for years about how I think the American stock market is massively overvalued and is set to crash. But when it's booming, no one wants to hear that message. So often you find that not only the companies, but also the people who are caught up in it, are just in denial. Even had the *Wall Street Journal* written about IPOs a year earlier, when the boom in them was on, people would have just ignored the message. (5 October 2000)

With the high-profile collapses such as Enron in 2002, media corporations suddenly changed tune (as did Greenspan and his ilk): the 'greed is good' era was gone forever. Michael Lewis in *The Money Culture* argues that all the news commentaries after the 1987 crash said exactly the same. Journalists were consistently ready to predict that the era of greed was not only over but that culprits were receiving just punishment. 'Beware false endings', he said (1991: 57–8). How correct also is his insight into the vagaries of newsworthiness: if bull markets come and go, the reporter should rather explain the longer-term context of these events. The problem, as above, is who would listen.

A QUESTION OF STATUS: FINANCE
JOURNALISTS VERSUS ANALYSTS

We have considered major problems in newspapers fulfilling their institutional trust role. A further issue is that financial news can attain high standards, as long as the sources of information are of high quality. In comparison to other news areas, 'the quality of business reporting is primarily dependent on the quality of information which is routinely produced by the institutions involved' (Tiffen 1989: 35). 'News is a reflective institution', Rod Tiffen rightly says. 'There is a 'balance between the news media's independence and dependence, their vulnerability as well as their limited autonomy.' Business and financial reporting face a host of different sources, a fragmented, highly secretive business world, and many of my interviews stressed how big firms were always ready to take out gag writs. In contrast, political journalism has a centralised focus on the government and opposition of the day, reporting is located in one national capital, leaks are common, and political accountability can be requested (Tiffen 1989: 197). Finance reporters must react to – and make sense of – many different business sources. Complications mount in impersonal trust problems, and every journalist confirmed this view.

Grant: The source of trust must be the accountants who audit and certify the integrity and accuracy of the numbers on which other decisions are based. And by the same token, the institution at the outer periphery of these concentric circles of trust is probably the financial press, which is the consumer of all preceding information and the re-packager of this information and the public validation of it. So Moody's and other rating agencies make judgements about credit on the strength of the perceived integrity and trustworthiness of the accountants. And bankers lend or withhold funds based, in part, upon the judgements preferred by Moody's, and the press reports on all the foregoing. (19 September 2000)

The press is reactive, and deeper probing requires proprietor support in lawsuits. Most interviews suggested that analysts, by and large, could not be trusted. Sceptical journalists were dismissed as 'bearish', well before the scandals among investment banks suffered the glare of full public light, as we saw earlier.

Before considering whether the financial news largely fails in its trust role, there is our major issue of uncertainty. Granted, journalists have outsider status, low pay (relative to many of their sources), limited numbers among their ranks, and long hours of work. Even so, the pressures on sceptical journalists just recounted are hardly conclusive; there are some, but their trust role and professional independence are defended. Most are highly educated and far from the low-status scribes of thirty years ago. The content of today's training is deemed a problem. (This is partly a responsibility of media corporations in hiring practices, as well as the fashion for MBAs, now diminishing somewhat along with hopes for the new century; see Chapter 9.) But media research resources are nothing to the billions of dollars poured into research by the financial sector itself. Journalists must report the whole business world. In the 1980s, the estimate was that 60 to 90 per cent of all information in newspapers came from routine channels (Tiffen 1989: 34). Research on Australian newspapers in 2002 found that 80 per cent of newspapers' business sections was generated by PR or corporate communications professionals (Chulov 2002). Beyond that, the primary source for journalists is analysts or stockbrokers of the major investment and merchant banks. A possibly innocent development, analysts are busybodies by definition about companies worth investing, a fruitful source as their own interests are presumably against distorted information (Tiffen 1989: 42). For reporters, they are the most accessible informants. This suits the analysts' interests in promoting their banking or broking firm, but formerly their research was independent (see Chapters 6 and 8). As we now know, during the Nasdaq boom, analysts gained star status (with salary bonus) if they attracted new business clients (and promoted them, rarely recommending that clients 'sell'). Open any page of a business paper or magazine after the new rules were introduced following the New York State fines in 2002 against Citigroup, J. P. Morgan Chase, Merrill Lynch, Morgan Stanley, and documented cases of institutional mendacity elsewhere. Quotes from analysts (not the ones now struck off) are 'back to normal'.

Why do journalists depend on analysts? It is not a matter only of their superior knowledge and research resources and their specialisation in specific companies. Of more interest is uncertainty. In as much as journalists are reliant on this knowledge and ignorant of uncertainty, they are also reliant on analysts' buy and sell recommendations. On what are these recommendations based, if not on stargazing into the future? This is where analysts are tempted to hype even without bonus policies – because their exaggerations are covered in the firm's fine print (see Chapter 6). Yet however honest, analysts claim to have techniques that are, for a time, successful in predicting future performance (Zuckerman 1999). To the extent that the methods actually control the firms they are so assessing, this social control is relatively predictable and reliable for journalists. Analysts are key targets of companies' efforts to attract investors and favourable comment, the front line for managers' regular visits, conference calls and announcements (Zuckerman 1999: 1407). Analysts gain status from knowing the owners and managers of firms in person, a familiarity denied to most journalists, who could be said to be ignorant, lacking status and legitimacy of contacts, and highly dependent on analysts as their source of close, gossipy information. Corporations use vast resources to control their public image and render top executives 'as inaccessible as CIA agents' (Kurtz 2000: 81). One US survey in 1998 found that 99 per cent of companies asked money managers to attend their conference calls, whereas only 14 per cent asked reporters – only to 'listen', uselessly off the record. The serious press, like the *Wall Street Journal,* often refuse to attend (Kurtz 2000: 96).

Ezra Zuckerman conducted research on public American firms between 1985 and 1994 to show that the homogeneity of many public firms reflects the analysts' use of a prevailing 'theory' – at the time, 'value' trading. If they are critics (the busybodies) of firms, their techniques at 'predicting' firm performance (denying uncertainty) was then to amass past data of all firms within a specific industry, say, car manufacturers or the restaurant industry. Analysts compared like with like within the whole area. Firms that diversify make it difficult to compare past performance in order to project or predict; therefore they were punished. The failure of a firm 'to attract coverage from the analysts who specialize in a firm's industries causes the firm's equity to trade at a discount' (Zuckerman 1999: 1401); they suffer what Zuckerman calls an 'illegitimacy discount'. Analysts must offer buy, hold or sell recommendations, and as they specialise by industry, 'diversified firms present a classificatory challenge'. Contrary to the idea that the de-diversification of the 1980s and 1990s was due to 'inefficiencies' in diversification, Zuckerman argues that these firms shed businesses because diversity hindered 'cross-product comparison' by investment analysts (1999: 1420). A newspaper article of 1995 criticised a diversified company: 'The hodgepodge of businesses it owns bothers Wall Street. Financial analysts can't categorize [it].' The CEO is quoted as saying, 'We're not going to get out of some business so we can make some analyst happy, so he can compare us with just the steel business or just the refractories business' (cited Zuckerman 1999: 1421).

Zuckerman's evidence contradicts orthodox views that there is no interdependency among investors. Clearly, finance dependencies are numerous among investment banks, their specialist analysts, and specific firms within each industry. Boundaries around information gained, or often defined through formulas for predicting future performance, keep journalists on the outside, trusting analysts. At the height of the Nasdaq inflation, the press eventually reported as 'fact', tips from star analysts engaging in 'pump and dump' – Wall Street jargon for talking up a firm's virtues in public, only to dump it when small investors are paying at the top. Interdependencies between Initial Public Offerings (IPOs were a 'fever' in 1999) and the investment banks are noted in the *Washington Post* in 2001 in an article titled 'Why insiders don't feel your pain':

> Some insiders would argue that they too have been hurt by the stockmarket's decline . . . But . . . not all stock losses are the same, because the insiders get their stock for pennies a share, if that . . . The truth is that little investors never stood a chance, because they simply don't have the same access, both to key information and to early deals, as big investors. One reason is the 'quiet period' mandated by the Securities and Exchange Commission, which requires a start-up company to shun any publicity regarding its finances for at least three months before its initial public offering. The law was intended to keep a company from hyping its stock, but in reality its main effect is to keep small investors in the dark. (Perkins & Nunez 2001)

Unintended effects of regulations are a problem noted here, another the secrecy or controlled hype fed to reporters. Few journalists, let alone modest investors, are equipped or able to question their prime sources, the analysts (or companies).

Kadlec: Generally you're going to find it at the biggest news organisations – the people at CNBC have been through it enough . . . and a place like *Time*. We [all] know what questions to ask, but there's a whole world out there of daily newspapers across the country, with just tons and tons of reporters . . . and they're really taking what they're given . . . I think that in terms of the internet boom many reporters were right out in front, cheerleading it on, quoting the analysts and giving rosy forecasts and talking about the 'New Age'. (26 February 2002)

Anya Schiffrin argued that 'the fact that reporters are dependent on financial institutions for their education about finance/economics is the number one reason for craven coverage . . . As a result, as one grows into the subject, one is inculcated' (E-mail, 18 May 2003). Journalists have few capacities to query institutional mendacity or guesswork.

A GLOBAL TREND OR NATIONAL DIFFERENCES?

Although Wall Street is the financial capital of the world, how global are these problems? Media policies are national, as are many financial regulations. Britain's media policy still requires high standards, which could be better (Curran & Seaton 1997). Australia has the worst of both worlds in concentration of ownership, failure to regulate commercial television, and lack of free and fair speech rules (Jones 2000). Few interviews disputed that manipulation of stock prices was common everywhere, or that American television finance news was basically dishonest. On whether the finance press behaved similarly everywhere, Brian Hale – initially a British stockbroker, and an experienced journalist before his location in New York – argued:

Hale: There's a lot of unthinking acceptance of what people say . . . At press conferences some will ask a question and you get an answer back, and people will accept it, and not so many ask – 'Just a minute, I seem to remember about three years ago you said something different and blah blah . . .' Everyone has a vested interest in sustaining the myth, whether it's a broking firm, whether it's the media. We now have financial TV channels which have become nothing basically but shills for the share market because they know from history that when indices rise, when people want to play the markets, their viewer figures go up. (13 September 2000)

Although the influence from the Wall Street hype spread to other stock exchanges, nevertheless, for Larry Elliott:

Elliott: I think what's been going on in America is borderline dishonest. If you go to the States and read the press and watch the channels like CNBC, they are constantly telling people, 'get into the stock market'. Every time the stock market falls, they say this is a good buying opportunity. The number of people who say this is very dangerous, you could lose a lot of money, is *minimal*, compared to the number who say very bullish things . . . They get people in from Mutual Funds, people trying to sell people equities or bonds with their own axe to grind. I think it's actually borderline dishonest to tell people that it's perfectly okay to invest in these markets when, for a lot of people, it's not going to be. (5 October 2000)

The people who were putting their savings for retirement into the stock market, he agreed, were likely to be the first to suffer, as they later did: 'I find the bubble mentality really quite scary in the States. A lot of it is generated partly by people's greed, but the financial media has fostered the greed.'

On 21 May 2001, *Fortune's* headline 'Can We Ever Trust Wall Street Again?', with Morgan Stanley's 'Internet analyst' Mary Meeker on the cover, offered to explain 'Where Mary went wrong; Inside the IPO racket; Plus: You're right – blame the media too'. As Graham Ingham said in commenting later on 'pump and dump': 'And there's no more sanctimonious journalists you could possibly get than in the US. They're all so pompous it's not true. And yet they make things up at the drop of a hat' (18 March 2002).

As one experienced in the Australian field, however, V. J. Carroll sees few cross-national variations in judgements about news values in business journalism. Speculative booms are simply not handled well by the finance press anywhere. Sceptics are not usually opposed to financial markets either:

Carroll: If the market is to work, it must be properly informed at all times. That is where journalism has a big role in the operations of all market economies, particularly in the money market. It will only work while the information is being spread, as rapidly as possible, and being analysed to see who is telling fibs, because to a large extent all corporate announcements are dressed up by the PR departments. They have to be discounted and analysed, and the sheer volume of information now has swamped the capacity to analyse the information. This particularly happens during booms. This is when all the shysters come in, all the company promoters come in, and they get away with murder. (18 January 2001)

THE FINANCE PRESS AS SHILLS FOR THE SYSTEM?

One charge by Brian Hale was that finance journalists were 'shills' for the confidence tricksters, the financial sector. These sceptics agreed that much financial reporting is ill informed. Even so, it is possible that certain aspects of journalism (reflective reporting) fostered the rise of *financial* public relations. If the finance press does fail in its critical role to dispute fibs and corporate spiel, if it fails in its institutional trust role to the public, the question arises as to why PR firms would be necessary. Other interpretations are equally plausible.

In exploring why financial PR emerged recently, I interviewed Jonathan Birt, who works for a PR firm in Britain:

Birt: From the experience of Financial Dynamics, there is if you like a corporate ethos about how we're expected to behave, that you do not lie to the press . . . You can't mislead journalists, but some people do, you see, and a lot of misleading goes on, but we say we can't. Once you start misleading journalists they'll never trust you again; they're never going to accept what you say again. So that's all your credibility gone. It takes a lot of time building that credibility up and it's quite agonising to lose because you can't put it back.

Financial PR firms in Europe and America face different reporting standards and corporate forms. According to Birt, financial PR started in the USA:

It's been stronger in the US and then the UK – as always the UK then Europe always follows the US. The UK is complex. We have a very vigorous press, we have ten national newspapers. They all do serious financial coverage, and they all have different slants . . . Take Germany. Germany is a much bigger economy than the UK and it has a vigorous press as well, but I think that up to now it has been a much more respectful press, as it has in France, so it hasn't been as difficult to deal with. The UK press is the opposite. They're always looking for the chink in the armour, for the downside or the bad news.

His comments highlight how German firms were stable and less 'global' for longer than Anglo-American ones:

Yes, Germany's now moving that way. Now they are all in the global game. Hoechst has merged; it's now listed in France as technically a French company. But a company like Hoechst has gone from being very German, used to dealing with the German press, [to being] an international globalised player and suddenly has to deal with the international global press. The press have become globalised as well. (22 March 2002)

Global players meet a global media, particularly CNN and the BBC, *The Economist* (which covers North America and Europe more than its British home base), *Time* and *Business Week*. However, a global game by corporations also has variable national impacts: perhaps a European press may be less respectful of, say, an Exxon or a British Petroleum. Elliott added a further reason for PR development.

Elliott: I think the level of sophistication in managing news has become much greater over the last ten or fifteen years. A lot of news management was fairly amateurish back in the 1980s. One of the funny things about the consumerist revolution unleashed by Thatcher and Reagan was that the consumers now bite back, so a bad press can do a company a lot of damage. You have to take a lot more care about your public image; it is very much consumer-driven. That is why the companies spend a lot of time and money getting a good press. (5 October 2000)

In the USA, pressures from financial PR companies, which developed during IPO floats, did not inspire Brian Hale's confidence:

Hale: Yes, there's an army of financial PR people out there – all trying to get their companies mentioned in the media and, more importantly, mentioned favourably. Same game as investor relations . . . All these people are trying to shape perceptions so that we walk around with a view of life that is not based on the reality that is out there. And their 'spin' works on most of the media in the US. (11 October 2000)

How far these are 'global' trends depends on national cultural differences and government policies. Although the 'Friday night drop' was made illegal in Britain to improve and defend journalist standards, Larry Elliott sees more impediments to papers' trust role:

Elliott: Well, you have big powerful organisations, be they governmental or non-governmental, using their power and influence to manipulate the press. They have teams of spin-doctors, press consultants who will do their utmost to get a good press. Particularly here on Sunday newspapers we used to have . . . the 'Friday night drop'. The Sunday newspapers are always looking for some big exclusive. So a representative of a public relations company, representing a big corporation, would drop a brown envelope off on a Friday night at the offices of selected journalists and they would find a juicy story sitting there for them. That sort of behaviour built up a very close relationship between certain journalists and certain companies. Quite often you can see that there's been a pattern there and this particular journalist is supporting a company through thick and thin. That relationship has been built up by a drip feed of stories over months or years

Expansion of British financial PR firms is not regarded with the scepticism of US journalists interviewed, even by a 'liberal' newspaper:

They're huge in Britain and they're incredibly profitable too. Most big corporations would have their own in-house PR deal with fairly routine things. But if there was a really big story they would subcontract out to one of the specialist PR firms. Citigate, Dew Rogerson are probably the biggest and incredibly effective . . . They'll be on the phone, lobbying me, not aggressive but incredibly assertive and they really, really want to make sure that their point of view is put across. You have to be quite strong to resist it. (5 October 2000)

On all the general constraints faced by financial journalists, PR is possibly the least of their problems, as it states its aims openly. Trevor Sykes recalls Australian corporate behaviour in the 1980s, an impressive catalogue of problems facing financial news reporting:

Sykes: The most distressing aspect of the 1980s was the way that the professions prostituted themselves to the corporate cowboys. Very, very few of the corporate collapses would have occurred on the scale they did if auditors and accountants, in particular, had been more vigilant at the start. You find me any corporate cowboy . . . in that era and I will find you within two years before that collapse, a balance sheet that's been given a teddy bear stamp by a respected firm of auditors, a top law firm that has endorsed the various schemes and manipulations to circumvent laws, a stockbroker with the Australian Stock Exchange who has cheerfully flogged and recommended the stock, and a financial journalist who has probably given the bastards an award, and I know them because I gave a couple of them. Now, taking things backwards there, as a financial journo I always felt I had a slight excuse in that I was relying on all the names on the bit of paper and if I couldn't rely on them, what could I do? . . . So the professions let the side down . . . these fellows prostituted their names . . . all the professions, the Merchant Banks, the lot. (19 January 2000)

The exact same problems of systemic mendacity recurred in the late 1990s, as James Grant insisted about US corporations in 2000: 'I think that a lot of companies manipulate the figures to present a better case for the stock market . . . It's called cheating and it's an intercontinental phenomenon' (19 September 2000).

From a PR perspective, Jonathan Birt defends the press, denying that its generally low reputation is deserved and rejecting the possibility that journalists might have uncovered the Enron case:

Birt: No, absolutely not. We're all in the dark, all relying on what other people are telling you, and the financial press is so overstretched that they write from press releases. Nobody really likes the press very much because they expose things, they ask difficult questions, but the best thing is to have a vigorous press for a healthy society. There is an issue that the financial press is often not well educated on financial issues, such as how to read a balance sheet, and also it is very powerful. Certain organs – the *Wall Street Journal*, the *Financial Times* – are particularly powerful. One story can be completely wrong but have huge and damaging impact. (22 March 2002)

If the press is overstretched, and liable to error, problems may be compounded, but not so much as to save organisations higher up the financial hierarchy:

Peston: The more investigative journalists become, the more it may be claimed that they have made mistakes. CEOs may not like this approach, as it's too critical. Since the collapse of the bubble, the authority of the *FT* and the *Wall Street Journal* diminished somewhat, but that was not confined to journalists, as even Greenspan had also climbed on the dot.com bandwagon. The reputation of the *FT* and the *Wall Street Journal* is high, but everyone's reputation got bashed by the Enron debacle and the collapse of the Nasdaq. Regulators were more damaged than journalists and of course the most damaged were the analysts and the investment banks. (26 March 2002)

Let us not focus on reporting the private sector alone. Very few people in the world understand central banks. Nor do many journalists, and constraints are many. The influence of government treasuries on financial news was formidable before the 1980s, and journalists complained of being mouthpieces of treasuries (Tiffen 1989: 45). With declining use of fiscal policy, and central banks more independent of democratic government, treasuries are less centre stage economic managers these days. Although central banks are formally responsible for macroeconomic management – and accountable per se, in contrast to the private sector – many finance news agencies readily assume the central banks are just neutral technicians.

Carroll: Another point about financial journalism – about the more serious journalists, particularly the economics correspondents. With few exceptions, they are snowed by the Reserve Bank [RBA] and the Treasury. The intellectual weight of those institutions is too much for them to counter, they can't handle it . . . It's not a criticism, it's just one of the facts of life. And they go to the Reserve Bank's conferences, which are full of Reserve Bank economists who've gone into the merchant banks and become *their* economists, and very few contrary views go into those conferences. Whereas I would say the role of the *Financial Review* is to be *sceptical* of the Bank, since the Bank is the power. The expert journalist has a great problem because he mixes with the Reserve Bank. (18 January 2001)

SHILLS ASSISTING THE SYSTEM

Much more could be said on the finance media, but that is a secondary focus. Advertising and news manipulate emotions so obviously, so blatantly, that it is easy to forget that financial institutions employ those advertisers. Ascribing a 'causal' role to the finance news media for the bull market surely overestimates their influence. Media corporations are not innocent since they have vested interests (advertising revenue; economic and political interests) in a bull market. But if, according to sceptical journalists, a large proportion of the financial press are shills for the system, trying to entice more investors and debtors for the confidence tricksters, it raises the question of who precisely are the con artists. Invariably, finance leaders, orthodox economists and politicians focus their critiques and cast blame on one corporate sector alone – not the finance sector but media corporations! Not media CEOs either, unless a public broadcaster, but 'the media' – not journalists working under pressures, not human beings in specific social relations but a piece of technology (a press, a camera, a 'media').

Apart from this technological tactic (determinism by 'information technology'), others skirt corporate trust. Even if all financial organisations were trustworthy, the field is treated as a market, or at least or worst as the 'business community'. This convenience means that rotten or overly emotional individuals are blamed, leaving unsullied those independent smart traders (and, until the 2002 cases by New York's Attorney-General, the investment banks). Any journalist who seriously investigates corporations constructs a more organisational view.

Rather than seeing media corporations and those share-touting media celebrities as merely benefiting parasitically from the rise in share-owning, as they did, Shiller's *Irrational Exuberance*, for example, ascribes to finance media an active role. It avoids Keynes's idea of *a reverse process whereby speculators are obsessed by 'the News' of finance.* Shiller considers finance reporting to be superficial with little analysis (none of my informed sceptics disagrees with that), citing the media's focus on new dizzy records of price changes as a problem of 'record overload'. But he ruins a reasonable case against celebrity analysts (now infamous) by attacking the MacNeil/Lehrer Show for fostering the panic of 1987 by interviewing a 'respected authority' who predicted a crash days before (Shiller 2000: 73). The now Lehrer Show (PBS) is a haven of calm reason on US television, but with tiny ratings. More revealing because problematic for Shiller is that crashes rarely occur from external events like a war or a new government policy.

Only orthodox economics would be surprised that stories of most relevance to investors during the 1987 crash were 'those about past price declines themselves' (Shiller 2000: 89). As in 1929 when 'relevant' news was solely on price movements, this finding leads him to attack the news media as 'fundamental propagators of speculative price movements' for disseminating ideas 'not supported by real evidence'. While acknowledging that audiences are not 'purely passive' (2000: 73, 95), his division between 'diffusion' (i.e. dumb, easily influenced) and 'smart' investors who independently use 'real' evidence is a far cry from Keynes's views on speculators' short-term focus on 'the News'. Since past evidence never shows the future, 'the News' is the latest finance news and is not generated by media corporations or finance journalists who get outsider, public, second-hand data. Speculators are trying to guess what average opinion about average opinion is, particularly of large investment firms. The importance of 'the News' to investors is evident in the fact that insider trading is unlawful because it provides an unfair advantage to buy or sell on 'news' – say from boardrooms – that is not yet public. The prevalence of insider trading implies that *any* finance news is constantly sought, whether corruptly or not, whether gossip or anecdote in the practice of speculation.

The fundamental aspect of finance routinely neglected in orthodox accounts is speculation. During a bull market, finance news ratings will be high as there will be an obsession with 'the News' about prices. Only the Keynesian tradition on uncertainty stresses that expectation is rarely 'knowledge' but rather 'imagination and hope' about future values (Shackle 1972: 432). Indeed, Keynes mainly cited 'the News' as an influence on expectations: the 'trading revenue earned by existing equipment in the immediate past' (Shackle 1972: 180). Today, television and print journalists may be the last to hear this 'News'. All finance 'News', in Keynes's sense, is unguessable and always remarkable; it reports as fact what was mere conjecture just before. News has an element of surprise, novelty and unexpectedness. The response is to assimilate it and reassess earlier knowledge. As Shackle says, the influence of 'the News' is magnified. In digesting 'the News', concentrated focus is given, it is dwelt upon and seen 'in magnified proportion to its background. We assume that news shows the direction of things' (Shackle 1972: 180) – as threat or opportunity – as 'the News' contains 'the counter-expected', 'the unentertained idea'. 'News may thus disrupt the former structure of a man's expectations, or may shift that structure bodily, as it were, towards the more sanguine or the less sanguine appraisal' (Shackle 1972: 181).

Conventional judgements, however, are adopted through an 'accidental coalescence of ideas'. Traders (employed by investment banks etc.) will agree with the majority as long as they can guess the majority's view just before the majority find it (Shackle 1972: 225). The price of a share rises when most believe it will rise and whether there is any 'objective' reason for a rise 'is of no concern to the short-term speculators' (1972: 185), because this is a game of musical chairs. In this interpretation of 'the market', 'the News' must be followed by all participants, less for clues about 'fundamentals' or some 'outside event' but merely to follow the current movement itself, to beat the gun. Interpretations and rationalisations are elaborately argued (as we see later), and merely reflected by financial journalists and compounded by media corporate policies.

Two main issues emerge: the private finance sector is hierarchically arranged in cores and peripheries; and most trading is highly speculative. To return to the finance media, modestly well-off populations with worthless dot.com shares stopped watching after 2000, with no point to their obsession with 'the News' let alone the press news. Some finance magazines no longer exist and layoffs were common, as elsewhere. Advertising revenue plummeted. American finance television was uncritical, at worst, dishonest. Clearly, professional, critical financial journalism was under enormous pressure over an unusually longer business cycle and, most crucially, however much senior journalists attempt to query financial claims, all argued that their words of caution are ignored. The 80 per cent of journalists who uncritically accepted the claims of the finance sector about investors' money being 'safe', played walk-on parts in a much bigger show where every trust relation was broken. Core financial players are more responsible yet are far more likely to emerge from a bear market with little loss. We consider later the organisations with more impact than finance media, with vast resources to deal with uncertainty, reliant, nevertheless on a stream of gullible and/or reluctant investors with neither any experience nor memorable somatic markers of a crash. Finance journalists face a diversity of financial sources of overwhelming scope (Tiffen 1989: 35–8). The finance sector sets the agenda; most financial journalists are prone to sycophancy and absorption in the world of their sources (Tiffen 1989: 45). Sceptics know that neo-classical economists and core practitioners use theories which rarely acknowledge or study organisation (Baker et al. 1998: 148), when sceptical journalists see organisations everywhere. The finance press reported losses for small investors, only while it was a 'fresh' story.

The activities of Merrill Lynch (like the others), so soon after its extensive 'Be Bullish' advertising campaign in early 2000, are the more capricious. By November 2000, an article entitled 'Merrill dumping mums and dads' said: 'In keeping with the traditional fickleness of the broking community, the Thundering Herd is tiptoeing quietly backwards in Australasia.' Merrill's Singapore 'retail' centre had ordered pulling out of New Zealand and partly out of Australia (Askew 2000). Similar retreats by US Wall Street firms occurred in London. Merrill's advertisements switched from its double-page 'Be Bullish' to a 2001 photograph of blindfolded (dumb?) investors needing 'advice'. But new firms are, in 2004, using the same old tricks.

To return to the question of what is money, the core actors in finance are those holding the more risk-free or balanced positions (this means an awful lot of bonds *and* stocks, swaps and so on). The hierarchical pattern varies: in the 1980s in the USA, the core consisted of securities dealers, employees of financial institutions (as they 'benefit from the insider information they are privy to': Baker 1987: 127), private investors, investment companies, institutional and other financial investors, real estate developers and builders, foreign exchange dealers and the futures industry. The semi-periphery comprised mainly commercial and mortgage banks. On the periphery was an assorted, atomised collection of investors from retail proprietors and employees, clerical and sales workers, physicians and housewives, retired persons, students, and military and civilian government workers (Baker 1987: 126–7). Central banks have greater importance, as we will see, and more concentrated private banks are back in the core in the early 21st century, mainly global European and American, now dominating the forex markets and so on, some making cheap purchases from recent debacles in insurance, mutual fund, financial adviser firms and forex trading firms, some failing from these ventures.

Baker argues that only the core actors 'control and define' money, as they hold 'dominant positions in the core supermarket where the assets closest to money are exchanged' (1987: 134). (Baker's 'core' in 1987 consisted of bonds and currencies, property, corporate equity, debt 'equity' or the petrodollars of the 1970s.) In contrast to orthodoxy's smart trader argument, the core are not smart but have massive resources compared to 'dumb' mum and dad investors. Those who do define money, by the same token, are also those who are saved from their own excesses and 'the follies of their own hubris' by the central banks – in most cases leading from behind (Carroll 2000). The 1998 collapse of Wall Street's cream hedge fund, Long Term Capital Management, proved there is no purely risk-free position, however massively powerful they were formerly. Whereas modest investors and mortgage holders bear the consequences of speculative asset decline, the powerful creators of near-money in LTCM were rescued by the US Federal Reserve's forcing the banks to bail it out (Lowenstein 2000). Journalists' sense of injustice about the inequality inherent in money in its own right is implied in Alan Abelson's concerns at the exposure of so many small investors, when the implications are 'not entirely salubrious if something happens'.

Finance news agencies are parasites on the financial sector while secrecy prevails, yet are used as shills. Journalists report speculation on 'the News' with its related emotions of trust, fear and distrust as these are generated by a finance sector routinely seeking 'direction' about the unknowable. Although institutional trust agencies, the finance media are largely incapable of maintaining trust relations with their mutually contradictory audiences, or of seriously questioning every dubious source, more so during a bull market. It is difficult to uncover scandals and cover-ups. Corporate finance only discloses when it *must*; whistleblowers, state regulators and investigative journalists are treated ruthlessly through corporate and libel law. Even so, when scandals are finally disclosed, orthodox news media offer a more adequate analysis than orthodox economics. In 1998, *Business Week* (5 October 1998) ran this headline: 'Who can you Trust? – When companies fudge their numbers – When accountants turn a blind eye – When analysts have a conflict of interest.' The self-styled 'sceptics', as the interviews with journalists show, engage in middle or meso-level analyses of inter-organisational relations of trust and distrust.

Trust and other anticipatory emotions are even less avoidable in the finance sector itself. After all, sceptical journalists are not deciding about future investment gain or monetary policy. They are reporters, not umpires, on the sidelines. Reporters can doubt or mistrust claims to a diverse and often too vaguely confident public. The next chapter considers evidence from the core players about emotions in decisions.

4 | Emotions in the Boardroom

KEYNES WAS FAIRLY scathing about the financial world of his day. Conventional judgements were formulated with flimsy assumptions – 'pretty, polite techniques, made for a well-panelled Board Room' – where 'the practice of calmness and immobility, of certainty and security' was always

> liable to collapse. At all times the vague panic fears and equally vague and unreasoned hopes are not really lulled, and lie but a little way below the surface . . . Tho this is how we behave in the market place . . . I accuse the classical economic theory of being itself one of these pretty, polite techniques which tries to deal with the present by abstracting from the fact that we know very little about the future. (Keynes 1937: 215)

Keynes is telling a story of social emotions in decisions, of emotional energy and polite rituals – never absent but rarely recognised or represented – until everyone explodes into contrary emotions. While the future remains, as always, unknowable, the size of today's global banking networks, financial markets and central banking institutions and the policy framework has made the organisational scale completely impersonal. Since today's organisations cannot rationally apprehend the future any better than then, reformulating Keynes's critique means exploring impersonal emotions in financial institutions.

This chapter is on decision-making inside some of these organisations. As interviews show, informed sceptics all accept uncertainty, so I suggested to them that in order to act they relied on trust. Their responses varied. Their jobs may require specific emotions to neutralise uncertainties or prevent hesitation. Public monetary policy committees and bank boardrooms, trading floors and treasuries are clearly poles apart in personnel, procedures and duties, though many are interdependent. Later chapters explore how internal decisions try to assess the integrity and credibility of other institutions. This chapter describes how trust and *esprit de corps* are developed and destroyed *within* organisations' decision-making procedures. Interviews attest to the same 'reckless and foolish' bank losses of other centuries (Bagehot 1962: 9). A conceptual framework derived from theories of attribution (e.g. Weiner 1986) on organisational definitions of success, competence and reliability helps to explain these issues. Praise and blame from outsiders create emotional feedbacks that insinuate themselves into the decision-making process, subtly under the boardroom glow of acclamation or distressingly under charges of blame and scapegoating. Gossip and rumour are rife in the financial world, but rather than seeking psychological insights about inherent dispositions of individual office-holders, I explore how procedures and decision-making duties shape emotional interactions.

INTERVIEWS WITH DECISION-MAKERS: THE EXPERTS

The core interviews were mostly former decision-makers. As Graham Ingham said, 'It's rare that a central banker is actually going to tell you something off the record, for very obvious reasons' (18 March 2002). Present office-bearers make official pronouncements, 'news-breaking', bound by rules of confidentiality. I sought people prepared to reflect on their decision-making over booms and busts.

Expertise, according to Harald Mieg, usually takes ten years of experience before knowledge (knowing what) of the field becomes ingrained procedural knowledge (know-how), about how to perform the cognitive activities nearly automatically (Mieg 2001: 20–1). Experts are never always correct, but have superior long-term recall and skills in seeing 'meaningful constellations' (2001: 18): 'they see more relevant things' than beginners (2001: 22–3). Yet asking experts means that their near-automatic performance is hard to explain: 'intuition' is a word used by many of the people I interviewed. Observers can try to become expert on why and how experts describe what they do (Heclo & Wildavsky 1981: lxvii).

In exploring the roles of emotions in formulating decisions, I showed the experts two diagrams. Figure 4.1 is Post-Keynesian (Dequech 1999: 418), where dispositions for 'animal spirits', knowledge and creativity create a 'state of expectations'. It rightly emphasises uncertainty, but only up to 'expectation', whereas my sociological Figure 4.2 includes the moment of action, *how decisions are launched into the unknown*, and the emotional effects of later outcomes on 'anticipatory emotions' which drive the next formulations of expectations.

Figure 4.1 describes creativity and knowledge, which are essential factors, and also personal dispositions or feelings – factors this chapter seriously questions. In contrast, Figure 4.2 emphasises social or organisational processes that shape specific emotions for deciding or acting. A number of 'anticipatory emotions' are drawn on in contemplating future decisions. The past and present elicit different emotions: past outcomes are recalled with optimism or pessimism (Kemper 1978: 74–5), whereas 'the News' of the immediate present generates confidence or lack of confidence in conjectures. Like Kemper, Dequech (Figure 4.1) rightly argues that a lack of confidence is not current pessimism, because pessimism is retrospective. Lack of confidence does not indicate character flaws but rather a greater recognition of uncertainty, even granted uncertainty, and even if armed with optimism from past successes. Where Figure 4.1 is a more static collection

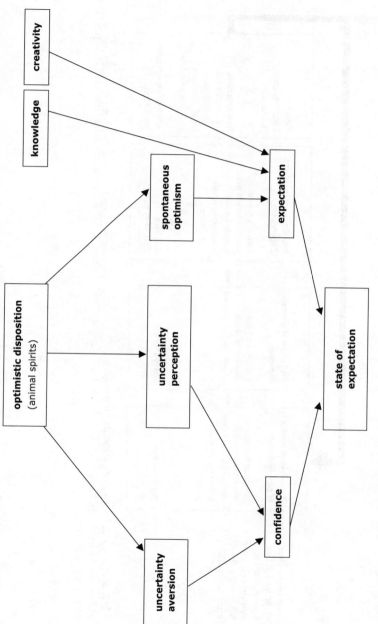

4.1 Determinants of the state of expectation

Source: From D. Dequech, 'Expectations and Confidence Under Uncertainty', *Journal of Post-Keynesian Economics*, vol. 21, no. 3 (Spring 1999): 418. Copyright © 1999 by M. E. Sharpe Inc. Reprinted with permission.

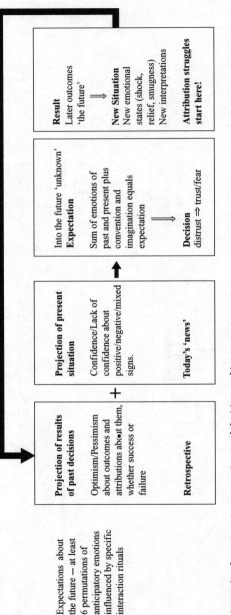

4.2 Role of emotions in expectations and decision-making
Author's model drawing on Kemper (1978); Luhman (1979); Collins (1990); Barbalet (1998). Economists: Shackle (1967; 1972); Keynes (1937). Myrdal in Shackle (1967).

of various attributes, 4.2 spans a continuous emotional process entailing many permutations. For example, an organisation may act on utter confidence about a certain grim present, compounded by deep pessimism from calamitous past outcomes, projected into a future via distrust. Decisions are inescapable, but if the outcome ends up OK, a response could be amazement. It may feed back to revive optimism, even arrogance.

Interviews assess these two formulations, and whether organisational relations are less personal, more impersonal. Some experts distinguish emotions from an 'art of judgement'; for others automatic or routine decisions remain contingent on unknowable outcomes. Habituation to the institution and ideological commitment – customary, seemingly rational action – are compared with learned aptitudes for decision-making, which are often felt as excitement or joy. The impact of the specific institution on personnel depends on rituals, with adaptation or cases of grovelling to the 'decisive' superior. The weight of political and economic institutions may make office-holders fearful of the slightest public mistake or ill-chosen phrase.

PERSONAL DISPOSITIONS OR SOCIALISATION?

Widespread individualism, particularly in the financial world, tends to make decisions seem personal: there is an invariable focus on leaders and financial gurus. Personal trust remains important, but contexts have changed. Heclo & Wildavsky called their research on the British Treasury of the 1970s *The Private Government of Public Money* (1981). They found a private, personal solidarity among the upper echelons, which lacked 'substantive rationality' due to Treasury's communal culture, traditions and customs (1981: l). In the USA, since the 1933 New Deal business regulations, private and public sectors focus on positions, not persons. Independent outside assessment of firms was required by SEC legislation and brought impersonal due process to prominence (Chapter 2). Even so, these impersonal processes are no more rational in the face of uncertainty than the former solidarity (which, more recently, has been called cronyism). In the 1970s, though this was a more regulated era, British Treasury was more personal than it is today. Kinship-like ties fostered a mutual confidence in which the 'nuclear family' of Treasury was in a 'village' relation with the wider civil service. As they say:

> However quaint and faintly ridiculous the idea may seem at first, the distinguishing feature of Treasury men . . . is not their intellect or their ideas but their emotions . . . When they succeed . . . it is because they recognise the overriding importance of giving and getting a personal commitment . . . [and] undergird[ing] the dictates of reason with the ties of emotions. (Heclo & Wildavsky 1981: lxiv–lxv)

The old school tie, rather than personal dispositions, mutually formed trust and internal training were the underpinnings of Treasury's decisions. In making rational decisions, mutual trust helps to overcome doubt.

In 1985 David Lazar interviewed London traders and stockjobbers in the private sector. Their remarks show a much harsher, impersonal process at work, yet one that also fostered 'trust' in competitive relationships. Memoirs of the financial world amplify this, such as *Liar's Poker* by Michael Lewis, or Frank Partnoy's tale of how traders learn ruthlessness, *F.I.A.S.C.O.* American traders at Morgan Stanley took part in weekend rituals like clay-shooting to heighten traders' collective aptitudes for making a killing. Socialisation usually fosters habituation and reduction of doubt. In the City of London such socialisation was intense even though personal ties of loyalty were eroding under Thatcher's neo-liberal policies and the disappearance of the City's 'gentlemanly capitalism' of family firms and cosy partnerships of merchant bankers and titled stockbrokers (Augar 2000; Ingham 2002: 154). Intolerance of dissent or egalitarian views was so marked that trainees could not express even mild political doubts (Lazar 1990: 90).

Although conformity was rigidly imposed, many younger informants with modest backgrounds arrived with neo-liberal views. The work's relentless, short-term focus, of success rewarded under highly competitive conditions, conforms exactly to neo-liberalism (Lazar 1990: 92). Wall Street arguably has the most brutal redundancy system to prevent employee theft of the firm's secrets and clients. These American techniques – a climate of cynicism or fleeting trust – are new to the City of London. However, Henry Dale, former banker at Crown Agents (a development bank), is not necessarily nostalgic:

Dale: The City worked in a kind of English way which built up over time inasmuch as regulation was very minimal, and a lot of it was to do with personal trust . . . If you were perceived as a bad lot, you would not be acceptable in the right sort of places. But there have been plenty of disasters in the City over the last hundred years before the 1970s. If you're a student of these things, Barings went bust in the 1890s, but it was rescued by the Bank of England and the City. Barings went actually bust and wasn't rescued by the City in 1995. (5 October 2000)

The public sector is (or was) motivated by different appeals. Roderick Chamberlain, a former London banker, supports this view:

Chamberlain: One of the fascinating things about working with regulators is to find people who do not work for power or money. This is a very strange feeling for those being regulated, who are generally in business for money allied with lots of power. (19 March 2002)

On the question of dispositions, comparisons of two chairmen of the US Federal Reserve hardly show personalities to be important. Many central bankers suggest that Paul Volcker and Alan Greenspan have very different personalities which are, however, irrelevant to their banking acumen: both are highly esteemed in the central banking world, as we will see.

Professor Alan Blinder's view on the personal disposition of Greenspan, and central banking environments, suggests that judgements give rise to the emotions.

For Blinder, former vice-chairman of the Fed during the mid-1990s in Greenspan's chairmanship, dispositions do not influence the impersonal emotions at all: the institution creates the emotions:

Blinder: In *these* environments – central banking – there's a very strong effort, largely successful but not entirely (we're all humans), to suppress these emotions about the future. Am I basically an optimist or a pessimist? What difference does it make? I think that if Alan Greenspan was given a battery of psychological tests, he would come out as a dour pessimist. Nonetheless, he was the herald of the 'New Economy', the productivity miracle, and he took a lot of risks with monetary policy. I think Greenspan proved much more correct than incorrect in promoting views that you'd associate with extreme optimism. I don't think that came out of his personality, it came out of his analysis and his judgement. So I would start there: the incredible importance of past experience and decisions. (22 February 2002)

Sir Alan Budd was formerly chief economist of HM Treasury and member of the Bank of England's Monetary Policy Committee (MPC). In considering the Post-Keynesian diagram (Figure 4.1) on expectations, personal dispositions of members were slightly relevant:

Budd: What the MPC process leads to is a state of expectation about the future path of inflation. There might possibly be a factor to do with people's temperament . . . but people are certainly optimistic or pessimistic. So disposition may be included. Also, far more important is knowledge. Knowledge means two things: there is knowledge of economics and knowledge of what is going on. So everyone in this process has their endowment of characteristics . . . I distinguish between knowledge – those with PhDs in economics, those with no training, etc. – and the enormous information stream that pours in. All the other things, [such as] uncertainty aversion [Figure 4.1] are not so important, as the MPC members are simply making a forecast. They are not deciding whether to set up a factory making widgets. This Dequech model really is a narrow decision-making process. (12 March 2002)

From 'adaptation' to 'grovelling' or the national interest?

Commitment to institutional values, socialisation and judgements of office-bearing are more important than dispositions. Various kinds of rapid adaptation to the institution by new appointments were also mentioned by some central bankers, the result of neither socialisation in the organisation nor personal or political attributes.

Some informed sceptics in the private sector suggest that self-interest (non-financial) within public organisations is about gaining recognition from superiors, such as praise for preparing sound analysis, or for defending the institution of central banking or their bank, in particular, to outside critics, primarily the elected politicians and the financial centre. Central bankers face pressure internally – the 'weight' of an institution such as the Fed – and externally from the White House, Congress or global concerns. When the first female Fed member, Keynesian economist Governor Nancy Teeters, took office, she was told by then Fed Chairman Arthur Burns, 'Within six months you will think just like a central banker' (cited in Greider 1987: 74). Whether this was so, or whether her economic credentials made a difference, Teeters consistently opposed the recessionary policies of 1980–82 as being unjust (Greider 1987: 465).

B. W. Fraser, former Governor of the Reserve Bank of Australia, draws a distinction between sectional interests and national concerns of members. During his time a president of the Australian Council of Trade Unions was on the RBA Board. Fraser prefers members being mindful of the national interest rather than merely being interest-based stakeholders. Institutional charters should also give central banks some discretion in decision-making, not a straitjacket like an inflation target:

Fraser: You talked about personalities and institutions. Institutions do have charters and objectives. If they are sensible, those charters and objectives will be expressed in very broad terms, like the Reserve Bank Act and the Federal Reserve, rather than a single, simple target. So, because they are expressed in broad terms they are capable of a wide range of reasonable interpretations. That's where the set of personalities and the make-up of the central bank and, to a lesser extent, the composition of the board is important . . . they can determine and influence the interpretation of the board's charter . . . I think it is important that [the board] consist of people from different backgrounds, but not consist of representatives of farmers or miners or manufacturers or whatever, because I think that just generates sectional pressures. But to get good people – that's always the hard thing . . . good people from different areas of business and the community who can pursue and have regard for the interests of the whole nation, rather than seek to protect their own sector. That's something that I've always had a close attachment to. That's not always the case in other places where governments specifically select people from particular sectors. Even here, some of the appointments in recent times have gone to sectoral groups – there's someone from the Farmers' Association and so on. (28 June 2002)

Fraser refers to the central bank's interpretation of the whole nation's interest. This partly depends on the appointment process which, in Australia's case, is by the government of the day. Former BoE Monetary Policy Committee member, Professor Charles Goodhart, compared academic economists such as himself to those with market experience and public service backgrounds, what he called the 'practitioners':

Goodhart: Academic economists are not necessarily representative of the central bank practitioners . . . there are differences between the two groups. Economists are much more analytical; they know less about the details of practical issues, and probably may have somewhat less intuition about political and practical constraints.

A problem for central bankers is to give differing weights to the qualitative commentary that one receives from businessmen, as compared with the quantitative approach . . . In practice . . . central bank practitioners – not the economists – [who] claim that they put no faith in the models, actually put *too much* faith in the point estimates of the models produced. They do not understand the uncertainty attaching to the models. The economists tend to be rather better at appreciating the inherent uncertainty of the models. What remains *very* uncertain is how much weight to give to the sort of gut feelings, the responses and the attitudes of businessmen. (27 March 2002)

Perhaps central bank practitioners are habituated to criticisms from private institutions and governments.

EMOTIONS AS SUCH?

The object to which an emotion is directed matters a great deal. Here future cost is the object, with organisations facing uncertainty about money and often obsessed with costs. In the private sector, the environment is highly charged, and few deny the presence of emotions. Central bank informants mostly denied emotions, while never denying uncertainty at the moment of decision. 'The future is always uncertain, and any decision is a leap of faith', says Goodhart. Alan Blinder agreed there was always a leap in the dark: 'Absolutely, you see that; everyone sees that all the time.' Incumbents can rarely admit that in their public statements and camouflage uncertainty in obfuscation such as 'Fedspeak'. Although analysts and journalists tend to laugh at Fedspeak as merely elitist jargon, I suggest that uncertainty is the more difficult (political) issue for public unelected officials. Greenspan publicly admits uncertainty only in face of external disasters like September 11 – 'nobody has the capacity to fathom fully how the effects of the tragedy will play out in our economy' – as though he could make other, fully fathomed predictions (cited in Parker 2001). In March 2003 he spoke of 'unusually large uncertainties clouding the geopolitical situation' – the coalition's invasion of Iraq – 'and their apparent effects on economic decision-making'. The Federal Open Market Committee (FOMC) of the US central bank, where the major decisions on monetary policy are made, acknowledged uncertainty in October 2003 as 'upside and downside risks' for the next few quarters' growth being 'roughly equal' (FOMC statements 2003). That is, Greenspan does not know the future; the Federal Reserve has no more clue than anyone. Bernie Fraser criticised plain speaking because it could lead to problems such as long-term predictions. He is referring here to the current Governor of the RBA:

Fraser: Ian Macfarlane might regret that he said a month or so ago that interest rates are likely to rise . . . over the next eighteen months, because that's a degree of precision that no one knows. We're talking about what might happen over the next eighteen months and no one knows that. So that's one thing – one shouldn't be overly candid because it can come back and haunt you, and it doesn't help matters because you're just guessing like everybody else. (28 June 2002)

Fraser stresses that no central bank official should imply they know the future. Emotions are freely admitted among money traders. This London stockjobber describes how he likes the work because

> really to sum it up, it makes the adrenalin flow. You can feel down in the dumps and then so elated it's not true . . . You get them wrong – of course, you get them wrong – and you do feel very depressed. But, my goodness, when it turns round! Every day is a new challenge. (cited Lazar 1990: 75)

Adrenalin charges are not always so enjoyable. Of his time at Quantum Hedge fund, George Soros says the following:

> As a fund manager, I depended a great deal on my emotions . . . The predominant feelings I operated with were doubt, uncertainty, and fear. I had moments of hope or even euphoria, but they made me feel insecure. By contrast, worrying made me feel safe . . . By and large, I found managing a hedge fund extremely painful. I could never acknowledge my success, because that might stop me from worrying, but I had no trouble recognizing my mistakes. [But] . . . [w]hen I looked around, I found that most people go to great lengths to deny or cover up their mistakes. (Soros 1998: 24)

Few public figures in the private sector seem as honest. Perhaps worry and doubt might engender a reverse-order 'trust' – negative views may make a positive decision to act more bearable. In considering my Figure 4.2, one senior manager of a large hedge fund did not, on the one hand, accept that trust played a part in his own decisions, or he had to *hope* the trade would work out. He said, 'It's not trust. What you've just described here, as far as I can see, is the process of calculating the expected value.' On the other hand, he said something else when talking about how hedge funds had invested in Russian bonds in 1998, when LTCM lost spectacularly (total $4.56 billion losses). LTCM stayed longest on grounds that 'nuclear countries don't default', which Russia did in August 1998 (Lowenstein 2000: 139). This manager in another fund talks not merely of the 'herd' argument but of fear.

Manager: We all suffer to some degree from a herd mentality. We all invested in Russia, for example, in the days of the GKO markets. GKOs [Russian government bonds, a rouble-denominated Treasury bill (Dunbar 2000: 199)] were paying 60 and 80 per cent interest per annum. I remember [another manager at the fund] . . . saying, 'We couldn't expect this to go on. Clearly no rational business, no rational economic system is going to be paying 60 and 80 per cent per annum interest; there has to be something wrong'. And yet all of us lined up to invest. You take the rational discount factor, and everything that says you shouldn't be there, or if you are there, you should be there on a very cautious basis and then it gets overruled by the fact that you're afraid not to be there because everybody else is there and you're going to look stupid. (27 February 2002)

Anxieties about looking stupid, mentioned by many, are rational emotions in an interdependent hothouse. Practically speaking from the 'floor', Chia Sieu Wong, a former investment manager – a woman with well over a decade of experience in large Wall Street banks and earlier in smaller firms – stresses the competitive, particularly aggressive nature of investment banks. By then, the early 1990s, everyone on Wall Street agreed that 'women have better gut feelings than men and act on them more than men'. Knowing that, her fear was not of looking stupid but of losing her job – even during the bull market:

Wong: I would say that however well you think you've analysed an issue . . . and you think you've covered all bases and nothing could go wrong – then four hours after you've bought the stock, it behaves in a way it really shouldn't. Instantly your self-confidence evaporates, and you're back in the fear mode. Any investment manager who's been through a couple of cycles, if he really is honest with himself or herself, would admit that a lot of the time they're living with fear. (28 May 2001)

In general, the evidence shows that emotions are ever-present but are of different kinds. Clearly private and public bodies operate at varying levels of intensity. Heightened emotions may be routine for one sector such as investment banking, and sporadic, if occasionally momentous, in others.

Decision-making in the private sector investment world

John Bogle, founder of Vanguard (well known as a genuine mutual fund) and with an academic background in Keynes, gave the classic statement about uncertainty. During the bull market he was saying it was over, and there was no 'new economy':

Bogle: Nobody ever listens but it doesn't keep me from saying it. But this is a very important point: if you read that speech, you'd think I knew what was coming, and in a funny way I did. In a funny way, anybody who's been around for more than twenty minutes did. You know *what's* going to happen, but you have absolutely no idea of *when*. So a lot of people are hesitant to speak out, because now might not be the moment. I probably would have given the same speech if I [had] happened to be talking about the same subject a year earlier. I would have said the same thing, and six months later they would have said 'Ha, ha, you're stupid'. So I certainly don't deserve any credit for my timing. (7 March 2002)

Picking the moment, he implies, is mere luck. His criticisms of the mutual fund industry were, by 2003, heard by Congress. He said to me that it was 'a system that sells funds on the emotions of past performance and future hope. But the past is never prologue, and hope often disappoints.'

Expertise in the face of uncertainty must include extensive due diligence procedures, according to a now former Director of the UN Pension Fund in New York. In a defined benefit plan, tightly structured and managed in-house by a salaried staff of international civil servants, caution is predominant. For the UN staff, fixed salaries and permanency are policies quite opposite to monthly star ratings and competitive bonuses for luck in investment banks. Decisions have strict accountability rules, justified daily by direct communication to the representative of the UN Secretary-General. The Fund's Director of Investments Director Investment, then Henry Ouma, nevertheless says this:

Ouma: There is an element of gut feeling that is not easy to quantify in the investment system, but a lot of it is there. There are cases when I come in here, and I say, boy, I want to sell this stock, [though] I really don't have any quantifiable reasons to. A perfect example we had was Lucent. Lucent had not really started to have a problem, but somehow – the numbers did not indicate that Lucent would have any major problem – but this feeling I had, and I talked to my managers, and we sold Lucent at its top. After that, bad news started surfacing and the stock price plummeted. It was not like I had this mysterious scientific way of knowing. (30 May 2001)

Lucent was one of the dot.com wrecks that dropped in January 2000, just before the rest of the Nasdaq plummeted.

Werner Frey is a former banker in Zürich (member of the Executive Board at Bank Leu, and later, when it merged with Credit Suisse Group). Frey is in no doubt about emotions for regular decisions:

Frey: It is probably a combination of rational and intuitive elements, for example when debating, typically with the Chief Economist at the bank and the Head of Trading on the Monday morning, the kind of proprietary trading positions we should enter into, say in buying or selling bond futures . . . Such a process . . . is heavily influenced by economic considerations, by political influences, by the state of the markets, and a variety of what seemed to us important aspects . . . I freely admit that . . . taking all this into consideration, and me taking at the end of the day the overall responsibility, I did, time and again, listen to a kind of an inner voice, call it intuition, in taking the final decision. (4 April 2002)

Georges Schorderet, an experienced chief financial officer, also in Zürich, said he was 'convinced that facts alone [were not sufficient] – if you put a decision on the table with good figures and people don't feel it with their stomach, they will not take the decision' (6 April 2002).

Of invariable finance scandals involving massive losses, that of Allied Irish Banks (AIB) occurred during my 2002 interviews, so it was a 'hot' example. For those who cannot follow every disaster, John Rusnak, a so-called 'rogue trader' working in Baltimore for AIB, incurred losses between 1997 and 2002 of US$691 million (£483 million). As in trader Nick Leeson's losses which led to Barings Bank collapse in 1995 and Leeson's time in jail, AIB did not 'discover' the loss for five years. 'Rusnak was singled out for berating the back office, and for threatening to have employees fired' (Ludwig Report, cited in Merrell 2002). Former banker Rod Chamberlain says managing uncertainty is a policy issue, an issue of correct processes throughout the organisation:

Chamberlain: The trick in all of this is keep your feet on the ground, and keep it simple. Recognising risk management as a strategic element of running your business is simply accepting that you are acting in uncertainty . . . We used to give seminars to back office staff when I was Chief Operating Officer of a big securities company. We said all of the kids in the back office ought to understand about risk: . . . 'you go bust in the back office'. It is the same for lending bankers: they do not go bust lending at the wrong price, they go bust lending to the wrong people. (19 March 2002)

Also discussing the Allied Irish case, Werner Frey explores emotional tensions that arise from traders' successes and failures. Many are below the threshold of individual cognition. As in Figure 4.2, management may not consider these problems if a firm has had a run of successes:

Frey: I've found time and again that traders have been highly successful for a certain period, others have been unsuccessful for a long period of time. It's been very important to neutralise an unsuccessful trader who took positions for the book of the bank by way of a cooling off period, because fear can also be stress, stress as a result of decisions that prove to be wrong. On the other hand, you would often see a typical . . . risk of over-exaggerating and overshooting, with people with a very good track record . . . Not usually, but quite often the positions become bigger and bigger [laughs] until the big, wrong decision is taken. This has been one of the more fascinating facets of a management duty to balance.

Frey also considered that if emotions are typically 'hot', the presentation of 'sober' or cool states may include aggressiveness, over-optimism, arrogance:

The successful run the risk of becoming arrogant. 'I'm the best anyhow; I know how to deal.' That's the over-optimism . . . And the result is that the trades and the positions become larger and larger. But let's quickly have a look at the negative side. A trader who has lost money often tends to increase the size of the transactions as well, and there is probably an additional word . . . *hoping* to reverse the bad results achieved before, and that's exactly where . . . limits imposing discipline come into play. (4 April 2002)

Frey agreed that the structure of competition among traders made those doing badly feel worse. This could encourage bullying as in the AIB case. In his view, the type of 'arrogance' at the firm level represented in LTCM and Drexel Burnham were 'outstanding examples'. These were firms lacking disciplinary limits which he supports (Chapter 9).

NON-DECISIONS: PRIVATE AND PUBLIC SECTORS COMPARED

By definition, elite office-bearers are decision-makers. In finance, decisions are routinely imposed, which suggests they are forced options. Uncertainty, Frey says, is always present. In the public sector (here, the BoE), an academic economist who appreciates uncertainty in analysis as well as decisions raised the issue of non-decisions:

Goodhart: Any decision is a leap of faith. But I remember a long time ago, when I was an official of the Bank [of England], having an enormous debate with a colleague about whether a decision to do nothing is just as much a decision . . . My colleague tended to take the line that you know so little about the world that you had better do nothing. I was arguing the other hand, that surely you know very little about the world, but you know something and you would do better to base your decision on your uncertain predictions than simply to sit there doing nothing because everything is too difficult. A decision to do nothing is just as much a decision as a decision to do something. Not everyone agrees with that. A lot of people believe that when you don't know what to do, it is better to do nothing. (27 March 2002)

Bernie Fraser argued that changes in monetary policy are rare, though equally he agrees that keeping a rate on hold is a decision. Are non-decisions more neutral in the private sector? Werner Frey talks of banking decisions: 'If the uncertainties were relatively dominant, it happened time and again that we simply did not enter into a position at all – just refrained from doing transactions or scaled them down in size.' Clearly Frey's is a cautious position, in contrast to the mass of foolish bank loans elsewhere. Considering Figure 4.2, on the influence of past successes, Frey argued that in reaching a decision, one could not easily separate confidence from expectations, or from creativity (in comparing Figure 4.1):

Frey: I think it's very important to have both, the trust and the fear. The fear [in Figure 4.2] would correlate to the uncertainty resulting from the mixed signal with respect to the more rational part of the decision process. It would clearly have an impact also on the intuitive part on the decision process. This then would lead to a non-decision, to do nothing . . . to defer any decision until the basis of the element of trust to be right is bigger . . . A non-decision is still a decision, which has a neutral characteristic because these decisions are not taken for joy of taking decisions but to make money. And whether by . . . a long position or a short position, if your assessment or your fear is . . . that the probability is bigger to lose money than to do nothing, [then doing nothing] is the better choice. (4 April 2002)

He doubted whether it was possible, at the point of decision, to distinguish the rational from the intuitive, or past experience, whether good or bad, from present assessment.

PERSONAL VERSUS ORGANISATIONAL – *ENTSCHEIDUNGSFREUDIG*

Although Frey argues that decisions in finance are not made out of joy but out of duty to make money, Rod Chamberlain introduced the idea of joy in another sense, with the German word *entscheidungsfreudig*, which means 'to be happy to make decisions', or joyful or just comfortable. It can also be used as 'decisive' (e.g. 'She's a decisive person' = *Sie ist entscheidungsfreudig*). That may imply adaptation or ritualised expectations from others against vacillation, perhaps acting the part with virtuosity. It shows there are definite roles to play in an organised drama. Whether or not it is a necessary personality trait for aspiring management virtuosi and leaders, the idea contradicts (instrumental) capacities for decision-making, by implying that an *entscheidungsfreudig* person can base decision processes on substantive values and emotions (e.g. joy or excitement), or must do so with pressing decisions.

Rod Chamberlain is a consultant advising executives. On lack of confidence and trust (Figure 4.2), he argued that the group must be considered.

Chamberlain: *Entscheidungsfreudig* . . . means I am quite joyful at making decisions. The amount of trust or fear I feel needs a prior filter. This is Rod the amateur psychologist. The prior filter is whether you are 'decision-joyful'. You can categorise people who will make decisions. Some are right, some are wrong, we do not lose sleep [over it]. Others are very unhappy making a decision in conditions of 120 per cent certainty, because who knows whether tomorrow something will change? To which I say, then we will make a different decision . . . As a hypothesis, one guy will decide or guess, and the other will say we will call a meeting, and we'll decide. (19 March 2002)

But he continues, in every firm 'the rituals will revolve around the individual, because that is what companies are all about. If you look, they are actually full of people and people behave in rituals.' The rituals can be markedly different between finance firms, even with no national-cultural differences. One US bank was 'a highly entrepreneurial culture – what is mine is mine, what is yours is negotiable'. Here 'a man is not a man until he has arbitraged three . . . dealing rooms against each other'. Another US bank is staffed like a diplomatic corps. Paul Chan at UBS in Zurich spoke of 'big cultural differences' between Americans, Europeans and Asians:

Chan: It's the perspective, I would say, of 'tolerance to failure'. It's not so much how you deal with success, it's how you deal with failure. I think the Americans tend to have a short memory about the failures. Bankruptcy? It's okay, it's one incident in many, life carries on. The Europeans are much less forgiving. Asia is also very, very unforgiving. (5 April 2002)

Many senior people Chamberlain advises have lost jobs because of a new boss. The superior–subordinate relationship is crucial:

Chamberlain: I have worked in a bank where the highly entrepreneurial chief executive left, and the 'diplomatic corps' chief executive came in, and guess what happened? Within six months he had changed the whole lot . . . because they just could not live with each other. [A former boss discussed technical issues on equal terms; the new one creates an 'emotional battle'.] You find people who have worked very successfully together for years and years . . . The subordinate does not have the language, let alone the understanding, or any votes, if a new boss arrives . . . [So] what [do] the rituals look like? One of the rituals is that the boss is decision-joyful, and has a mask. The boss says 'I am the boss, so there are no questions because I have all the answers.' That can create a climate of fear. Alternatively you can have a climate of all trust and no action. 'We are frightfully nice chaps here, gosh everyone gets on so well, we are so inclusive, embracing, consultative . . . Unfortunately, we have not decided anything for a decade, and someone just took us over' . . . It is an interesting balance of trust and fear. (19 March 2002)

A triangle exists between leadership roles played well or not, confidence among subordinates, and trust or fear. Here decisions are ultimately forced options. Virtuosity in decision-making is a role learned, but team rituals take time to rebuild: building is easier with a new team. A balance exists, says Schorderet, in trust within teams. 'If the trust relationship becomes good, it starts to become dangerous. If you have blind trust, this is not good any more. People need to stay critical . . . If you are all of the same opinion, that's never good . . . Good decisions have always been taken because there has been heavy questioning' (6 April 2002).

PUBLIC SECTOR DECISIONS: EMOTIONS OR THE 'ART OF JUDGEMENT'?

No expert sees decisions as scientific. However, the public sector is less forthcoming about emotions. Professionalism in uncertainty is uneasily bound to concepts of public service. In a book written mainly by former central bankers, *How Do Central Bankers Talk?* (2001), Alan Blinder, Charles Goodhart and colleagues state the well-known cliché: 'Outsiders understand that policy-making is more of an art than a science. Some even call it a gamble' (2001: 18). Interviews with Budd, Fraser and Flemming support the cliché. Blinder and colleagues stress that 'forecasts are educated guesses' (2001: 112). For Goodhart, confidence is hardly an emotion in judgements.

Goodhart's was the most robust criticism of including emotion as an aspect of expectations, though possibly a semantic point: he was considering Figure 4.2:

Goodhart: I think if you ask central bankers, people like DeAnne Julius, people like myself, we wouldn't say we had emotions about the future. We would agree we had prognostications about the future, a word that fits in better with our mental state.

However, the idea that emotions may be embarrassing seemed not the issue, and he agreed that journalists used these terms all the time:

I don't think that we would say that we went through interactional rituals . . . Inter-action procedures . . . I don't know how much past success necessarily makes one that much more confident, thinking of success in terms of forecasting accurately, achieving a good outcome, that is neither optimistic nor pessimistic. Since the outcome that is forecast may be rather bad, one can be pessimistic about the economy, but quite optimistic about one's ability to forecast that the economy will be bad. Optimism, or confidence in terms of one's ability either to predict or to influence the outcome can be compared with optimism or confidence in what the outcome is going to be. I don't regard pessimism as an emotion, or optimism as an emotion. Attitudes of mind, again I'm happy with. You won't find many of us keen on the word 'emotions' . . .

Your summary – to make a semantic point, some of the phrases you use, like emotions and rituals, I am sure they are used in sociology. It grates against the way a central banker and probably academic economists would see themselves. (27 March 2002)

Another British view has emotions as a residuum. A former chief economist of the BoE, John Flemming, thought that 'emotions should stay out of rationality even though Hume did say "passion drives reason"'.

Flemming: It is not surprising that people don't get calculations right. Whether you describe the residual [conjecture over and above rationality] as an emotion or what, I am not sure, but there has to be something that people rely on, or that drives them, or guides them, or whatever which is not simply rational calculation. (13 March 2002)

Some central bankers were more open to the idea of emotions. It seems a matter of national cultural difference, thus another academic economist, Professor Blinder drew attention to long-tenure rules and long-term views of central banks providing calming rituals:

Blinder: If you see a trading pit, emotional energy is expended and people are acting on gut instinct and emotion. When you get up to the central bank, which is where you started talking, every effort is made to suppress any of that – and I think largely successfully. They are aloof and cloistered away; they look at the facts . . . It's not so much different data, I think, as a deeper and a longer time perspective. These things have happened before, they'll happen again, and we shouldn't get too carried away with the situation at the moment. All these clichés are actually practised in central banks. And when they fail, when they get swept up in the moment, that's when they tend to make mistakes . . .

Independent central bankers with long tenure in office have the luxury to do that in a way that investment bankers or mutual fund managers – who are marked to market [i.e. to current market valuation of their firm] and graded on a quarterly basis (on their relative performance), if not more frequently – cannot. [These assessments] induced some people to jump into these internet stocks against their better judgement. (22 February 2002)

In the Federal Reserve's transcripts of central bankers' formal discussions there is an open acknowledgement of emotions. Governor Rivlin notes at an FOMC meeting: 'The worried faces around this table . . . are worrying about the best set of problems that we could think of having' (FOMC, 24 September 1996: 22; all FOMC transcripts are now released after five years). Her use of the word 'worry' may well be about facing uncertainty.

Some central bankers discuss the fact that monetary policy committee meetings reach a decision most typically by consensus. Many committees aim for public consensus as we will see, because these monetary meetings are watched closely by the financial world, by politicians, and sometimes by the public. Other reasons that consensus tends to be the norm are to do with the particular ritual and how the meeting is run, whereas in the BoE's fairly new Monetary Policy Committee, each member votes and majority rules. A 'stunning example' of dissent within the Fed's monetary committee is mentioned in Blinder and colleagues (2001). In a February 1994 meeting, members strongly opposed the Chairman's recommendation in the policy discussion, but collapsed at the formal vote, after 'Greenspan demanded – and got – unanimous support' (2001: 113). The FOMC transcript shows other processes, including the way Greenspan violated the rituals, his appeal to members to trust the Chair's long experience, and his previous successes as so attributed. The denouement appears to be highly charged emotionally.

At this 1994 meeting, a rate change was proposed after years of policy inaction. The 1987 stock market crash was (maybe) the market's response to Greenspan's first major decision as Chair. He raised interest rates and the stock market promptly fell on 'Black Monday'. Perhaps traders feared a massive recession similar to Volcker's clamp-down in 1980 (Smithin 1994). Greenspan's instant turn to monetary easing after the 1987 crash allegedly saved the day by averting a repeat recession. This, in any case, is the dominant, positive attribution in which Greenspan gained intellectual acclaim from 1987.

Monetary meetings (interest rate decisions) are highly formalised rituals, which vary from bank to bank. FOMC members start by debating 'policy' in light of estimates on their own region if presidents of Fed district banks. Governors of the Federal Reserve discuss economic data for the whole country.

After this anecdotal 'go-round', the Chair puts his view on the decision first. Then each member responds, like a straw poll before the formal vote. In February 1994, Greenspan's preference was that the FOMC should raise the short-term interest rates by '25 basis points' – 0.25 per cent. President of the New York Federal Reserve Bank McDonough goes next and agrees. In this meeting, Greenspan breaks ritual to intervene before polling the others.

As the straw poll moves on, Melzer then Jordan disagree by favouring 50 basis points, but Jordan gives way after Greenspan again interjects (President Melzer disagrees [50 basis points] as does President Jordan, but Jordan gives way to 25). By the time Governor Lindsey opposes him, Greenspan more forcefully interrupts the 'ritual' (or so it seems), because Lindsey asks him, 'You want to correct my sense of history?' (FOMC, February 1994: 51). (They debate policies enacted in the 1960s, in a similar fashion to the way that the 1994 situation is, with hindsight, often extrapolated to that in 2004.) As more members support 50 points rather than his 25, Greenspan again intervenes – after gaining a supporter. What does Greenspan say in stemming the majority opposition?

CHAIRMAN GREENSPAN: Well, I've been around a long time watching markets behave and I will tell you that if we do 50 basis points today, we have a very high probability of cracking these markets . . . Having stuck with an unchanged policy for so long, it is going to be far easier for us to get on an accelerated path if we need to . . . later. To go more than 25 . . . would be a bad mistake. It could generate surprising counterproductive responses in this market . . .

I would feel very uncomfortable . . . I think it's the wrong pattern and I must say it would make me really uncomfortable.

VICE-CHAIRMAN MCDONOUGH: Could I make a comment? [He has already had his turn]

GREENSPAN: Certainly.

MCDONOUGH: I very much share the view that the effect of a 50 basis point move today in the marketplace is highly unpredictable. It's sufficiently likely to be damaging in cracking the markets. (FOMC, February 1994: 53)

The straw poll is completed with three more members (including the sole female member) still unpersuaded. Greenspan is facing widespread disagreement, and responds:

GREENSPAN: You know I rarely feel strongly about an issue, and I very rarely sort of press this committee. But let me tell you something about what's gnawing at me here. [whether growth may 'simmer down' etc.].

I would be very concerned . . . because I don't think the markets expect it. You want to hit a market when it needs to be hit . . . Were we to go the 50 basis points with the announcement effect and the shock effect, I am telling you that these markets will not hold still. I've been in the economic forecasting business since 1948, and I have been on Wall Street since 1948, and I am telling you that I have a pain in the pit of my stomach, which in the past I've been very successful in alluding to. I am telling you – and I've seen these markets – this is not the time to do this . . . I really request that we not do this . . .

I also would be concerned if this Committee were not in concert . . . If we are perceived to be split on an issue as significant as this, I think we're risking some very serious problems for this organization. (FOMC, February 1994: 55)

The 'announcement effect' was an innovation at the time, as previously Wall Street insiders could infer the policy sooner than outsiders: now policy was announced. The 'shock effect' is after the years of inaction. After this plea, this threat, opponents like Lindsey made a few face-saving gestures to tie Greenspan down to a further telephone meeting. These proposals were rejected by McDonough for setting a bad precedent for 'particularly this Chairman' and for 'demeaning the process' (FOMC, February 1994: 56). The formal roll then gained unanimous agreement.

It is hardly overstating the case to take this transcript as evidence of a highly charged discussion. Woodward's Maestro – Greenspan – apparently talked of physical pains in his stomach 'many times', pains about 'feeling' a danger, or his 'fear' about making an 'absurd statement' in public, 'before he was intellectually aware of the problem' (2000: 120). Greenspan's appeal on grounds of his reputation required their accepting public attributions that Greenspan was indeed experienced and 'successful' in the past: He basically said 'trust me', into the future, according to Blinder: 'There's no way he could have done that' unless he had made many such successful judgements in the past. 'If he'd had a spotty record of often being wrong, the others would have said "Why should I concede?"' (22 February 2002)

Other CB informants said to me that Greenspan totally dominates meetings. Two years later, Governor Lindsey makes a backhanded compliment at an FOMC discussion where he forcefully requested CB action against the speculative boom (see Chapter 5). He compares 'mainstream academic thinking' to Greenspan:

> MR. LINDSEY: What you [Mr Chairman] are proposing is more reflective of what I would call an entrepreneurial, hands-on approach. I think it is built frankly out of self-confidence and nimbleness, and you have earned the capacity to have self-confidence and to be a little more nimble in the conduct of policy. I will be supporting your recommendation based on . . . a very well-earned reputation of success. (FOMC, 24 September 1996: 38)

Decision-making structures vary. Before central banks had independence from treasuries, a typical situation was governor and/or sole treasurer decisions (Blinder et al. 2001: 113). Blinder discusses Committee decisions compared with 'unitary' decision structures as formerly at the BoE.

Blinder: The incredible importance of past experience and decisions, I think, can't be over-estimated. That's where, in a group, the leader gets a lot of his authority. In another context, when I was in the Clinton administration, Bob Rubin, first as Head of the National Economic Council and later as Secretary of the Treasury, used to start conversations by saying 'Well, I was in the markets for twenty-six years and . . .' So now who around the table would say, 'Well, I was in the market for twenty-six *days* and I have a different view'? It just didn't work. It just shut every body else up. So who else has twenty-six years [of experience]? That's usually important in group decision-making. (22 February 2002)

Intellectual financial acclaim can heighten emotional energy in a field of intellectuals competing over reputations. For a novice, the requisite emotion may be grovelling. Mistakes are often made. In the private sector, innumerable studies attest to stockbrokers' poor decision records, as with any professionals dealing with human behaviour (Mieg 2001: 30). Interviews highlight anxiety about making mistakes. FOMC meetings interminably recall past decisions and attributions as to whether outcomes were from skill or mere luck – the most damning description. Given his dourness, Greenspan's form of *entscheidungsfreudig* may be suited to a traditional mystique of central bankers. Practitioners like Greenspan, experienced in the private sector's logic of competitive second-guessing and secrecy, and his public servant experience of political power and policy disasters, over-rule the mere luck ascribed to the Fed by those who speak more plainly about uncertainty.

Organisational Memory

Fear of making mistakes, or looking stupid to a huge audience, or oblivion to potential errors is driven by specific corporate memories. Personal dispositions are as irrelevant as orthodox assumptions of 'independent' – uninfluenced – actors. Lack of memory is a hallmark of trading floors, whereas Blinder stressed the long-term nature of central banking where, however cloistered, memory is crucially interpretive, conjectural. Considering my Figure 4.2, a former Bank of England informant said:

Budd: You learn from the past. There is something else. Knowledge is made up of training and experience. For example, I often used to divide the members of the Monetary Policy Committee over whether they had been involved in some of the great policy disasters of the United Kingdom. If you had been involved in those policy disasters you had a very different take on life. (12 March 2002)

While it could result in greater timidity (see Chapter 5), long memories foster skills – the ubiquitous 'art of judgement' – in picking which historical event is most similar to the present. As no past event is ever the same, former luck, intuition and conviction, as well as somatic markers from experiencing some disaster, cannot be avoided in extrapolation. In contrast, short-term thinking is so prevalent in the private sector that everyone added refinements. In criticising private sector greed, Chamberlain's suggestion was that 'the restraining factor on greed is fear'. However, this fear was about fear of being caught by regulators. Long-term fears, say about a severe downturn, were, in his view, not sufficiently prominent in financial markets.

Short-term thinking is not only about lack of experience of collapses. For Chamberlain the City's scandals need assessing for ethical failures and also for plain 'human fallibility and incompetence'. Optimistic and pessimistic dispositions can easily 'flip' inside the boardroom, but also:

Chamberlain: People do not *learn* about the past. Sometimes they don't forget and they don't learn, like the Bourbons. Sometimes they don't know, and therefore are doomed before they start . . . I can remember in my twenties the first time a major bank suffered catastrophic foreign exchange losses at an overseas branch, and it still happens today. They are no cleverer . . . in fact the tricks that they are up to are no cleverer . . . There is that lack of collective memory in the City. Lloyd's Bank in the Chiasso case lost tons and tons of money; a nice man called Mark Colombo put it straight down the tubes. That was back in the early 1970s. What was different between him and John Rusnak in his Baltimore branch [the AIB case of 2002]? As far as I can make out nothing except the year. (19 March 2002)

Some successes can lead to collective failures to examine cautious strategies: 'unless you knew . . . whether the due diligence before you decided was skill, or was it luck. If it was all luck then you better keep kicking the tyres.'

The 'Chiasso Affair' was the biggest affair in the financial industry in Switzerland for decades, when Lloyd's lost significantly; Credit Suisse wrote off a billion Swiss francs. Such countless swindles, according to Kindleberger (1989: 104–5) – here a trader speculating with illegally exported Italian capital and a fraudulently guaranteed dividend – are evidence that banks are as reckless today in lending for foolish or dubious schemes as they were in the 1920s. Of the USA, Henry Kaufman says twelve years of expansion and no real stock market setback are other factors in forgetfulness.

Kaufman: New credit instruments [and] the globalisation of the financial markets has really brought with it . . . the mathematical quantification of risks. It has brought into the business a lot of younger people . . . [with] limited historical knowledge, and they are risk-motivated, risk-orientated. They have not experienced any real travails. (29 May 2001)

Werner Frey characterises organisational errors more forcefully. But he, like Blinder, insists that central banks were doomsayers during the dot.com boom: 'It's been the Fed that time and again warned [about not merely irrational exuberance] but . . . insane developments.' Such insane errors are not necessarily from arrogance. Negligence or poor professionalism are causal factors, since arrogance, he argues, expresses 'a behaviour' and not expertise.

Frey: It's definitely the combination of lack of corporate memory, or that those who have only seen the 1990s in their professional life simply didn't have that memory. There is then a second category: those who had the memory but were of the opinion that the economic rules had been rewritten in the 1990s and therefore the experience of the 1970s and 1980s [was] of no value. Then there is certainly the third element which was just too stupid or too arrogant to take into consideration the experience of the 1970s and 1980s.

Competition among bankers to get on the new economy bandwagon, even while not believing it, for fear they might lose money or look stupid, was the fourth factor.

Or they mustn't even lose money if their performance is lower than their competitors, though on the positive side, they will have a hard time as well . . . UBS [Union Bank of Switzerland] as a management in the late 1990s . . . continued to primarily apply the value approach in selecting the securities to be purchased, missing the heydays of the technology boom. Not only got heavily criticised therefore, but customers withdrew their portfolios before waking up when it fizzled. (4 April 2002)

On British banks in the 1980s, the same issues of incompetence and structure of competition point to forced options. Mike Lazar, trained as a stockbroker, worked for several banks briefly, before Britain's 1990 housing-bank loans disaster:

Lazar: I was astonished at how incompetent they were [and] . . . at how little they understood the securities industry. I thought they were actually very limited people, and did I think they were any more honest than anyone else? . . . This is again the market response, you see: they feel they have to. They are in competition to lend, and money is . . . something you sell and you've got to sell it because you've got too much of it on your hands. (4 June 2001)

Incompetence in overlending is depicted as organisational pressure, not an individual disposition. Floor traders are positioned by their firms, although Graham Ingham suggests they operate at a distance from their organisation:

Ingham: Traders on the whole work pretty much alone. They're expected not to lose money. Traders are held to be responsible for their own decisions. If a trader makes a lot of money he gets a fat bonus, and if he doesn't make a lot of money he gets the sack . . . I don't think an individual trader would ever be following slavishly a corporate view of whether to buy or sell. If they did, you wouldn't need them. The corporation could decide, press a button. (18 March 2002)

Traders are employed to make rapid decisions which investment firms rely on, because there cannot be a fixed 'house view' under the daily conditions of selling and buying. But national differences in corporate policies cannot be ignored, here in bank decisions:

Chan: The punishment system is very important as well. You can be worth a million dollars for making one decision in America, but in Switzerland or Germany you get a salary, so why the hell would you take the risk? If you make a mistake you're punished a lot. People make rational decisions ultimately because in the one case, if you lose money it's the bank's money, if you make money it's your own bonus. (5 April 2002)

That fosters a particular emotional outlook in the USA – recklessness, not caution. Traders, John Flemming says, are hired for a narrow skill that they may not be able to describe:

Flemming: The stereotype in London is that smart traders are not well educated, or know much about the fundamentals. They are professionals at what they are doing. There is an interesting study on billiards. You can teach people about bisecting angles and so forth, but if you do, they play billiards less well. The same may be true of the market, but late in the cycle, when the professional and slightly smarter people have made a lot of money, a lot of mugs come in. (13 March 2002)

Traders bring skills not informed by analytical economics. In Mike Lazar's words, 'dealers are like fish in the sea. They don't think about anything, they only think about the next mouthful'. However, another issue was raised by a Wall Street journalist. A stark example of latent emotions in private organisations, memory is no requisite, rather fearlessness is a standard operating emotion. Hale's comments were when the Nasdaq was starting its slow decline:

Hale: I've had conversations with some of the still older people who run the big mutual funds and you say . . . how are you going to manage things and what they say is, the next time there's a big blow-out, next time there's a big crash, we will have to fire 90 per cent of our fund managers because at the time of the crash in 1987 most of them were in school, they were still at university. They have no fear. Once they've been burned incredibly badly and they've learned fear, they'll be useless to us; we'll have to get rid of most of them and we'll hire a whole new breed . . . who've got no fear, because the old lot once they've learned that things can go down as well as up, they're too frightened – ah, but that comes down to the psychology. (13 September 2000)

Emotions of fearlessness are below the threshold of awareness, until events intervene. Caution and anxious memories of previous collapses (say in central banking) are the last emotions American firms require for traders. Although it is possible that traders could unlearn their fear and recover from being burned, investment firms prefer the less time-consuming, less costly process of hiring a new staff with the requisite emotion: no somatic markers of a disaster. Turnover in the financial world is not solely a function of booms and busts, or of 'skill', but of emotions.

WHO GETS THE BLAME?

Attributions of success or failure which foster emotions towards how to succeed the next time are recurring processes (Weiner 1986). Evidence from social psychology shows that unexpected outcomes tend to give rise to a far more extensive search for attributions than in cases where actual outcomes are expected (Figure 4.2). If the result is unexpectedly good – a surprising gain, an unusual win, an inconsistent rise in profits – slightly less search for causes goes on than for an unexpected defeat or failure (Weiner 1986: 32–3).

Rod Chamberlain, in discussing floor traders, drew an analogy with politics:

Chamberlain: Somebody once asked Macmillan, 'What is the biggest danger to governments in implementing their policies?' He looked [at him] and said, 'Events, dear boy, events'. What happens in the dealing room is that these kids start with a position and they have events pumped at them all of the time simultaneously, instantaneously, all around the world, and they crunch it. (19 March 2002)

No big outside 'events' halt this frenetic activity on a trading floor; each day's position ends from luck. But with unexpected internal (financial) events, the more the search for causes turns into a thorough post-mortem. Crucially, attributions – whether a cause is set down to internal or external sources, how stable or controllable the cause is deemed to be – have a strong bearing on emotions about the next decisions and actions. Attributions are as relevant (and emotion-laden) to an organisation as to an individual. So if success is attributed to internal sources such as skill and competence (stable, positive internal factors) or failure to plain lack of effort or a mere incorrect strategy (unstable internal factors), an optimistic, positive outlook is inspired for future chances: improvement is possible. However, if success or failure is set down to simple luck (unstable external factors) or to complete incompetence and lack of skills and ability (stable internal factors) (Weiner 1986: 175–6), a negative, pessimistic feedback loop can set in. As Chamberlain suggested, if outcomes are continually attributed to mere luck, a firm may as well give up. The feedback varies according to the attribution – with a successful outcome, the emotion may be pride in competence, confidence, gratitude, happiness, relief, surprise or satisfaction. After poor results, it can be anger, pessimism, disappointment, disgust, fear and paralysis, incompetence, resignation, gloom (Weiner 1986: 124–5).

These debates highlight later motivational effects of attributions. But social psychology neglects how attributions are formulated. Its impact comes back to haunt or encourage the boardroom or committee in their next decisions (Figure 4.2). More important is which attribution prevails in the first place? How do attributions about an 'event' get settled into being the 'accepted' prevailing attribution? One Fed transcript gives a particularly apt example. This institution is watched by the world – traders, the press, investment analysts – and is answerable to Congress in televised hearings. The Fed's responsibility for successful or 'wrong' moves is constantly debated. When Alan Blinder attended his first meeting of the FOMC as Fed Vice-Chair, it was just after Greenspan gained control of the February 1994 decision, cited earlier. His statements ascribe the outcome of Greenspan's decision to external, unpredictable, unstable causes. In July 1994 he said:

> MR. BLINDER: As all of you know, I wasn't here when this tightening started, and I was trying to imagine, if I had been here . . . what I would have wished for . . . I think what we have today is very, very close to what I would have wished for . . . which is to say better than anyone reasonably should have hoped for, because wishes don't usually come true . . . It looks to me like a three bears economy: not too hot, not too cold, it's just about right. It seems that the Committee was very, very lucky – [laughter] – skilfully lucky! Let me say for the record that you can do the right thing and be unlucky and come out in terrible shape.
>
> CHAIRMAN GREENSPAN: You can do the right thing and turn out right.
>
> MR. BLINDER: And you can do the right thing and turn out right. . . . (FOMC transcript 5–6 July 1994: 36–7)

When the meeting resumed the next day, a similar exchange occurred over econometric models versus 'intuition'.

Greenspan rejects Blinder's attribution of sheer luck instead of skill, experience and the 'art' of judgement (FOMC transcript 5–6 July 1994: 42). They debate different interpretations of past events involving mistakes. Greenspan refuses to accept that his decisions only succeeded from luck and failed (the 1990 recession) from poor judgement or flippant, 'irrational' analysis. He argues that inflation was not perceived irrationally as 'sinful' but 'truly undermining' stability at that time. Greenspan calls on the authority of his being present then, not Blinder; he criticises economic models – Blinder is an academic economist, not a 'practitioner' in 'playing the world' and its unpredictable complexity. Blinder must accept: Greenspan has the last word. Take also Governor Lindsey's attribution of 1996:

> MR. LINDSEY: Last night one of the TV news magazine shows had a story about people who won the mega bucks lotteries . . . and ruined their lives . . . [It] reminded me that we have been having a string of what appears to be good luck, although the people at this table all know it is the result of our skill at managing the economy! I would like to comment on the possibility that our luck may be running out. (FOMC Transcript, 24 September 1996: 23)

As we see in Chapter 5, Lindsey did not win the struggle over this attribution either. Greenspan refused to stem the speculative boom (beyond jawboning about insane developments), instead reinforcing *esprit de corps* via acquiescence to his triumphant definition of skilfully crafted outcomes, not lucky ones.

CONCLUSION

This chapter describes the emotions in finance organisations generated by internal decision-making procedures. Many emotions are *involuntarily* induced by the context. Evidence contradicts the conventional view that financial decisions are 'cool', instrumental and calculating, with no place for emotions, which are 'embarrassing' – as implying impulsiveness and lack of reason.

In contrast, *future-oriented* emotions are inescapable, because of the obsession with costs under extreme uncertainty. The promise of success is enclosed by insecurity of loss, whether of money or credibility. What is admitted is that decisions are often guesswork: neither a 'science' nor an 'art of judgement'. Many have great experience, and yet ways of taking decisions are dependent on particular emotions; some are explicit managerial requirements. 'Fearlessness' is a standard operating procedure for traders which cannot be cognitively managed. Cool aloofness with formal rituals and intellectual competition over reputation are required in central bank decisions to face down their diverse audiences.

I am not taking a normative view. Emotions are either good or bad: in specifically facing the unknown, rational calculation draws on a blasé indifference, a low-lying, ever-present form of emotional energy, but decisions are difficult: coolness heats up into stark, obvious emotions, even inside quiet central banks.

The experts are faster at seeing relevance in the data, but many of them acknowledged mistakes. Public sector decisions are far from private concerns about profits. Similarities emerged on how emotions are induced within organisations. Personal old school tie relations, now known as 'restrictive practices', are less important than impersonal positions. Playing the part is a key, but personal dispositions are irrelevant compared with rapid institutional adaptation under continual decision-making. Under competitive banking pressures, trust of the superior's experience becomes more necessary but reduces diverse opinions and can lead to scapegoating of those in weaker positions. Although longevity helps to develop an esteemed 'art of judgement', it silences other views; because successful outcomes are truly a matter of luck, the reputation must inevitably fail. Central bankers are least likely to accept emotions in decisions, despite evidence of constant battles over attributions about luck or skill. Interpretations of past outcomes shape emotional feedbacks about 'successful' decisions. A major difference was memory and incentive structures. Where the private sector has very little 'corporate memory' and rejects its role for engendering fear, the public sector engages in constant institutional recall, perhaps also disabling. Memory, intuition and a run of successfully 'won' attributions interact to gain trust. 'Unintended consequences' are a deficient concept since 'intended' effects are as unknowable as those unimagined. If US banks foster reckless traders, some banks later regret intended incentive structures, as collapses prove.

This chapter emphasises the extent to which anticipatory emotions generate expectations: impersonal relations of trust and fear in taking a leap to a decision. Praise or blame is not settled by appeals to the 'fundamentals', because money is not neutral but involves uncertain relations of promises and claims of trustworthiness to an external chain of banks, investment funds, and central banks. In the following chapters, we explore trust and distrust relations *between* organisations.

5 | Credibility and Confidence in the Central Banks

EMOTIONAL ENERGY IS generated within organisations. Internally, managerial control over rational and emotional norms gives some predictability to executives, though not necessarily fostering caution. Far more fraught are assessments of likely responses of other relevant institutions. These decisions are guesswork. Guesses are publicly framed in scientistic terms or, more modestly, as professional judgements, but reputations for good guesswork are bound to falter. Given that elites know this, what do reputation and credibility mean? Public institutions like central banks fret openly about their credibility. Economic researchers meanwhile attempt to measure the credibility of central bank monetary policies.

This chapter and the next two argue that credibility is uncontrollable and cannot be measured. Credibility arises in relational contexts of emotions at the organisation level. It is fleeting because it is created and also tarnished by continual struggles over attributions of success among these entities. Emotions cannot be managed indefinitely but, since trust is so predominant in this competitive era of selling money as a private commodity, credibility becomes implicitly mistaken as certainty. Every institution investigates how credible are others' reputations; moreover each fosters external perceptions of its own success, competence and reliability. Professional standards and legal, fiduciary and regulatory structures frame and support the attribution processes. When prevalent emotions like distrust shape these standards and structures, they can easily be overwhelmed by blame and counter-blame.

Judgements are unavoidable and elicit involuntary emotions. We saw this occurring within boardrooms, but all organisations are influenced by and negotiate with many others. Committees can split between advocates of trust and distrust about external claims and promises. In deciding, committees or boards must imagine the future behaviour of their opponents, allies or public/private counterparts. They must project debated or less explicit emotions of trust into possible futures. The trust position so decided – as rationally as possible – is always liable to revision, as trust depends on the lack of contrary evidence.

In these chapters I show trust issues in a new light by asking financiers and retired central bankers about their specific hierarchy of trustworthiness in the financial field. Chapter 5 explores old and new roles of central banks to see how their own credibility preoccupies them today. Central banks have statutory duties over entire national economies; prominent central banks are now burdened both with economic management of global proportions and with the requirement to be neutral technicians over an inherently political, value-laden task. Although central bank survival is assumed, their credibility is not. Chapter 6 is devoted to hierarchies of credibility *between* public and private financial institutions, and the reputation problems of private firms. Since reputation can only be retrospective, the entire financial sector relies heavily on past data. Chapter 7 considers dependency on information from data-collecting agencies. These aspects of credibility are difficult to separate, but my categories are not arbitrary, since public and private sector tasks and decisions are based on different principles, with constituencies broad (citizens) or narrow (buyers and sellers). All three chapters explore the same theme: various emotions for coping with diverse uncertainties.

Uncertainty is such that seemingly irrelevant constituencies can suddenly become relevant to institutional credibility. The gulf between the decision announced (Chapter 4) is only bridged after conjectured 'announcement effects' become actual effects, fraught with short and long horizons. In the public sector, central bankers use a jargon often called 'Fedspeak' in the USA. Without fear for their institutional credibility, bank officials could admit uncertainty to their core audiences. This is our focus here.

PUBLIC RELATIONS TO PRIVATE OR PERSONAL TO IMPERSONAL

In the 1930s, central bank reputations were low from abject policy failures in supervision. Constructive rescue was beyond their powers, but far more despised was private finance. To recall, Wall Street's 1929 crash reverberated into a global depression, the pound could no longer be supported as the most trusted world currency; the 1930s debt-deflation proved impossible to cure with monetary policy, however low central banks set interest rates (Chapter 1). World crises focused Anglo-American political leaders away from being dominated by private money as a commodity, towards long-term stability: American state management of the most trusted money, the dollar, was also more public than 19th-century Bank of England arrangements. The US Federal Reserve System (the Fed) and, in part, the 1945 institutions of the IMF and World Bank dominated globally over private financial networks. Also World War II severed many international banking networks and the 1933 New Deal SEC and Glass-Steagall Act minimised financial speculation (Galbraith 1974; Arrighi 1994: 278; Braithwaite & Drahos 2000: 133–8).

After the war, private banks redeveloped global networks, partly as Wall Street entered the City of London. Private control outside and over state money production was restarted by British merchant banks finding loopholes in Bretton Woods exchange rate controls, in eurodollar markets. Private creditors' demands for credibility in the central banks grew. By the 1980s many began to mimic the postwar Bundesbank, later the Fed arrangements: central bank 'independence' from governments over monetary policy was one change; another separated bank supervisory functions off to other prudential agencies. Relations became more impersonal, and while the balance of power shifted, it was more about the onus of credibility shifting onto central banks: and yet, should they lose it, the financial sector can and does face far deeper credit problems.

Some interviews compared private sector relations with central banks over the two policy eras, starting with notable regulatory changes. Sir Alan Budd describes previous Bank of England policies towards the then major British commercial ('clearing') banks (Barclays, NatWest, Lloyds, Midland). In his view, BoE relations with the private sector were personal:

Budd: Institutions are trusted to a greater or lesser extent, obviously. The former system in Britain very much worked on a fairly close relationship between the [central] bank and a small number of commercial banks. It was very important that there were a small number who *knew* each other and, I think one could say, trusted each other. There could be a shared objective, even though the Bank of England was trying to control inflation, let's say, and the commercial banks were trying to make money.

In that era, he argues, the profit motive was relative:

They were there to make money, but their willingness to make money was very much constrained by their feeling of a public duty. Not only a public duty, but also a feeling that if they didn't behave properly, the Bank of England could punish them in one way or another. Of course, that system has collapsed completely and utterly . . . There has been a process of change ever since the war. It accelerated with Big Bang in 1986. We still have the large UK banks which dominate retail banking, but the investment banks are largely foreign-owned; the old system could not survive. (12 March 2002)

The commercial banks took a restrained approach to making money, partly due to BoE regulatory discipline but also from 'public duty' – a rare term today. The key policy change in Britain, the so-called 'Big Bang', and its repercussions for personal ties between the City and BoE, is discussed by a former stockbroker who worked from 1989 to 1994 in HM Treasury:

Lazar: Big Bang was in 1986. It resulted from a change in policy under the 1974–79 Labour Government, adopted by the succeeding Tory lot, the aim of which was to break down restrictive practices in the City of London. It did this very effectively. Every British city firm is now owned by US or German or Japanese or some other foreign financial conglomerate. The City of London is probably a more efficient place, but no more honest, and arguably less decent – there was quite a lot in the old City idea of gentlemanly behaviour. In my first firm, there were still three Second World War veterans, none of whom would have dreamt of doing anything dishonourable in their business lives. (E-mail correspondence, 24 June 2002)

This seems less a nostalgia for 'gentlemen' than a defence of honest standards and public duties and a tempered approach to profitability under personal, restrictive control by government. Regulations to increase competition among banks and copy NYSE stockbroking rules, to reduce central bank oversight and expand foreign ownership, created a dramatic shift from these personal relations, so too the further US policy changes in the 1990s. In talking about global financial crises and the Nasdaq inflation in the USA, the late Mr John Flemming, a former chief economist of the BoE, argued:

Flemming: Some of those excesses are characteristic of a boom. He [Greenspan] tolerated a boom, and to some extent fed it. I don't know whether they are cause and effect, but the speed with which things went wrong after the effective repeal of Glass-Steagall is quite extraordinary. Of course one of the areas of excesses was in the pushing of IPOs and in things which should have been across Chinese walls. (13 March 2002)

He refers to Roosevelt's Glass-Steagall Act, which had kept commercial and investment banking separate during this temperate era, and rules against conflicts of interest (in the USA sometimes called firewalls, in Britain, Chinese walls). After waivers or exceptions were permitted by the Fed (Mayer 1997: 27) Glass-Steagall was rescinded in 1998. New Deal reforms had initiated impersonal trust relations in the States. The impersonal employment of external accountancy firms, the oversight of NYSE, Glass-Steagall rules, the Fed and SEC provided a trustworthy environment for highly competitive financial firms in a much more decentralised market than the UK model. When impersonal trust as embedded in these New Deal legal and statutory procedures moved to Britain, the policy environment was unable to cope: this is not about 'gentlemen' (such as Augar's *The Death of Gentlemanly Capitalism*, 2000) but the relentless selling of money as a commodity. Neither this competitive selling nor the financial sector's demands for external certainty was historically new; rather, it was the impersonal forms they took that were new. In Britain, the Thatcher Government imposed shock therapy in the form of the aptly named Big Bang, at first without even a comparable SEC or tough independent regulator. Too late, other financial centres copied the procedural remnants of New Deal impersonal trust from Wall Street. Gone was the close 'epistemic community' (Braithwaite & Drahos 2000: 124) where the City of London accepted BoE 'gentlemanly' control, at a personal level of shared regulatory and technical knowledge. Thus Budd compares British public institutions in an era of 'shared objectives' and relations of trust with private finance. Back then, it was personal and impersonal:

Budd: It was both, it's very important. People knew each other. It was a club. They met each other all the time . . . It cannot [now happen], there are too many, and they don't have a national interest . . . They know *some* of them, but there are just too many. It is a much more objective and impersonal relationship; it has to be. So this is impersonal trust in a way. If it is trust, it has to be impersonal. Whereas, as I said, in the old days the chairmen of Midland Bank, Barclays Bank, they all knew each other. They moved between jobs. The Governor of the Bank of England very often had been a clearing banker, that sort of thing. Everybody moved around, and they also told each other things which now we would regard as *completely* scandalous.

[Because of the personal trust] they did not have to be too greedy. They were basically told what was going to happen. If you do that now people can be shot, because not everybody can be told. There would be very angry people out there. The Germans went on doing this longer than most. The Germans still told their friends what they were up to. But the system worked. To make a familiar distinction, it is now much more of a market relationship than a community relationship. (12 March 2002)

Rule-bound, impersonal relations and exit capital market control demolished the 'English' inner circle of an 'epistemic community of finance', perhaps cosy but, during the postwar era, cautious and temperate. Implicit emotional commitments of 'Treasury man' in relation to the 'family village' of the wider civil service (Chapter 4) was analogous to how the BoE prevailed over the City: in 1957 the BoE Governor said: 'If I want to talk to the representatives of the British banks, or indeed of the whole financial community, we can usually get together in one room in about half an hour' (cited Braithwaite & Drahos 2000: 124). Today in the UK, while personal links are always forged among office-holders, global impersonal relations predominate:

Chamberlain: This is correct in the history, which gave rise to the immortal phrase that regulation was 'chaps letting chaps off over lunch', the days when people talked about the 'governor's eyebrows' – and if you were actually invited for tea at the Bank of England you really knew that you were in trouble. It actually worked. But that was then and this now . . . You now have five hundred and thirty something banks alone in the City. The Bank of England now has no regulatory role any more, of course. The FSA [Financial Services Authority] regulates God knows how many thousands of organisations. You cannot have nod and wink relationships with all of those, nor should you. The lawyers won't let you, for a start.

If the City is less 'the tight-knit and homogenous community of decent chaps it once was' – whether it remains more tight-knit than Wall Street (Braithwaite & Drahos 2000: 161) is a moot question. The 'new' City of London relations to the state are reversed; routine personal trust has vanished. Rod Chamberlain speaks of the Barings collapse in 1995:

Apparently when they went bust, the biggest problem the regulators faced was that none of them knew whom to call, or what the phone numbers of their colleagues were around the world – it's just that the logistical level is always hard for nationally bounded regulators dealing with a global industry. It is twenty years since anyone in Goldman Sachs reported to anybody in London. They all report to New York. What does the top guy in London do – looks after pay and rations, stops them harassing the secretaries, and meets and greets for Britain, or America. (19 March 2002)

Fed watchers employed by Wall Street investment banks are often trained within the Fed and maintain close contacts. Many central bankers trained as academic economists, bankers or regulators. Greenspan started on Wall Street, as we saw, in 1948; Blinder is back at Princeton, and Governor Bernanke is from Princeton. Naturally they all know each other and conferences are regular. Interviews with former Fed members mentioned inter-bank connections at meetings like the Bank of International Settlements in Basle. They provide a commonality among central bankers, particularly, as one said, given the unpopularity of their decisions at times. Some connections among G7 central banks are over global finance crises, but ordinary meetings raise other issues:

Budd: I do not know how important that is. It helps. I am not impressed by seeing a great group of central bankers all gathered together. I think, who is paying for all of this? That is my main reaction to it. (12 March 2002)

University conferences, numerous public speeches and televised press releases are far from traditional intimate secrecy and personal ties. While rightly less cosy, the impersonal, public relationships of central banks are dominated by trying to maintain credibility, because market rules now dominate.

INDEPENDENCE: FROM THE GOVERNOR'S EYEBROWS TO THE FED'S BRIEFCASE

Whether British Treasury was subservient to the City in the 19th century, the BoE was clearly 'independent' of government. Only between the 1930s and 1970s were private financial networks and central banks controlled by governments and international rules to reduce financial asset trading. Bernie Fraser emphasises further factors:

Fraser: Let's remember what the breakdown of Bretton Woods meant. It meant a more volatile system, with floating exchange rates replacing the fixed exchange rate regime and, in a way, changes in exchange rates have similar effects to changes in interest rates. I see the breakdown of Bretton Woods *and* the emergence of financial deregulation as part and parcel of the same process . . . one contributed to the other. But as things became more deregulated they became more volatile, and capital flows more significant. Capital flows increasingly affected exchange rates, whereas previously trade flows led to rather infrequent changes in exchange rates. But as the whole system was freed up, it became a more volatile environment, a more difficult environment for policy-makers in a way, but that led to a greater reliance on monetary policy because of the greater potency of monetary policy within the deregulated environment. (28 June 2002)

Central banks gained novel prominence after this dual unravelling. More than twenty major monetary, securities and banking crises have occurred since the 1970s: international monetary and national banking crises and numerous individual bank failures (Braithwaite & Drahos 2000: 135). Stability from the hegemonic dollar ended with Nixon's float of 1971 – the Bretton Woods breakdown – and in 1975 when competitive regulations replaced control-type restrictive practices on the NYSE. Overnight, every other stock exchange became globally uncompetitive and foreign investment flowed into Wall Street (Ingham 2002: 153). In what became an anti-state era, central banks expanded responsibilities economy-wide – not necessarily effectively – while under enormous pressure to rescue private network banking breakdowns. Whether central banks formed a symbiotic relation to the finance sector's demands for 'certainty' and stable money, governments were standing aside. Also banking evasion of Bretton Woods controls had become expensive for central banks to police. The public responsibilities of private banks were unravelling. Meantime, both right and left-wing governments – Reagan and Nixon as well as Johnson – exerted pressure on central banks. Looking back at political pressure applied to the Fed by Nixon, Graham Ingham recounts:

Ingham: [There are] plenty of examples of pressure of one kind or another being applied to the Fed. You don't have to go very far back to look at Arthur Burns, William Miller . . . I think for a central banker what matters is being perceived as taking decisions for the right motives. There's nothing damages a central banker so much as the suspicion that that person has responded to some kind of pressure. Of course, it's possible that those things aren't apparent at the time. A classic example is Arthur Burns expanding the money supply in 1972 so that Nixon would get re-elected and no one quite noticed it until after the event. So Arthur Burns' reputation wasn't quite so badly damaged as it might have been. (15 March 2002)

Politicising central banks appeared so flagrant that it perhaps legitimated a shift in trust about elected governments and their banks, as both seemed to have deceived the finance sector and electorates. Financial actors could effect their complete mistrust of treasuries by requiring 'credible' central banks that were independent of government – a distrust strategy. Monetarists claimed that banks were pressured into inflation. Credibility here demanded central bank independence, and for treasuries to surrender their discretionary powers to unelected central banks, partly from a simplistic equation between German economic success and the inflationary conservatism of the independent Bundesbank. In 1979 Volcker demanded, and by the 1990s nearly all banks had, greater operational independence. As they regained responsibilities over treasuries, this might include making monetary policy *appear* to be effective, as Galbraith (1958: 189) argued long ago. Certainly, the experienced American financier Henry Kaufman ('Dr Gloom' of Wall Street) sees two sides to renewed central bank prominence:

Kaufman: You can argue that in the United States when we don't have strong political leadership, the central bank becomes very strong. The Federal Reserve still lags behind many of the things that are going on. It is actually the entrepreneurship in the financial markets that is very strong. (29 May 2001)

Others agree that central bank independence leads to 'following' the market (Grahl 2001), or at least runs the risk of replacing the 'short-termism of politicians' by dependence on the short-termism of financial market pressures, in Governor Fraser's words (Fraser 1996: 589). Central bankers acknowledge that their influence over markets is uncertain (Blinder et al. 2001: 9). Kaufman (2000: 190) frequently stresses the need for an 'attentive state' rather than the weak, passive governments sought by monetarists. Central bank loss of regulatory oversight is also a concern to Fraser: Kaufman points forcefully to the inconsistency of keeping government out of finance until asked to bail out those 'too big to fail' (1986: 46).

One of many journalist books, *The Confidence Game* (1995), counters these diverse critics: Steven Solomon says central banks 'govern' but through a 'confidence game'. His idea implies a dynamic process, which in my view is an implicit reference to the growing dominance in central banking of attribution struggles and the 'personality cult'. In Solomon's breathless prose about Volcker's use of monetarist doctrine in 1979, 'winning credibility with financial markets was the central bankers' philosophers' stone . . . to creating a favorable power curve of market expectations' (Solomon 1995: 135). Kaufman's less sanguine view is that if Volcker had used monetarism to effect control over inflation, the 'rise and rise' of monetary policy emerged because 'policymakers had lacked the will to make Keynesian policy work'. By the 1990 recession, fiscal countermeasures were simply not available due to the 'staggering Federal debt' and Reagan budget deficits of the 1980s (Kaufman 2000: 199). In 2004, the IMF warned that the Bush Adminsistration's federal debt is a far greater straitjacket.

In conventional accounts, Volcker 'restored' the reputation of the Fed. Its distrusted role in allegedly succumbing to pressure from weak politicians could be mended by independence: it would be burdened with economic management; government fiscal policy and welfare expenditure must take minimal roles. Henceforth the Fed became a global model. Formerly in the UK, France and Spain, Treasury set monetary policy. Both the Bank of Japan in 1998, and the Bank of England in 1997 set up monetary policy committees that were independent from treasuries (Blinder et al. 2001: 113). Mandated price stability through inflation targets was introduced for the Reserve Bank of New Zealand in 1989; the BoE, Mexico, Brazil and the European Central Bank (ECB) followed with more or less tight targets. Even so, after controlling inflation (and the dollar flight) as 'the cure' and route to credibility, two decades on, the Fed faces deflation much like the Bank of Japan during the 1990s: having squeezed out uncertainty in one arena at the cost of mass unemployment (and more low-wage work), it emerges, as a Fed governor suggests, in speculative booms, corporate collapses and deflation (Bernanke 2003: 74–5). Central banking tends to retreat into the present, to recall the most previous loss of reputation, despite long historical memories. Although they aim against short-term thinking, 'independence' may be detrimental to this, as credibility is socially contingent. With monetary policy the sole tool, and supervision so reduced or thinly spread, the Governor's personal control over banks is over. In the new era, the size of the Fed Chairman's briefcase became a source for taking a punt on monetary change. Personal trust is now replaced by impersonal distrust/trust policies.

LEADING BY IMPRESSION MANAGEMENT?

After independence, the next demand was for central banks to overcome their traditional secrecy by moving to 'transparency'. In frustration at expensive US bailouts (e.g. the Mexican debt crisis 1982, the S & L crisis in 1989) where market rules were immediately overturned by rescue operations, elected representatives became uneasy. Starting with the US Congress, they demanded that central banks disclose their decisions to the public: orthodox economic theories also supported full announcements. Transparency has created further problems. It is supposed to increase central banks' credibility. But to whom?

Transparency is the theme of *How Do Central Bankers Talk?* Written by an Anglo-American-European cast of leading bankers and economists (Blinder et al. 2001), its partly inadvertent agenda is the credibility problems of the central banks. Central bank 'opacity' is redundant, they say, now that these banks are independent from government. The 1970s monetarists promoted transparency because central banks were allegedly biased to inflation. Banks should not be secretive, because they will not win credibility by taking popular public positions like reducing unemployment. In the monetarists' view, they gain credibility and a 'hard-won reputation' only from the financial markets. Blinder and his colleagues reject the idea that central banks have ever supported 'inflation surprises', even under pressures from financially hard-pressed governments (2001: 14).

Independence, Blinder and his co-authors argue, requires accountability and accountability requires transparency (2001: 16). This seems democratic even if 'the financial markets constitute the channel through which monetary policy actions are transmitted to the economy . . . Since this channel is dominated by expectations, "convincing the markets" is part and parcel of monetary policy-making' (2001: 25). They support transparency because 'a more predictable monetary policy – better understood by the private sector which ultimately sets prices – is also more effective in maintaining its inflation objective' (2001: 8). Central banks' control over interest rates is at 'the shorter end of the maturity spectrum' but it affects 'market expectations' which 'works through' to longer term interest rates, asset prices and exchange rates. They use the metaphor of a dog's leash, 'transmitting the owner's (the central bank's) command to the dog (the economy)' (Blinder et al. 2001: 9), which neglects how pushing a leash is ineffectual for a sleeping dog or a depressed economy. Critical views would use the 1930s string metaphor rather than the leash and add fiscal policy (directed at stemming inflationary or deflationary spirals), agreements among governments, business and unions on income, wage and price controls (attempted under Australian Labor governments), and banking supervision, not just short-term adjustments to the interest rate that central banks charge private banks.

Blinder and his co-authors also urge transparency to 'the public'. In this difficult defence, they shift positions. In the first, banks are accountable to the public and to elected officials. They are required to gain credibility from the markets and the public. In the second, the public and politicians suffer from myopia. They cite how 'debtors, homeowners, industrialists and equity holders routinely welcome interest rate cuts . . . almost independently of the prevailing conditions' (2001: 14–15).

If the public is myopic, the market is different: 'a goal of a fully trusting relationship between monetary authorities and financial markets is likely to remain elusive' as 'misunderstandings can occur' and markets may react 'incorrectly' (2001: 17). A transparent bank could become 'hostage to market sentiment', which might occur from 'herding' or financial crises (2001: 15). Banks cannot appear to be 'responding to the whims of the market' as their 'carefully designed strategy, the focal point of their communication efforts, would lose credibility' – even if 'adjustments' in 'rare circumstances' are necessary like the 1998 crisis of the elite hedge fund LTCM (2001: 25). What they call the Fed's 'modest but conspicuous' intervention – in arranging for LTCM's private counterparties (major Swiss, US and British banks) to recapitalise the firm, and the FOMC's rapid lowering of rates in three successive moves – was cause, they admit, of many 'concerns' as to whether it had a 'compelling public interest' (2001: 45). Why was this massively leveraged, elite firm of hardened Wall Streeters and Nobel laureates (Merton and Scholes) 'too big to fail'? As a British journalist said:

Elliott: Markets are very volatile, very unpredictable places. Attempts by people like Merton and Scholes to say you can trust these markets because we can tell you what is going to happen to them, are just fatally flawed . . . That is what the LTCM problem exemplified, that the free marketeers had completely overestimated the extent to which they could understand markets. They came to a Keynesian-type solution run by this man who was a devotee of free-market economics, Greenspan. He said, I am going to have to intervene in this market. [He] tears up the free market textbook, and goes for an old-fashioned interventionist approach, which is bail it out. (5 October 2000)

The FOMC minutes of 28 September 1998 barely mention it (Blinder et al. 2001: 45), but the full transcript, released in 2004, devotes many pages (97–119) to explanations by McDonough, FOMC Vice-Chairman and President of the Federal Reserve Bank of New York, and to numerous questions by members, often simply trying to understand the whole issue. Back then, headlines about glasshouses and stones (in *The New York Times*, for example: Stevenson 1998) crossed a world just then insulted by the IMF's and US Treasury's condescension about Southeast Asia's so-called 'crony capitalism' – not about the aggressive investment banks which left the region in chaos. Greenspan had opposed regulation of hedge funds to Congress only weeks before the scandal broke. The Fed's credibility also became dubious to non-financial corporations, as to whether moral hazard is distinguishable from 'systemic threat':

Dale: Take Long Term Capital Management. I've heard people in the Bank of England talk about this. The argument is that if a bank like Natwest is going to fail, it poses such a threat to the public financial system that it cannot be permitted to fail. But if some highly sophisticated esoteric player in the market is going to fail, it shouldn't pose a threat to the whole financial system. Players like that can't be allowed to be effectively supported just because they make a complete mess of it. Why should they be? I've heard many senior industrialists say 'I ran a major manufacturing company in England. We had huge problems. We were going bankrupt.' In some cases they went bankrupt. Did the Bank of England come along and say 'We may have had to let go ten thousand workers'? Why shouldn't we have been supported? Why should a bank which makes a complete mess of everything be supported? Who draws the line as to what is systemic and what isn't? (5 October 2000)

Yet the Fed's credibility continued to rise in the financial sector. According to *How Do Central Bankers Talk?*, the main distinction between publics and markets is this:

> What is good for markets is not necessarily good for the public. *The markets thrive on volatility while the public dislikes it quite intensely* . . . The markets ultimately see monetary policy as affecting their bottom lines, but monetary policy has wider redistributive and therefore political implications . . . The danger, then, is that central banks become too preoccupied with their communication to the financial markets and occasionally overlook their other constituencies. This danger diminishes the more open the central bank . . . First, transparency reduces the market value of central bank information, which allows for a more arm's-length relationship with the financial markets. Second, transparency allows outside, reasonably neutral observers to interfere if the relationship becomes too cosy. (Blinder et al. 2001: 26; my emphasis)

What form 'interference' might take is obscure. Take distinctions between public and private: 'It is both patently unfair and profoundly undemocratic to give certain market insiders an edge in learning about changes in central bank policy' (Blinder et al. 2001: 36). In other words, formerly only Wall Street Fed watchers deciphered Fed movements, whereas transparency is 'fairer' (*or* speculative trading less publicly repulsive) for minimising Fed watchers' exclusive know-how. As for the public, Blinder and colleagues suggest that 'citizens care little for monetary policy', do not understand it and make little effort to grasp its arcane language (2001: 23): we saw this failure of the financial press to translate Fedspeak. As the public does indeed see that bank policy affects growth and employment, banks 'must create and maintain an impression of competence' which, they say, generates 'quiet acquiescence'. But since central banks try 'to distance themselves, mostly unsuccessfully, from the real economy' (Blinder et al. 2001: 23), acquiescence is not automatic.

Full transparency to the public is dismissed, however. Bankers' technocratic worldviews were dominated (then) by private financial attachment to the 'certainty' of low inflation: for them, 'greater candour' does not require a central bank to use 'blunt language like, "The Bank of X wants the unemployment rate to go higher." More polite euphemisms have always sufficed in the past and they will continue to do so in the future' (Blinder et al. 2001: 31).

Volcker hinted at 'necessary pain' or 'substantial adjustments', avoiding publicly stating that the Fed deliberately provoked a recession in 1981 (Greider 1987: 394). Volcker's secret repudiation of monetarism in 1982 was even more evasive, in order to forestall monetarist and private finance criticism (1987: 506). Nevertheless, this more recent transparency seems to call for more public presentations couched in euphemisms of technocratic neutrality – to 'the public'. In 1997, the statement by a hawkish governor (Meyer) that 'inflation is caused by too many people working', in the *Wall Street Journal*'s summary, seemed a 'PR disaster' to other FOMC members (cited Woodward 2000: 186).

It is difficult to avoid inferring that central bankers' talk (according to Blinder et al.) has the object of building impersonal trust relations with financial firms and their orthodox economists who dominate public commentary with the latest, most 'credible' predictive theory. The exception to transparency (i.e. when central banks dissimulate) is the use of 'sterilised' foreign exchange interventions by central banks to surprise the Forex market – even if central bank attempts to manage their currencies are mostly in vain (Henwood 1998: 23). Only in dire events is the public included as an audience that assesses central bank credibility. Leading by impression management and condescension to the public is an openly admitted consequence of transparency. Governor Fraser argued in a National Press Club speech (1996: 590): 'A lot of what is written about the Reserve Bank [of Australia]'s "credibility" is in the narrow context of the Bank's credibility with the financial markets for delivering low inflation', and 'their (understandable) priorities for weak economic activity and employment numbers' because 'they imply lower inflation and higher bond prices'. He reminded journalists that the Bank has 'multiple objectives' and needed to build credibility in 'labour and other markets' as much as with financial actors who have 'more ready access to the media' than others.

But is credibility, in the sense of predictability, a further problem? For Blinder and his co-authors, 'interest smoothing' or small steps may help banks cope with fears or 'significant uncertainty': they can appear to be 'fearful of acting too strongly and having to reverse gears', and they may be in 'fear of criticism' of erratic behaviour (from market actors). Yet a 'small steps' policy is to surrender to private banks, hardly an arm's-length relation. When banks are consistent, 'markets can easily anticipate further moves' (Blinder et al. 2001: 21). 'Consistency' (the publicised research 'measurement' of credibility) is a straitjacket. Maintaining credibility is impossible if central banks are required to be prescient.

What all this means is that central banks occasionally carry out sub-optimal policies because they fear not to be understood and care for their credibility to the point of affecting their actions . . . Acknowledgment that a mistake was made, and then explaining why, does not have to provoke a loss of reputation. But then, maybe it does. (Blinder et al. 2001: 22)

The new European Central Bank's credibility to the private financial sector 'mattered' but was difficult to build. Its structure is unlike any other, yet an apparent lack of discretion in monetary policy was no help in managing the process of attribution. It had no central democratic government to answer or to play off, since each ECB member is accountable to their national government. It began when Greenspan's Fed was revered. The ECB took up a low inflation target but financial actors focused on the uncertainties of each member country. The euro reduced the number of trading currencies and therefore scope for market deals. In technical literature that attempts to measure credibility (Weber 1991), credibility is defined as 'consistency', where expectations (from economic forecasts) match subsequent policy announcements. The idea was that the ECB was to copy the credibility of the Bundesbank as a consistent inflation fighter. In this further depoliticisation of money, the financial sector held the ECB hostage to credibility, in the absence of a specific government to blame. In *How Do Central Bankers Talk?* one view was that 'acting' was a key to central banking: the 'markets' unjustly accused the ECB of 'misleading markets'. Although the Fed took the markets by surprise twice in 2001 (credibility measurements count this as detracting from reputation), it was then unfashionable to criticise the Fed (Woodall, cited in Blinder et al. 2001: 104). This is hardly surprising, because after 2000, Wall Street appeared reliant on the Fed for reassurance following the Nasdaq decline (even down to the size of Greenspan's briefcase). In Europe, the private finance sector cast scorn even though the ECB did not stray from its rigorous inflation target. Although the new President Trichet expressed deflation fears openly in 2004, the first ECB President, Duisenberg, was 'allegedly' unable to make 'decisive' announcements to markets.

The late John Flemming put an institutional view on the reputation-building problems of the ECB. The capacity to act is less important than the lack of a European treasury from which the ECB could prove its independence and make claims for success:

Flemming: The Fed is operating on Keynesian legislation [like the RBA, with inflation *and* employment objectives]. This makes the Fed arrangements a bit fuzzier than the Bank of England arrangements, not to mention the worst of both worlds, which I think is probably the ECB. They managed to make a bit of a mess of the definition of the target; they do not publish minutes . . . They select their own target so that they do not have external constraint . . . I do think that the crucial element of independence is independence of the central bank from the treasury. That is, a lot of the discussion in the context of the European Monetary Union was really pretty pointless, because in the absence of a European treasury the European central bank's independence was never in question. To mimic a number of the arrangements that have been found necessary in national governments was a waste of time. There is no European central treasury, so end of story really. There are some reasons why you might want to strengthen the European Parliament because of the absence of any other kind of control . . . I think that there are dangers in the question of how they should be held to account. (13 March 2002)

Flemming highlights what are in my view simplistic efforts to assume an automatic or spuriously measured reputation. The ECB's lack of a strong European Parliament and each government's loss of monetary sovereignty was bound to hamper finding a unified political mystique with which to present guesswork as mere technical matters. The ECB cannot monetise state debt as ordinary CBs do, nor does it necessarily have the capacity to intervene to avert private banking defaults (Ingham 2004: 188–96). Credibility was completely narrowed to indirect control of short-term interest rates, with an obsession about inflation:

Fraser: They do have a fair bit of credibility for fighting inflation, and from Duisenberg down, they're all inflation fighters – they see inflation as the main concern. That's probably the reason why Germany and other continental European economies are struggling a bit. Monetary policy is tight and it's kept tighter than it should have been for that reason.

The Bundesbank was not the only institution in Germany to provide stability in the postwar era. It was, like Britain's, a cosy epistemic community, yet the German welfare state expanded, and German corporations and banking institutions were under stable government influence:

Yes, but the culture of the central banking fraternity influences perspectives. The Bundesbank people to a man would believe that their stability, in fighting inflation, contributed to the recovery of Germany and everything that's gone with it. There's something in that, but there's more – it's not the whole answer. (28 June 2002)

For Japan's long decade of debt-deflation, the Bank of Japan and the Ministry of Finance responded not unlike the Fed and Bush Administration from 2000 on. In Paul Krugman's opinion (2003: 86), a firm Fed response was important because 'Mr. Greenspan is the only economic policy maker we have'. Japan's decade of failures after reckless domestic credit expansion elicited distrust, but possibly it is the lack of government and of BoJ credibility with *the public* that ultimately matters.

Flemming: Well, they have been expanding the money supply like nobody's business. They have been borrowing like crazy; they have been spending, until recently, like crazy . . . The one that they could do, but they would get a bad press, though they have done a bit of it recently, would be to trigger a devaluation of the yen. That would be characterised as a beggar-my-neighbour policy before, but they have been doing all the sort of closed economy Keynesian sort of things. They are in a liquidity trap . . . Right from the start they have presented it wrongly. They have undertaken bursts of public expenditure, mostly on pouring concrete, each of which was said to be [such a] large pump-priming operation that things would then become self-sustaining. They have tried that once, twice, three, four, five times, and it has never worked. So obviously their credibility and reputation is under question. As a result of which, when they do the next one, everyone says, well, why should I believe that this works? Maybe it just means that things are even worse than they had realised before so I should save, stack, push even more money into my piggy bank. (13 March 2002)

Central bank credibility seems to rely on apparent success, apparent 'control' in fostering economic activity and getting a good press globally. Pulling the monetary string to keep inflation down affects employment and so on (the ECB), whereas pushing the string to forestall deflation (the BoJ) is ineffectual or worse. After America's 1990s boom was over, a former Fed governor suggested another plank to the Fed's public reputation:

Gramley: As their understanding of the Fed has grown, their trust in the Fed has grown , . . In the financial world right now, [laughs] completely the opposite is developing. A significant amount of concern and suspicion is that firms are not being honest, that their earnings are misstated; no one knows what to say about them or how deeply to have confidence in them. So the Federal Reserve has become quite a revered institution relative to any one that you might select in the private sector. (7 March 2002)

Greenspan's Fed has faced the 'bitter Bushes' – bitter from losing to Clinton during the last recession; conjectures have swirled about alleged Republican influence on the Fed. The second Bush Administration's financial regulatory laxity, before Enron, and other factors, might work in favour of the Fed's own reputation: it all highlights the tenuous nature of credibility. Treasury's 2003 claims to thousands of new US jobs – hardly in sight – and a housing boom on more credit, only restored Wall Street's faith in the Fed. But what about the public's? Since Fraser supports governments' role in fiscal policy, he also sees a futility in central banks appeasing the markets:

Fraser: Central banks have been moving more to what I would regard as my position, that they have to do more than just appease the market. They must satisfy the broader community and the Parliament, and I think that's increasingly the case. Certainly the Reserve Bank here has continued to have regard to employment and economic activity. The US Fed has done that and even some of the European central banks have given more weight to non-inflationary considerations lately. This is what you'd expect, given that inflation is no longer a significant problem . . . at least for the time being . . . [Also] more people and more and more central banks are coming to agree that as well as being very, very short-term, markets – probably it's the same thing – change their views very quickly. Central banks shouldn't be bluffed and governments shouldn't be bluffed by the markets. If central banks are following a sensible long-term course, they should stick to it and they will find that the markets will eventually fall in behind them. They might express disappointment . . . but the next day they're looking for something else. (28 June 2002)

If central banks seek credibility with the finance sector alone, they will be bluffed.

LEADING BY GUESSWORK OR STICKING TO CONFIDENCE GAMES

Central banks may seem to fear the big private banks; they are rarely brave or aggressive. In 2004, for example, Fed governor Ben Bernanke supported 'aggressive and pre-emptive' acts by the Fed to ward off what he argues is potential debt-deflation in the USA (Kennedy 2004). Yet whether a decisive 'strategy' will actually work is one fear. Another is whether the chosen strategy will preserve, or detract from, the 'credibility' of the institution. These concerns are difficult to untangle, particularly when 'consistency', as defined by CB watchers, cannot maintain credibility if it proves a mistake. Past success is the fragile basis of credibility. But effectiveness is relative, constrained by investment traders and dependent on attribution processes disputed by other sectors and short-term versus 'potential' long-term outcomes.

During those booming 1990s, the levels of impersonal trust in 'Alan Greenspan', the embodiment of central banking mystique, had reached extraordinary proportions. FOMC members with little personal experience to match Greenspan's claim 'I have been on Wall Street since 1948' were unlikely to prevail (Chapter 4). Guessing correctly a few times is sanctified as 'skill'. One Fed official said: 'Decisions that the Federal Reserve make differ from conventional decisions, because it is not so such what *I* think but what the *market* thinks. It is very hard to know how the market comes to these results, and it is a big mystery' (interview, official in the Federal Reserve System, 2001).

Global private actors, for example Swiss banker Paul Chan, have reasons for the high reputation of the Fed, in comparison here with the Bank of Japan:

Chan: The Fed governs a much wider territory. It's much more dynamic, so they can learn and also source people better. They can find people to work for the Fed who know the market because of their training. The Bank of Japan operates in an environment which is extremely regulated, with few people moving back and forth; their environment is very uniform, non-dynamic . . . They want to bring themselves up to date, but structurally cannot find staff. The banks that they regulate are not quite as dynamic and open. They don't have the right information to tell them what's going on. (5 April 2002)

Though far from the personal club days among the City and Bank of England, a Wall Street or City experience gains approval, credibility from finance audiences as well as internal authority over committees. FOMC transcripts show how members' two concerns, guessing and reputation, are at the forefront:

MR. SYRON: What does the market think we are going to do tomorrow? (FOMC, 3–4 February 1994: 6)

MR. FORRESTAL: The credibility of the central bank is a very, very important element at this time, and I think we will gain credibility by moving now. (p. 49)

At this 1994 meeting, Greenspan and McDonough said their own predictions would prove correct and anything else would be highly 'damaging in cracking the markets' (p. 53). Later that year, more fears were expressed about investment traders:

> CHAIRMAN GREENSPAN: I am a little nervous about raising the rate more than 50 basis points . . . It's very important . . . that we not give the impression that somehow we anticipate major accelerations . . . If the markets believe that, then I think we have a very serious potential of creating a major negative market reaction. I think we have to be very careful to avoid giving that impression. (FOMC, 16 August 1994, p. 32)

> MR. BLINDER: If we are going to make this kind of policy credible . . . it has to be with a statement that indicates as clearly as we can state within the limits of Fedspeak that our oars are out of the water. That does not mean that we have thrown the oars overboard; we still have the oars [Laughter]. (p. 33)

Markets 'think'. One vital transcript was of a meeting three months before Greenspan made his celebrated 'irrational exuberance' speech in December 1996. Traders said then: 'Instead of raising rates, he is going to make speeches.' This is called 'jawboning', and according to John Cassidy (2002: 134), 'Wall Street had taken the measure of the man'. Thereafter, during the dot.com inflation, Greenspan stated publicly that the Fed could do nothing concrete about asset inflation. *How Do Central Bankers Talk?* includes it as a 'fundamental principle' to guide bank action: 'keeping inflation below some threshold, avoiding large output gaps, smoothing interest and exchange rates, containing asset volatility, etc.' (2001: 17). In Blinder's own view:

Blinder: I agree with what is the broad consensus – which is that it's not the central bank's business to manage the stock market. What is the central bank's business is making sure that banks are not proliferating credit unduly, because that is inflationary. That is all the central bank's business. But to make a judgement about whether the Dow Jones industrial average should be 10 000 or 8000 or 12 000, and then to act on that judgement, way oversteps the bounds of what a central bank should do. Not to mention what it's capable of doing, as you could be grotesquely wrong. Let me remind you that the great seer, Alan Greenspan, raised 'irrational exuberance' when the Dow Jones industrial average was around 6400; even now it's 9900. (22 February 2002)

In the September meeting of 1996, one FOMC member spoke of stock market 'recovery' and private banks 'making money' again (FOMC 24 September 1996: 18). Only Governor Lindsey stresses the opposite:

> MR. LINDSEY: What worries me . . . is that our luck is about to run out in the financial markets because of what I would consider a gambler's curse: We have won this long, let us keep the money on the table. You can see the early signs of this.

It includes real estate appreciation in the Hamptons, Connecticut, and Manhattan . . . The IBES earnings expectations survey for 5-year projected earnings hit a 12-year high in August . . . Readers of this transcript five years from now can check this fearless prediction: Profits will fall short of this expectation. Unfortunately, optimism is ripe in the markets. Excessive optimism is also necessary to justify current levels of IPO activity and valuations of highly speculative stock . . . This emerging bubble is . . . real. As a survivor of the so-called Massachusetts miracle . . . I can attest that everyone enjoys an economic party. But the long-term costs of a bubble to the economy and society are potentially great. They include a reduction in the long-term saving rate, a seemingly random redistribution of wealth, and the diversion of scarce financial human capital into the acquisition of wealth. As in the United States in the late 1920s and Japan in the later 1980s, the case for a central bank ultimately to burst that bubble becomes overwhelming. I think it is far better that we do so while the bubble still resembles surface froth and before the bubble carries the economy to stratospheric heights. Whenever we do it, it is going to be painful, however. (FOMC, 24 September 1996: 24–5)

Others see a bright future, but Lindsey's attribution of luck seems an attempt to dampen FOMC confidence; few investment firms will get out while the prices continue to rise, given their competitors and debt situation, therefore the Fed should act. After further debate, Greenspan turns to Lindsey:

CHAIRMAN GREENSPAN: I recognize that there is a stock market bubble problem at this point, and I agree with Governor Lindsey that this is a problem that we should keep an eye on. We have a very great difficulty in monetary policy when we confront stock market bubbles. That is because, to the extent that we are successful in keeping product price inflation down, history tells us that price-earnings ratios under those conditions go through the roof. What is really needed to keep stock market bubbles from occurring is a lot of product price inflation, which historically has tended to undercut stock markets everywhere. There is a clear tradeoff. If monetary policy succeeds in one, it fails in the other. Now . . . it is not obvious to me that there is a simple set of monetary policy solutions that deflate the bubble. We do have the possibility of raising major concerns by increasing margin requirements. I guarantee that if you want to get rid of the bubble, whatever it is, that will do it. My concern is that I am not sure what else it will do. But there are other ways that one can contemplate. (FOMC, 24 September 1996: 30–1)

Little more was said about 'bubbles', and Greenspan never did raise the margin requirements on stock investors. (Margin loans are extended by brokers to purchase more shares. The Fed, since 1934, has powers to limit margin lending. During the 1990s investors were required to provide 50 per cent of cash to pay for their stock purchases. Senator Schumer wanted it raised to 60 per cent. Greenspan refused [Cassidy 2002: 265]). Margin debt soared before the Nasdaq crashed in April 2000. Some argue that the transcript shows duplicity on Greenspan's part. As asset inflation rose far more, Greenspan repeatedly argued against various senators, that raising margin requirements would be ineffective, or 'unfair to small investors' (cited Cassidy 2002: 265). At a Senate Banking Committee in January 2000, he testified that 'the reason over the years that we have been reluctant to use the margin authorities which we currently have is that all of the studies have suggested that the level of stock prices have nothing to do with margin requirements' (Greider 2002: 6). By February 2000, the FOMC raised interest rates, acknowledging asset inflation, and the dot.com inflation declined, as did the whole economy. As a former editor of *Barrons* said, a year later:

Abelson: Well, I prefer Volcker by all means. I think Volcker was much more sensitive to the Federal Reserve's role. He was worried about excess to a much greater extent; he didn't consider himself as much a cheerleader as Greenspan does, for either the markets or the economy. He came in at a much more difficult time and he did a very good job . . . He was someone who believed that the Federal Reserve had to act as a countervailing force in the economy. When things got out of hand, 'too exuberant' as Greenspan would say, his job was to cool things off. When things were limp, in need of resuscitation, his job was to do that. His was an almost puritanical, and in the true sense of the word, conservative, attitude. (24 May 2001)

Even though Greenspan recognised asset inflation, the Fed's reputation seems the overriding issue, maybe also the credibility of so-called financial 'markets'. In August 2002, Greenspan argued against strenuous Congressional questions. It had been 'very difficult to definitively identify a bubble' (Greenspan 2002), but in the transcript he is unable to act for fear of other consequences. Early in 2004, Greenspan argued that 'our strategy of addressing the bubble's consequence rather than the bubble itself has been successful'; he was referring in particular to his 'highly aggressive monetary ease' (cited Aylmer 2004). In Abelson's words, in 'delivering a glowing tribute to himself' Greenspan, like everyone 'in exalted office . . . is concerned about his legacy' and posterity's treatment of his reign (Abelson 2004).

6 | Hierarchies of Trust

EMOTIONS DRIVING THE most significant decisions arise from assessments of each finance organisation. Their constantly monitored relationships generate trust and distrust, which are rarely fixed for long. The interviews show how differently knowledgeable actors order their hierarchies and define the trustworthiness of investment banks, credit-rating agencies, accountancy firms, pension funds, mutuals and the financial press, on the private side; and central banks, treasuries and prudential agencies on the public side. Fiduciary and other agent–principal relations are grounded on past evidence of impartiality, competence and trustworthiness. Often credibility is mistakenly attributed to a 'personality' for successful judgement.

Having explored central banks' internal concerns about credibility and their historical legacies, this chapter shows how their external worries are not comparable with those of the private sector. They are more obsessed with keeping their reputation, also measuring it as a 'thing'. With private firms, trustworthiness is defended in lawsuits, massaged and peddled as commercial good will. Whereas we, the people, may read transcripts of FOMC meetings (from the federalreserve. gov website) and watch parliamentary debates of our elected representatives – where emotions invariably rise and fall – the mighty private corporation is above such democratic scrutiny. Publicly listed corporations are marginally less so. How convenient. Reputation has a disputable, alienable and therefore alienating price. Each organisation is moulded by and moulds others: credibility – 'believability' – is assessed, misjudged and re-fashioned against other firms whose reputation is climbing, slipping, or in tatters. Credibility is relational, inherently conjectural. Confidence gained from attributions of success is sometimes routinised, holding long after institutions sustain failures. Whole sectors such as accountancy or mutual funds suddenly become a dubious source of respectability.

Problematic trust is neither observable nor measurable, least of all the shifting trust relations which keep recycling out of private wreckage. Reputations may parallel structural (or constraining) hierarchies, but not necessarily. High finance is not a 'system' because there are too many ignominious crises, too little restraint. Corporations thought impregnable just vanish; their allegedly measurable power (stock value: conjectural) no longer counts. Although central banks face none of this, the Fed's reputation was recently somewhat tarnished. This chapter explores whether these huge organisations depend on trust and on suppressing fear in global attribution struggles for credibility and trustworthiness. As the hierarchy changes, so do capacities and constraints. Impersonal trust is possibly the predominant relationship, easily becoming the contrary in impersonal disputes over loss of trustworthiness or sudden lack of credibility.

AVOIDING THE ODIUM

Central banks' obsession with credibility is about routine private sector assessments. Just as the Nasdaq crashed in 2000, some FOMC members thought Greenspan wanted to avoid the fate of the 1929 Fed Chairman by claiming that aggressive interest rates cuts would forestall a catastrophe (Cassidy 2002: 160). John Flemming, a former central banker, had this to say:

Flemming: When these great Ponzi finance schemes emerge, what should the government do? In the case of the Fed and the American bubble . . . there was no doubt in my mind that it was a bubble. If you believe it is a bubble and you let it go that far, there is a simple cost benefit for the central banker which points towards not pricking. If you are seen to prick it, two things happen. One is that *there are likely to be a lot of losers*, and if it has got very big they lose a lot. *You get a lot of odium.* The classic statement about central bankers is to take away the punch bowl when the party is warming up, not when a riot is about to break out. You take it away early. If you fail as Greenspan failed – given that his 'irrational exuberance' speech failed to arrest the process – then, if you think it is about to burst, the choice is this: either you attract an enormous amount of odium, or, if you have some confidence in yourself, [you] earn a lot of brownie points for statesmanship in picking up the pieces. It seems quite clear that if it is going to burst on its own tomorrow there is absolutely no point in attracting any odium for pricking it today. You would be far better to pick up the pieces afterwards. Now if that is what he was doing, the mistake was to make the irrational exuberance speech. People wondered why he did buy in, as he seemed to subsequently, to the new economy. There were also these allegations about the Greenspan put. It was a one-way bet, that was the point about the put. If it went up you took the gains and if it went down you sold, in effect to Greenspan. (13 March 2002; my emphases)

Gaining attributions of success, reliability, timing and futile 'forecasting ability' is a constant battle, yet there is fear of attracting odium even from 'the public', finger-pointing from everywhere. What could the Fed do? The Fed, the traders, and Fed watchers employed by financial firms watch each other. Records show the Fed is very sensitive to 'bad' commentary. Financial journalists (on the *FT*, for example) used the term 'Greenspan put' to imply that the Fed was encouraging complacency (metaphorical soft landings), that it would be a 'friend' to investment banks, saving them from market rules (cited Brenner 2002: 174). The institution walks a tightrope among its constituencies. One is the government of the day:

Fraser: Politicians will never change their spots and they will say when it suits them, when interest rates are rising, 'the central bank is doing it'. When interest rates are coming down they'll claim the credit for it. Politicians will always do that. The significant thing is who in reality is pulling the strings – is it markets, is it the government, is it the community? Who is pulling the strings? I don't think there's any doubt now that here and in the US and probably in the UK as well, the central bank is seen as the rightful and actual institution calling the shots, and that the institution is going to be held accountable for those shots. (28 June 2002)

To financial actors at that time, 1996, when Lindsey urged action to temper the speculative boom, the central bank was still meant to fight inflation. The problem for unelected civil servants was which *kind* of inflation – asset prices or wage prices? This is exactly the situation where less orthodox critics call monetary policy a 'blunt tool', and it also has different, but invariably global effects on bond markets: traders may be over-extended on bets (their demand for 'certainty') whether over low or high interest rates; global crises may necessitate lower rates (though 1996 was relatively crisis-free) or, as by 2004, higher rates, but only for global bond and currency buyers, *not* for domestic debtors like the US Administration or households. Perhaps if Greenspan continued to talk up that 'new economy' the Fed could avoid raising interest rates as employment rose. Perhaps his 'new economy' talk was intended to cure the most recent (neoclassical) belief that more jobs cause inflation (the NAIRU was still fashionable; by early 1998, however, news of rising employment caused such stock declines that it dented the public reputation of Wall Street, momentarily). Thus, inside the Fed, the 'doves' quietly accepted (Woodward 2000: 175–7) what was well known to labour researchers, let alone anyone who glimpsed Wall Street's own barrow-sellers and beggars: that most new jobs were very low-wage jobs. Yet Greenspan's confidence game further strengthened asset inflation and consumer debt, fed by the 'wealth effect'. In 1996, as we saw, Lindsey and Greenspan indicate comprehension. Republican 'Fed-bashing' against Greenspan's 'irrational exuberance' speech of 1996 was more debated during the fallout after 2000, so too his treatment at congressional hearings, which was far softer than Volcker's (Hartcher 2003).

At the opposite pole from eighteen years of speculation, Volcker faced contradictory demands from Reagan's Administration and its faith in monetarist doctrine. Some argue that the Fed's 'independence' was gained *against* monetarism and Reagan's regressive tax cuts (Greider 1987; Krugman 1997). Evidence of problems then about credibility to different constituencies – the public, the Administration, Congress and global financial markets – is from Lyle Gramley, a governor during Volcker's time:

Gramley: When you're there internally making these decisions, you're well aware of the fact that's there's an *enormous* amount of short-run pain involved. People lose their jobs, businesses go bankrupt. Families break up, people commit suicide. You can't go home at night when you're involved in something like this, without feeling *deeply* that this is something that has to be done. If you don't really understand that it *has* to be done you could not do it. At the time we were there, the housing industry was suffering to the point where builders around the country were encouraged by their trade association to get pieces of two-by-four, put their name on the corner, put Paul Volcker's name on it, stamp it and send it to the Federal Reserve. And these came in, in large trash buckets, huge things. I still have one at home, as a souvenir. It can be very difficult, politically, to conduct a campaign of this kind. You are doing something that is very unpopular. At that time, Congressman Henry Gonzales of Texas introduced a bill to impeach all of the members of the Federal Open Market Committee. And I saw that bill, and I saw my name, one of the persons he wanted to impeach. He didn't get anywhere.

Maintaining credibility with Wall Street was one issue. Avoiding the public odium while scotching economic fashions was another Volcker strategy, as Gramley attests in retrospect, though impeachment threats and builders' campaigns suggest it was not entirely successful:

One of the things the Federal Reserve did, during that period, to try to insulate itself from what was clearly going to be a lot of public resentment, was to change its modus operandi of monetary policy. You may remember the famous change on 6 October 1979, when the Federal Reserve said, 'We will stop setting interest rates, instead we will target the money supply, and our objective is to slow down the growth of the money supply in the interests of controlling inflation.' Now, no one said so at the time, but this was purely a façade . . . Studies beforehand had indicated that you could control the growth of the money supply just as easily by setting interest rates as by setting a path for non-borrowed reserves. Studies that were made *immediately* before the decision confirmed that judgement. The Fed went ahead anyway. It went ahead because it knew it was going to have to raise interest rates so high that if it took *credit* for this, it would bring down the wrath of the public, Congress, everybody, the Administration. So what, in effect, it said was, 'Look, we're not setting interest rates, we're determining the growth of the money supply', and there were not too many people who really understood what was happening. But this was a cover, to do what had to be done, and it was effective. (7 March 2002)

In other words, monetarism could be blamed and Milton Friedman's reputation and influence on Thatcher and Reagan would suffer, as it did.

ATTRIBUTION STRUGGLES OVER 'REPUTATION'

Gaining attributions of 'success' encourages further confidence (higher motivation to succeed in the same way), in a recurring process. Attributions are significant for their emotional feedback to those held responsible for a particular outcome. The struggle is a continuous juggling act around constituencies assessing central bank effectiveness and reputation. Unexpected outcomes – 'bad' news – gives rise to a feverish search for causes and a far more extensive search for attributions (Weiner 1986). With unusual successes, amazement turns to self-congratulation amid millions of 'winners', leading to implausible claims of sagacity, prescience. After a collapse, central banks try to continue with expected policy (predictable). As Bernie Fraser argues about 2001:

Fraser: The Fed has been a bit guilty, during its long series of reductions over the last twelve or eighteen months, of telegraphing its moves so precisely that the markets and everyone else knew what was going to happen, how rates were going to move, when they were going to move and by how much. I think that ran the risk of reducing the impact of those changes. I think it's still important for central banks to jolt the market from time to time, to give them a bit of a surprise... When you're very predictable you remove that opportunity to be truly pre-emptive... If you jolt, you mightn't be in for so many changes. I think five or six years ago there was a lot of favour for monetary policy being pre-emptive, for central banks getting in early, but in the last four or five years it's become more predictable. (28 June 2002)

Fear of 'announcement effects' – when unexpected by the market – seems to shape too many moves of central banks. Credibility concerns can lead, not to brave policy, but to providing mere predictability for investment banks. A surprise is only effective if secret or stonewalling. Central bankers who try to avoid dishonest representations suffer the odium of accusations of 'misleading' markets. The 1994 FOMC meeting when most Committee members wanted an unexpected decision – a brave 'jolt' – was contentious. Investment banks now feared monetarist and other 'hawks' because their memory of rate rises was Volcker's 1979 recession, which virtually halted economic activity. These were the fears that prompted the 1987 crash. After the recovery from 1987, borrowing levels for new financial products had risen under the assumption that the Fed would keep interest rates low. In 1994 Greenspan's timidity won, on his market expertise and alleged credibility from 1987, in his insistence that the majority trust his judgement. Before he 'won', the dramatic split and possible surprise had to remain secret. Greenspan had proposed 'drastic measures' (FOMC, 3–4 February 1994: 40) if a leak occurred in the middle of that divisive meeting:

CHAIRMAN GREENSPAN: If we end up tomorrow morning with anything in the newspapers . . . of what it is we've discussed today in any respect, I think it will do very grave damage to this institution. And the *Wall Street Journal*, the *Post*, and the *Times* . . . know it's a crucial meeting. There will be all sorts of endeavors to get some *information* directly, indirectly, or otherwise. I just beseech you to be as careful as you possibly can and not even tell your doorman where you've been! (FOMC, 3–4 February 1994: 40)

Journalists are usually the last to hear leaks and here, Greenspan suspects that they bribe doormen. As we saw, the independence of central banks from governments developed from contested attributions of distrust about the relation between treasuries and central banks. Credibility or trustworthiness is a social form through which an organisation gains a reputation as trustworthy, but what counts as credibility is socially contingent (Mieg 2001: 56, 178). Any sign of division within the FOMC might detract from the credibility carefully built up. Those who gave universal acclaim to Greenspan's 1987 credit-loosening forgot how, after 1929, Federal Reserve credit rose more quickly and rapidly than after 1987. The plain good luck of expanding rather than declining conditions was a different attribution that failed to gain much publicity (Eichengreen 1990: 246). If success is due to mere luck, an exaggerated public acclaim may give rise to a collective sense of shame inside a beleaguered central bank. Constant public questions, congressional inquiries and even, perhaps, this shame may foster inability to act, providing little further optimism about controlling the future. Hence since the mid-1990s central banks made creeping, predictable changes. According to V. J. Carroll,

Carroll: It's no good pussyfooting because the markets will just say 'Oh, you know, okay – tomorrow's rise will take care of that' . . . The effect of their decisions – whether they follow or lead the market – often is not clear cut, *unless* they are bold, and central bankers are rarely bold, you see. They don't want to rock the boat. (18 January 2001)

How the reputation of the central bank is created is less a matter of which debate is the more 'correct' than of how the attribution process creates feedbacks into the meaning of 'sound reputation', or unravels it into a 'confidence game'. With the sole focus on monetary policy, rather than fiscal policy made by elected officials, trust in unelected central banks becomes increasingly necessary. Given the limitations of monetary policy (particularly after a crash and its trail of debts) attested to by Bernie Fraser as much as by Abelson, Kaufman and Carroll (see Chapter 9), central bankers have constructed new forms of mystique.

THE 'CULT' OF PERSONALITY

The cult of personality emerged in this competitive policy era of impression management required of unelected public bodies. Central bankers now regularly give interviews to journalists, whose 'tick-tock' books recount every hourly move of prominent figures: 'now' talking to family, 'then' seeing the President. In Woodward's *Maestro* (2000), the cult of wise governance was located in one man, Greenspan. Although mystique remains the rule, *visibility* was not at issue during the heady 1990s. According to a British journalist,

Ziegler: Greenspan is someone who very carefully cultivates his relations with the press (always off the record), and who cares very much about how the press depicts him . . . He does see them often and speaks quite frankly to them – off the record. For example, when I was Washington correspondent for *The Economist* in the early 1990s, I would arrange to see him perhaps once a month. He was also a great party animal, and there was rarely a cocktail reception in Washington where one didn't bump into him. The central bank might be independent, but its executives are part of the same old government–press–lobbying nexus. (E-mail, 1 May 2003)

Yet not quite the traditional lobbying nexus. By 2000, traders regularly gambled on the size of Dr Greenspan's briefcase (an 'omen'), zoomed in on by the television cameras before Greenspan's entry at each meeting. This is a far cry from the days when BoE Governor Montague Norman (1920–44) travelled incognito, with cloak, top hat and even a pseudonym. Some central bankers were concerned about the omnipotence surrounding central banking in the 1990s, rather than simple competence (Grenville, cited Blinder et al. 2001: 102). That is open to interpretation by journalists who are less impressed by finance's 'epistemic community' or the transparency that still conceals what matters most:

Abelson: I never associate much intellect with the central bank. Here the central bank, Mr Greenspan and his friends have become extremely publicity minded, and the press is accommodating them . . . The other point is that central bankers are very devious types; they don't want to tell people what they are doing or why they are doing it. The cliché of the times is transparency and there has been an attempt to give things the appearance of transparency. Whether that means much, I don't think so . . . Transparency is a good thing, but things can be so transparent they are invisible. (24 May 2001)

Paradoxes and dilemmas face central banks. When agreeing about the Fed's place at the peak of impersonal trust in the financial world of 2002, Alan Blinder had these suggestions:

Blinder: The one place I would take issue with you slightly is that the definition of trust that borders on confidence is probably most fitting and, over the last decade, this confidence has been very personalised in the man . . . It's really personalised in that the Fed's position nationally and internationally will change when he retires. Think of this question: 'Who do you trust to run the world economy?' Everyone says Alan Greenspan, whereas if 'Smith' is running the Fed after Alan Greenspan, not everyone will say 'Smith' . . . To the extent that sitting in the Chair is so personalised in Alan Greenspan, [the Fed's reputation] is not automatically transferable. To the extent that it's institutional, it's automatically transferred. So part of it is institutional. But the cult of personality around Greenspan is so strong that a fair amount of trust, prestige and confidence will not be automatically waiting at the desk when the new chairman arrives. (22 February 2002)

One British central banking view of the Fed's reputation is institutional:

Budd: In what I would call monetary policy, there is great trust in the Federal Reserve, in the sense that people trust it to do the best it can, to behave honestly and mainly competently in its tasks. By and large, its tasks are to stabilise the American economy . . . So people trust Alan Greenspan. He is a decent and modest man, and whenever anybody says it is Alan Greenspan, he always says that it is not me, it is the Open Market Committee [FOMC]. What the Fed has at the moment is a trust in the way the institution does things, and trust with the present chap . . . The Fed has not always had a good reputation, but it has had a good reputation for some time. It had a good one under Volcker, and this has continued under Greenspan. It is an institutional reputation. (12 March 2002)

The cult of omnipotence is, therefore, bestowed from outside. Others suggest that the context was as responsible for creating the cult, and that the heightened reverence for central banks is a recent phenomenon:

Abelson: He [Greenspan] came in at the right time, and essentially his temperament is to do very little, which in this particular circumstance has been extremely good. I mean he's acted once or twice, as in Long Term Capital Management, and I think properly so. Essentially this deification is absurd; he's not even the best Federal Reserve chairman we have ever had. He is by no means an infallible person as far as economic acumen goes. All Federal Reserve chairmen have managed somehow to keep a certain aura about them.

On whether Greenspan 'believed', at that time, in 'new economy' claims, Abelson says:

That I am incapable of answering. You certainly can't tell, because there are days when he seems to and days when he doesn't. It depends on which day of the week you are asking about. There is a lot of Wizard of Oz about this fellow. He has seen the movie more than once, but never read the book I am sure. [*The Wizard of Oz* is] about a phoney wizard essentially, who had all the confidence that you are talking about. (21 September 2000)

The institutional reputation (the dominant leader, the best at Fedspeak) bestowed on Greenspan was possibly from heightened tensions at the end of a bull market. Fashionable theories about anonymous markets seemed, ironically, to require a mythical figurehead to assuage the uncertainties of what finance journalists suspected were huge Ponzi firms (Chapter 3). Fed watchers inside Wall Street became reliant on Greenspan's predictions. Since these invariably fail (Chapter 7), emotions cannot be managed indefinitely either by financial markets or central banks. Once caricatures appeared in the *New Yorker*, like 'Saving Face' (Blitt 2002), a cartoon about a mythical financial disaster caused purely by the fanciful idea that Greenspan might 'Botox' his face to erase his famous wrinkles, everyone knew that speculators were gambling on facial clues. Impression management by unelected entities is obviously unavoidable if public facial expressions are included in the aura. Market actors seemed to require public claims to technical infallibility: uncertainty must be denied, contained, albeit heavily qualified by jargon; when central banks finally say 'upside or downside symmetrical', that means they do not know if future inflation risks lie in deflation or inflation. The 1990s cult of personality surrounding Greenspan gave an aura to monetary policy as always 'effective'. The carefully 'earned' reputations of central banks focused exclusively on inflation, which limits their potential to reverse policy, supervise foolish hedge funds or admit the contingency surrounding their earlier reputation for success. As confidence in such a trusted institution dwindles, though holding long after a series of failures, organisational sensitivity turns to panic, and defensiveness turns to spin, on a downward spiral. The attribution process is always contested, but if forex or investment firms require central banks to predict the future, to validate every expectation, such omnipotence was bound to fail.

PRIVATE/PUBLIC CREDIBILITY: HIERARCHIES OF DISTRUST

Having looked at central bank problems of credibility with the private sector, we now turn to the private financial sector's trust relations and reputation problems. Conventional optimists (who see money as neutral in the long run) argue that global designs emanating from rational market processes will correct investor mis-judgements such as speculative booms and crashes. Orthodox economists call this mere 'herding' behaviour which has no lasting economic significance. Pessimists see sinister conspiracies or a Washington–Wall Street consensus that is hegemonic. Financial cross-sector frauds and catastrophes from selling esoteric financial in-struments as risk-free undermine these diverse views (for a while). In looking at *normal operations* of finance among ethically driven public and private entities, we ask whether continual interplays of impersonal emotions between organisations are unrecognised until they turn badly to the contrary. Uncertainties created by money relations are hardly trivial but involve vulnerability and insecurity. With collapses, uncertainties are 'intolerable', anger and fear are expressed, until optimism (revived, so often, by we, the people paying in fees, taxes or deflation) sweeps away lurking doubts. How do switches in credibility occur? Most publicised scandals are inten-tional deceptions or massive foolishness, but there are many grey areas which are legally untouchable even if similarly dubious. More interesting are latent distrust strategies leading to confident expectations of certainty, even when uncertainty is acknowledged through insurance.

For central bankers, most are not so naive as to 'trust' large segments of private finance. Alan Blinder's ranking was similar to other central bankers interviewed:

Blinder: From the Fed's view, the financial press rank lowly [in the finance world], the investment banks probably very low, the mutual funds and pension funds higher. But how to rate each of them vis-à-vis the banks? The Fed has the most contact with and the most nuanced view of the banks, which leads to a wide range.

There are straight, honest, trustworthy banks; and there are some bad players. That's the nature of being a regulator of those banks. (22 February 2002)

A similar hierarchy exists among the cautious and sceptical private bankers.

DISTRUST STRATEGIES TO DISHONESTY

Trust is an inescapable element of finance, completely paradoxical. As John Edwards, Chief Economist of the HSBC for Australia and NZ sees it, there are two elements, trust and distrust:

Edwards: The entire financial business is completely dependent on trust. I work in a Treasury where almost all of our traders are engaged in the inter-bank market and they work on the assumption that the trades that they make will be honoured. Deals will be honoured within a market. From the bank's point of view, the first circle of trust would be other banks, identified by reputation. We do categorise banks, so it's not entirely trust. Edicts are issued about the extent to which other banks can be given credit lines. (12 February 2002)

HSBC was built in Asia and is one of the conservative banks with caution its global criterion. It refused to lend to hedge funds long before LTCM, due to lack of clarity about their obligations and the likelihood of over-leverage. Elsewhere, in these decades of financial pre-eminence, firms' credibility and claims to trustworthiness emerged out of two trust strategies. The first was that governments should leave the private sector to regulate itself: everyone should trust the free market since markets can reach perfectibility. Second, a range of distrust strategies developed towards every organisation, in particular corporations. But, consider the failures. What is striking is that no firm or sector trusts any other, yet they depend on trust. Money, a social relation of promises, is merely a believable promise (to the creditors) made by others (debtors) that the issuers (creditors) also promise they will accept: credibility is tautological except that it seeks future certainty. Credit-rating agencies provide credibility for a time, central banks at times, with the major exception that central banks are the issuers of liabilities which are the most credible, acceptable promises (Chapter 1) *if* 'we' pay taxes. Orthodoxy pretends money is a 'thing' dependent on 'real' measurable goods and not fragile promises. Do they have to pretend? If money does not matter, why are there constant assessments of public and private creditworthiness? Cycles of government intrusion (grandly called 'new financial architecture' in 1998, 'governance' in 2002–04) impose a standard for each previous catastrophe from leaving the private sector to self-regulate or new yardsticks to tether money on thing-like, neutral fundamentals (Chapter 7). Regulatory tinkering fails from massive expense, new loopholes discovered, or officials succumbing to bribery from finance's august institutions (as a London banker remarked). New sources of credibility emerge from the wreckage of attribution struggles.

White-collar crime is mostly located in financial firms, fostered and often concocted by the firms (Shapiro 1984), but cases of embezzlement, bribery or financial loopholes are a symptom of today's larger world of impersonal trust organisations. Corporate raids, downsizing and mergers are now misnamed 'growth' in this increasing commodification of financial assets and securities among all corporations. In essence, all are about a distrust that corporate management will keep its promise: namely that management will increase investor stock value. These unrecognised emotions – self-deceptions like distrust which assume greed in a context of self-regulation – lead to firms 'living down' to the distrust so imposed. Economist Paul Krugman said that when he started as a journalist on the *New York Times* he received letters saying 'Corporate America is full of Ponzi schemes and some of our biggest corporations are false fronts' (*Texas Observer*, 10 October 2003). He suffered what many journalists 'continue to suffer . . . that it was just too hard to believe': that a 'company with the eighth-largest stock valuation' like Enron could be just a Ponzi.

Regulators cannot assess future promises any more presciently, and private assessors take turns with public agencies as sources of credible scrutineers. Who guards these guardians? Like the trustees, the guardians of trust have opportunities for abuse. In Enron's case, Andersen's accountancy firm proved untrustworthy. The area is always ripe for corruption: a truthful negative audit is hardly favoured by a corporation wanting to cover up huge debts or secret profits. Most relevant, even the most honest guardians are asked to do the impossible, namely to predict the future.

THE FINANCIAL PRESS OR THE INVESTMENT BANKS?

Sceptical journalists argued that only 20 per cent of financial journalists were well informed, that financial media organisations failed their institutional trust role, and that many journalists were shills. Overwhelmingly, from central bankers to investment bankers, a consensus among these informed sceptics was that the finance press was the least trustworthy, the most excluded ('that's their lot', said a British central banker). Many qualified this, in considering the leading players of stock booms, by citing stockbroking and investment banks. In Zürich, Werner Frey agreed that the press's standards were very low:

Frey: There are very, very few exceptions among them, probably two British, the *Financial Times* and *The Economist*, but the rest . . . are not of a high credibility. But this is, to be fair, mirroring a phenomenon which I call 'the financial peepshow'. I do not know any other industry that is so person-oriented, so story-oriented as is the financial industry . . . I mean, clearly the investment banks earned most of the money, in that time, with ideas and yes indeed, they had the vested interest in talking it up. So I would rather blame the investment banks leading the new issues, setting up the new markets, than the financial press or Wall Street. What is Wall Street? Wall Street is the marketplace. Do you blame the marketplace for the bad salad you get? It's probably the man who sells you this salad . . . who is to be blamed that it's rotten. (4 April 2002)

If vendors are concocting a Ponzi with producers, public exposure needs media proprietor support – media corporations with deep pockets. Henry Dale's description of global bank lending and investment around the 1998 collapse of LTCM clearly illustrates Frey's view that emotions are not exclusive to journalists:

Dale: Take Russia. Everybody was talking about going into Russia, then people lose their shirts. Banks have *an infinite capacity for losing money* with such crass actions . . . And it takes a very brave banker to say 'No, I don't think we should be doing that', and stick to it. A few have done in the past – some of the ones that I find very interesting people. But of course if they're all quoted companies and they're all driven by the kind of fever that inhabits them – 'Why aren't we all in Russia, why aren't we all investing in Russia, everyone's talking about Russia, we're all going to make lots of money in Russia, this huge bank is doing this in Russia' etc. (5 October 2000)

Public regulators may be the braver institutions, at least for publicising misdemeanours. Yet British finance journalists eventually uncovered the 1980s scandals because supervision was unfashionable. In the case of Wall Street's 'exuberance', only the New York State Attorney General office had sufficient legal protection to uncover Wall Street's misdemeanours over the 1990s, despite the best efforts of sceptics. It came too late, possibly because the Fed's defence of LTCM fostered a collective emotion of invincibility on Wall Street – a barely distanced, lender-of-last-resort case of 'too much, too early' (Kindleberger 1989: 197).

Errors of prudential regulators – which have nothing like the wealth of central banks – is primarily starvation of government funds (interviews cited the SEC, APRA, FSA, many sympathetically; also FOMC 1998: 110). No technical solution is available: all have the impossible task of guessing the timing (with its attendant later 'excuses'). 'Too little, too late' brings down honest, solvent firms (and ignites public wrath). Following press exposure, the Bank of England closed British branches of Bank of Credit and Commerce International (BCCI), a bank responsible for the world's largest banking fraud. Although this was a case of 'global vulnerability' to global money (Davies 1994: 428), the liquidator of BCCI, Deloitte & Touche (of Deloitte Touche Tohmatsu), sued the Bank of England for £550 million and interest, accusing it of being 'deliberately or recklessly negligent'. The ten-year case, fought in Britain's highest courts, is being heard in 2004. It may prove a PR disaster for the BoE's reputation, given cited memos of BoE officials claiming that BCCI's founder was a 'slippery customer', yet licensing BCCI in 1980 (Vina 2004).

In comparison, on Wall Street, investment banks like Merrill Lynch were fined $US100 million in June 2002. The New York State Attorney General in taking court action said: 'This was a shocking betrayal of trust by one of Wall Street's most trusted names. The case must be a catalyst for reform throughout the entire industry.' Internal e-mails were strong evidence of duplicity. One analyst called an internet company's stock 'a piece of junk', yet as the company was a major client, he gave it Merrill's highest stock rating. Some expressed concern for individual investors, thus a research analyst giving a 'buy' rating to a poor investment said: 'I don't think it is the right thing to do. John and Mary Smith are losing their retirement because we don't want a client's CEO to be mad at us' (E-mail within Merrill Lynch). Such doubts sometimes lead to brave whistleblowing.

Merrill Lynch could not scapegoat a single individual or unit, Eliot Spitzer's suit argues. The head of the equity division had conducted a survey to find out 'the complete details' of every analyst's work in bringing in business, such as 'the degree [to which] your research played a role in originating . . . [banking business]'. That is, the firm was keenly interested in analysts who talked up firms to gain those firms as clients (Office of the Attorney General 2002). In trying to shift the attribution of corruption and negligible firewalls, finance firms used various unsubtle defences: about rogues or 'mum and dad' emotional exuberance. LTCM's collapse in October 1998 was quickly forgotten: the same could happen for stockbroking scandals. LTCM intimidated major banks (from Merrill Lynch to UBS and Chase [FOMC 1998]) into lending huge sums while refusing to admit its extraordinary leverage ($US1 trillion):

Abelson: The interesting thing in that case just reinforces what I say of the level of intelligence and gullibility. Gullibility is as high in the most successful people in Wall Street as it is among those several rungs down the ladder. So LTCM is a very illustrative case, I think. (21 September 2000)

Henry Kaufman highlights the contradictory roles of investment bank businesses. Trust is primary but profitability is often too overwhelming:

Kaufman: I continue to feel . . . that financial institutions have a kind of a balancing act to perform. They have a fiduciary responsibility and an entrepreneurial drive. This is a difficult balance because . . . financial institutions by their very nature are highly leveraged, with small capital and large liabilities. The more you can leverage, the higher risks you can take, with potentially higher rates of return on the thin capital. Since you are dealing with other people's money, either in deposits or in the form of borrowing – it doesn't make any difference – you have a kind of quasi-public responsibility. In a highly motivated world, a risk-orientated world, an entrepreneurial world, it is very difficult to balance this, and that is where official supervisory responsibility has to come in. (29 May 2001)

Financial firms are highly leveraged, and have a fiduciary relation to those entrusting their money in the purchase of competitive entrepreneurial services. But gullibility is easily re-created. Money, in Dominic Ziegler's account, seems to circle around the financial sector's credibility.

Ziegler: It was always my assumption that if you're dealing with money, if you're close to it, some of it sticks to your palms, and that's why people in the City of London earn such fabulous amounts. Traditionally financiers have been able to do that by pretending to be alchemists, and good alchemists don't show the admiring public exactly what they do to produce the gold. [In 2002] there's now a lot less trust in the guardians of your money. (14 March 2002)

Despite scandals, investment banks retain immense influence on firms' credibility – because selling stock is a threat which makes CEOs panic and boards collapse in acrimony. Firms that give confusing signals are punished or threatened by analysts' reports, for example Telstra's 'Agitated confusion gets on market's nerves' (*Australian*, 4–5 May 2002) remain common headlines. During 2002, when analysts might have tempered their sagacity, French efforts to revive Vivendi were criticised for avoiding the question of whether corporate elites can 'buck the market'. The idea that French capitalism could neglect market disciplines of 'le capitalisme sauvage du modèle anglo-saxon' was, *The Economist* anonymously thundered (5 October 2002: 66), ludicrous. 'Investors will stick with a France Telecom or a Vivendi only if they trust bosses to spell out clearly how they are proceeding – and to do what the markets want. If not, they can take their money elsewhere.' Why investment banks know the future any better than corporations is not a consideration.

Yet every bull market collapse brings scepticism into high relief, where formerly it had been censored. The change is very simple:

Abelson: There is nothing like four trillion dollars worth of losses to increase one's scepticism, and that has happened. Wall Street's oxygen is hype, so it is not going to ever disappear completely; it has its moments of relaxation and lapse. (21 May 2001)

ACCOUNTANCY FIRMS

Most large public corporations employ high-profile accountancy firms. Before 2002, Andersen and the other 'Big Five' seemed at the peak of the attribution chain. During Andersen's demise, previous, 'reliable' information became a frightening fiction, though long experience casts a shadow:

Abelson: This is a process of, you might say, quiet corruption. Accountancy firms have always been the handmaidens of corporations. And I remember the 1960s particularly, which was the last great speculative epic, and what you find is that then the accountants were willing servants of whatever the corporations wanted them to do, to bend accountancy to their purposes. Accountants have no longer restricted themselves to auditing functions, but have gone into consultancy, which has led to conflict of interest. There are hearings as we speak. The SEC says you can't have this double role and it's not clear. The SEC is doing a good job, it's come under enormous pressure, and as the Republicans have always been closer to big business, the firms have become very adept at lobbying Congress; this has never happened before. (21 September 2000)

Each decade's accounting scandals has brought inquiries, reports, 'reforms' and new accounting standards. No interview yielded a flattering portrait of accountancy firms. Coopers Lybrand was the auditor of British tycoon Robert Maxwell's firm which defrauded £400 million from thousands of pensioners in 1991. In 1999 Coopers was fined barely a single year of Maxwell's audit fee, complained Simon Jenkins in *The Times* – calling them 'Maxwell's Backroom Boys' (Jenkins 1999). Michael Lazar tells a similar story of another British firm:

Lazar: I would not trust them as far as I would spit at them, and I will tell you lots of stories about them. I won't bore you, but stories about the rank dishonesty of the top firms . . . I can give you one example where the person who did the auditing told me that they never checked the say-so of a man who was notoriously dishonest. He used to keep his books in a locked room and he wouldn't allow the accountant guy into that room. (4 June 2001).

As in other accountancy scandals, the accountancy firm did nothing: 'Because who pays the bills?' asks Lazar. 'I would put the accountancy firms bottom actually; they are the biggest crooks.'

A host of panels – US committees, royal commissions in Canada, Australia and Britain – have explored accounting standards since the 1970s. In 1999, one proposal that a company's financial statements be 'fairly' presented was roundly condemned by 'the corporate and legal' sector (Schuetze 2001: 7). Unfortunately, since the 1930s, the SEC has argued that 'fair values' are 'too soft' (2001: 27). Accounting standards permit corporate practices like the 'disease' of 'earnings management' (2001: 6). Arthur Levitt Jr, then Chair of the SEC, criticised 'earnings management' in 1998: 'big bath restructuring charges, creative acquisition accounting, cookie jar reserves, improper revenue recognition and abuse of materiality.' Massive overstatements by management are matched by massive understatements. Loading losses into one year is also misleading because it is intended to make the next year's results look 'stronger'. According to a former chief accountant of the SEC, corporate manipulation of earnings faces no objection from external auditors. It goes on 'in broad daylight'.

> Everyone on Wall Street knows it is going on. The SEC knows it is going on . . . Every institutional investor knows it is going on. But, the individual investor who is not part of the Wall Street in-the-know crowd doesn't know it is going on . . . Maybe members of Congress don't know it is going on . . . Because the accounting rules allow for earnings management, the SEC can't stop it. (Schuetze 2001: 10–11)

Auditors are often only 'handmaidens' or 'client pleasers'. In one case, the 'self-confessed shredder who wanted only to please', Andersen's employee, had his own office in the Enron building, and allegedly destroyed the documents used to audit Enron. He became bold from success, 'amply rewarded and pushed by an ever-demanding client' yet reluctant to be confrontational. 'He is not the kind of person in a business meeting to be disrespectful' (Raghavan 2002). Since then, some argue that the Big Four survivors cut Andersen's loose, allowing it to take the brunt of criticism of auditors (Clarke et al. 2003: 216), and little has changed.

Rotating the whole firm of auditors from firms, such as Grant Thornton's rotation off Parmalat Finanziaria, did not prevent the Italian multinational's unexpected bankruptcy in January 2004 amid allegations of questionable reporting. Although Prime Minister Berlosconi had decriminalised accounting manipulations just previously, the auditors of Parmalat were not consultants either (a lack of firewalls was the criticism of the 2002 scandals). Other recent rules about 'independence' appear impotent over contemporary corporate structures and the social loyalties required of paid 'outsiders' like directors and auditors (Clarke & Dean 2004; see Chapters 7 and 9).

DISTRUST AND STOCK OPTIONS

Hierarchies of trust shift, often rapidly, from these agent–principal scandals, but there is more to it. The other 2002 scandal about CEOs of collapsed firms taking huge share options was at the time described as an 'alignment of interests' between share-owners' and CEOs' interests that went fatally wrong. Top managements formed a 'conspiracy of interests' and abused their insider information positions as agents for the principals. These asymmetries of information between insiders and outsiders allowed numerous CEOs to sell out in the nick of time. Severe problems are, however, involved. Stock options are a distrust strategy aimed at maintaining and raising shareholder value but, in imputing greed but little or no loss for failure, they foster increased greed and recklessness.

Fraser: It offends me that so many CEOs and directors take a large part of their income through share options – i.e. through capital gains which are lower taxed, so it's tax-driven. That's one point that's offensive. The second point is that many of these share options are totally without any performance criteria. They're without risk, because they're options they don't have to take up. And thirdly they're not usually expensed in these companies' accounts. There's more evidence now that if they were expensed, profit numbers would be 4 or 5 per cent lower than have been recorded. And while I can't prove it, a fourth reason is that I suspect that share options and the drive to hold up share prices lie behind some of these WorldCom and Enron debacles that have been going on. (28 June 2002)

The principals do not trust that the agents will prove to be trustworthy in the future, but distrust itself encourages deceit. Even if management does not succumb to deceit, it still faces uncertainty – heightened by positioning management to take greater risks. There may have been no 'abuse' but still a collapse, as the firm was fine until the share market dropped or the exchange rate shifted. Excuses may not be dishonesty, but distrust is an aim for certainty, a projection of a controllable future.

Some corporations complain that constant pressure for shareholder value makes long-term investment decisions far more difficult:

Abelson: What they're saying is true. They put it in a different way, because anybody paying so much attention, as the investment world does, to quarterly or daily developments can't possibly plan for more than a day or a quarter. That also reflects the fact that the corporate titans are not immune to this whole business. The stock options were certainly the nectar of the gods as far as they were concerned, and they contributed to this – they were very much a contributor. They couldn't wait to get on television themselves to say how great their companies and implicitly their stock was. A lot of their decisions were made with an eye on Wall Street, rather than an eye on the bottom line or on Main Street where their customers are. There has always been an undercurrent or disenchantment with people who thought they should be running a company rather than running a stock. But this was a distinct minority view. (24 May 2001)

MUTUAL FUNDS

The principle of mutual funds as mutually owned by each member survives in very few cases, Vanguard in the USA being notable. Most non-mutual funds and retail funds are highly competitive. They publish monthly performances on the assumption that small investors continually shop around.

Lazar: This causes lots and lots of problems. For instance, the way in which retail funds sell themselves is to point to the fact that they have funds which invest in the flavour of the month, quite literally. All the adverts you'll see in the Saturday *Daily Telegraph*, financial section, will be, say, about technology funds: 'our technology fund' came top of fourteen tables, 'our technology fund' has won this and that practically worthless award . . . As far as I'm concerned, investment is a matter of what happens over the next ten or twenty years, not what happens over the one month or three months or a year . . . These people are supposedly professionals, are supposedly thinking in responsible terms about the funds of their clients, and they're not at all. What they're thinking about is performance, what they're thinking about is their own salaries, what they're thinking about, if they're senior enough management, is profitability and dividends and bonuses.

This is not to say that the former mutual funds in Britain were 'perfect', but competition, performance and managers' salaries are all-important now:

One of the great tragedies is the collapse of the mutual system (such as building societies and mutual insurance), because the mutual system was fuddy-duddy, comfortable and smug . . . The managers made things very comfortable for them-selves, but they also did very good business for their pensioners, and the whole system worked well. It built up large reserves for the very good reason that they were prudent . . . You could criticise all this as being a sub-optimal allocation of capital, and all that (economic rubbish), but the fact is, it was safe. (4 June 2001)

Global investigations into mutual funds began in 2003, some by Eliot Spitzer in New York, which uncovered abuses where insider investors and fund managers made money at the expense of their everyday shareholders. According to the founder of a remaining, genuine mutual fund:

Bogle: When I created Vanguard, I wanted it to be operated in the interests of those we were serving. I wanted it to be more involved in stewardship than in marketing. This industry has become a marketing business and when you cross the line – well, we all cross the line sometimes – between business and profession the consequences may be unfortunate . . . So we created a firm with a structure that made it mandatory to focus on the needs of our fund shareholders. That is to say, the fund shareholders own our management company. Our mutual fund strategy follows that structure.

As 'a fiduciary entrusted with the responsibility for other people's money', Bogle says that Vanguard's key aims were to reduce the costs by having no sales force and by creating three businesses: money market funds, bond funds and index funds. Their lower costs, in not paying for guessing the markets, have been a great part of their success, as Bogle points out in the case of Vanguard's Index Funds, 'where there are only marginal differences in the ability to precisely match the index. The main difference is that we're charging eighteen basis points and someone else may be charging 150. We will give you 1.32 per cent in extra return year after year after year.'

Bogle's view of the other funds was rather different from the cautious philosophy at Vanguard:

Bogle: Well, I will make two simple statements. Point A, I have never met a corrupt person in the mutual fund industry. And Point B, the mutual fund industry is a corrupt industry. We're all part of a system that just isn't right. It's a system that doesn't give the investors what they deserve. It's a system that offers investors a lot of funds with buzz when they're hot. It's a system that sells funds on the emotions of past performance and future hope. But the past is never prologue, and hope often disappoints. We create new funds to meet investors' demands, to advertise performance. The one-year performance of the funds that were averaged in *Money Magazine* in March 2000 was plus 85.6 per cent. We're pandering to the public taste. Why? Because it brings in money. But these aren't people who think they are doing anything *wrong*. They say, 'Well, we didn't say that 85.6 per cent would happen again. Indeed if you look at our ads, it will say at the bottom in tiny type, "Past performance is no guarantee of the future."' Well, let's just think about that for a minute. If they don't think it has anything to do with the future, why did they put it in there? Because the *readers* think it has something to do with the future. They want the hottest performers. It's a business that's based on marketing and not stewardship. (7 March 2002)

In the middle of 2002, the US stock market went down to the biggest fall for many years – some argue since the 1930s. In 2003, John Bogle provided evidence to Congress about the corrupt situation in the non-mutual 'mutual' funds he had publicly criticised for years. This example shows up the importance of the concept of fiduciary duty to fund shareholders (which Bogle would like to see enshrined in federal statute), and Vanguard's policy towards the future: it is never certain: for him short-term speculation 'makes no sense' (Interview, PBS TV, 4 November 2003).

CONCLUSION

We have seen in this chapter a different way of understanding the dynamics of change in the financial world, through analysing the problems of uncertainty which explain rapid changes in reputation or credibility. Clues appear in how these organisations continually create and recreate hierarchies of impersonal trust and other emotional relations. Central banks defend their reputation so closely that their decisions are hamstrung; whatever happens, it is odium they fear most. As for the private sector, the New Deal set up impersonal hierarchies of trust agents to guard against 'cosiness' and to scrutinise other organisations. That stability was undermined long before its repeal, as firms learned to manage credibility problems, not well, but in a spiral of impersonal trust, failure of trust, invention of new rules and new distrust, and cycles of sectors with more (and less) credibility. In any one year, no firm and no sector trusts any other. By the next year a new chain of trustworthy, credible, 'scientific' strategies arises from the survivors.

Institutional investors and pension funds demanded that management consultants 'prove' that firms are increasing shareholder value, so firms hire the same accounting firm as consultants to 'clean up' the firm's management reputation to investors. Certified accountants hired to validate firms' finances must apply impenetrable, thousand-page standards, with increasingly damaging effects, because the 'true and fair' override is too imprecise; it admits uncertainty. Rules against conflict of interest for accountancy, consultant and legal firms may be insoluble because uncertainty is the underlying issue.

Shifting trust relationships do not necessarily *parallel* the hierarchies of power or the social structure of markets; indeed they may dominate. Here we highlight an obsession with the future in strategies to gain control over it, to validate former trust. Hierarchies switch suddenly, sometimes from an event but mostly in processes of attribution conflicts. The reputation earned becomes so apparently manipulated that a former source of confidence becomes liable to outside suspicions of playing a con game when outcomes turn out poorly. No firm can guarantee certainty. A good reputation – the attribution of trustworthiness (rather than luck) – is difficult to build and easy to lose whether deserved or not. Also, whether they are public (central banks) or private (investment houses), each failed outcome leads to further organisations of trust, or resurrection of formerly disgraced ones. Examples not mentioned here abound, such as the IMF's deep credibility problems (Pixley 1999a). Demands for more trustworthy standards and procedures for full disclosure of information ebb and flow in an effort to achieve the unattainable – certainty. The relentless use of distrust strategies switches – one year credit-raters, another year management consultants – as long as they promise that the brand new innovation in risk is *safe*. Aggressive instruments and new struggles over attributions of success arise until failures re-emerge. Then a new spiral of guardians submerges what are momentarily acknowledged uncertainties back to unsayable and unacknowledged dangers. Impersonal trust is constantly reworked and reclaimed in layers of new meanings, but as the management of reputation becomes too managed, too alienating, the next distrust strategy fails.

Emotions are prevalent, ultimately, because capitalism is future-oriented towards profit. Yet today's struggles to gain an attribution as a credible institution are increasingly uncontrollable. Projections of 'value' are dependent on reputation. The meaning of the value given to particular numbers depends on context, and is in part reliant on trust that uncertainty may be only risk. In the next chapter, we explore the extent to which numbers are a matter of trust.

7

Overwhelmed by Numbers

FINANCIAL ORGANISATIONS ARE completely reliant on past data; although no assessment can be anything but retrospective, this has not diminished the sector's trust in numbers and the repression of uncertainty through redefinition. This chapter is about the trust – in risk and hopes for predictability – placed in accountancy and insurance firms, banks and credit-raters, and in forecasting and confidence survey data.

THE PERFECT CALCULATING MACHINE: THE FIRM

Why is information so important? Or, in other words, what does information mean here? A very prominent orthodox theory of the firm puts information at the heart of all corporate activities except, strangely, in the financial sector. In this theory, luck and trust are ruled out as firms use information with 'guile'. For several decades, Oliver Williamson dominated neo-classical economics by conceding (three centuries on) the existence of *the* capitalist institution – namely 'firms'. Firms must imply more than the independent, opportunistic agents of classical economics, whose economic activity is coordinated through market price signals. (The 'firm' is a word Williamson uses interchangeably with 'hierarchies', in a simple contrast with 'markets'.) Since firms do exist, this success story is, allegedly, because they can minimise the transaction costs of market exchanges. Williamson construes the origins and functions of 'opportunistic firms' as the answer to the 'hazards' created from and by opportunistic individuals. (I might note, in passing here, that these individuals sound very like those untrustworthy agents we saw in Chapter 2.) Market failures from hazards and externalities like 'information asymmetries, uncertainty, incomplete contracting . . . have transaction cost origins' which hierarchies (firms) can overcome (Williamson 1991a: 4). Uncertainty is mainly an issue because all agents behave opportunistically at all times, with guile. This framework accepts that agents can only be 'boundedly rational' in a prevalent situation where hazards occur in transactions – all of which seem to suggest cheating and lying – because 'contract as promise is naïve' (Williamson 1991b: 93). Therefore, 'promises to behave responsibly' apparently need 'credible commitments' (1991b: 92). Opportunistic organisations can build divisional safeguards against the risks of external opportunism, something far beyond the capacity of opportunistic individuals.

Firms save the costs of cumbersome individual contracts designed to reduce market opportunism, with what Williamson calls 'crafted safeguards'. They economise on bounded rationality – complex contracts are, he says, unavoidably incomplete – by deploying forms of 'adapted sequential decision making' (Williamson 1991b: 92–3). Does this presuppose not only adapting to uncertainty but also breaking promises? Williamson (1993: 460) claims that economics could 'design control systems with reference to all consequences', even unintended ones. Accepting bounded rationality, he does not claim that firms possess divine foreknowledge, but that 'a farsighted approach is often feasible'. Any problem with contracts or credible commitments can be treated as 'a (broadly) foreseeable condition' (1993: 460–1). According to Williamson, although there may be bad outcomes, most can be 'mitigated' by 'competent calculativeness' (1993: 467). As long as this was the case, the parties to a contract would be 'aware of the range of possible outcomes and their associated probabilities' in order to reduce the hazards, project the expected net gains (1993: 467), and 'factor in' possible future changes (1993: 460).

If corporate origins and purposes are merely transaction-cost efficiencies, a constant stream of profits is presupposed in Williamson's definition of the firm (hence success). He concedes that trust – 'culture' or 'atmosphere' – may further help firms minimise costs. But trust is merely an external bonus, not implicated in calculative transactions (1993: 467, 476). This is because he sees the future only as a matter of risk, not uncertainty. And if trust simply means risk, a 'subjective probability' that our expectation will be correct, trust is, he says, only a calculation about risk; 'calculated trust' is unnecessary (1993: 43–4). Although Williamson is correct to argue that rational choice accounts of trust (see Chapter 2) equate trust with risk, Keynesians, such as Shackle onwards, argue that this equation is a dubious move. Where I argue that trust is needed to face uncertainty and more so distrust – given the context of universal opportunism that the neo-classical tradition assumes – Williamson rejects uncertainty. In his view, Keynesians see economic actors as myopic or unable to 'project' (1993: 460). His model of calculativeness has firms overcoming risks of transaction costs via superior access to information. Uncertainty is relegated to myopia.

Such myopia trivialises the impossibility for organisations of predicting, despite firms' overwhelming aims of pursuing efficiency and profitability. Williamson neglects the millions that fail. For him, firms are not lucky (even honest) but rational, with a farsighted opportunism which builds safeguards against 'poor outcomes' before the future unfolds (Williamson 1993: 467). If we reject Williamson's view, firms must juggle mutually exclusive projections and give a spurious air of authority to probability 'weights' (Shackle 1972: 22), but they cannot project the actual future, however trustworthy they may be. Well known in practice, as Werner Frey explains, often a perception of uncertainty arises from conflicting evidence. Rival hypotheses are obvious:

Frey: Yes, when it was clear on the negative or the positive side you could act accordingly. When the signals and information were conflicting, or the often-quoted 'mixed signals', this would clearly have an influence on the basic question: do we enter into transactions at all and what should be the size of those transactions? (4 April 2002)

Mixed signals are not resolved by 'calculated risk'. The implication is caution, not profit-seeking at all times: transactions are here seen as binding. In dealing with uncertainty, sceptical bankers are adamant. A sole aim of profit puts a bank out of business (as it has, often). To survive, safety must be banks' overriding aim. A London banker insists that banks should take their debt-holders' view (a bank's core fiduciary role) about unforeseeable events over the typical, day-to-day shareholder view (about a stock's value today), where probability *may* sometimes apply:

Shepheard-Walwyn: To a significant degree, what you're looking to do is to assure yourself that in the event that something like that occurs, the bank would still be in business. In a sense, it's a debt-holder's view of the firm. The reason that's important is because the debt-holder view for a bank *should be pre-eminent*. In other words, somebody who has lent this organisation money wants to know that they are going to get that money back, that the bank is solvent in all credible circumstances. (22 March 2002)

Ironically, for Williamson credibility is an objective factor as much open to calculation as hazards, safeguards and net benefits. But credibility is impossible to dissociate from a trustworthy past record and legal fiduciary obligations. More seriously, opportunism and guile, imply an *institutionalised norm of lying*, which possibly explains why Williamson's framework must avoid the financial sector by and large: banks can hardly claim a reputation for opportunism. Attempts to reformulate corporate ethics and fiduciary duties against the flagrant opportunism of firms, as we saw in Chapter 6, are often mired by agency theory with its neo-classical basis (e.g. in distrust and in money's neutrality; see Chapter 9). Corporate opportunism is ethically dubious, partly because it misconstrues the future as available in information. As a consequence, specific data is institutionalised by norms of distrust and opportunism.

SKYSCRAPERS OF DATA

Williamson only described an environment congenial to such views. Robert Haugen (1997: 621–2), an American professor of finance, dates the start of Wall Street's hopes for predicting firms' expected future growth at 1924: these 'new era' hopes revived, following their deep disfavour after 1929's calamity, in 1964, and have grown steadily ever since. Just as the prestige and power of quantitative methods (Porter 1995: viii) became entrenched in the financial firms, so too did positivist hopes for faster, even prescient calculations from information technology.

Although such models of rational decisions and monitoring control are possible only under conditions 'close to certainty', this has been a theoretical point (Parker & Stacey 1995: 38) completely lost to the armies of managers, number crunchers and consultants of the past thirty years. Widespread faith in a future of mere risk has gone hand in glove with a deployment of numbers to calculate probable future benefits and 'credible commitments'. Williamson's notion that firms have significant capacities to remedy uncertainty basically rests on information searches (Ingham 1996b: 263); these searches have been amplified into exaggerated claims about a contemporary 'information society' but they merely describe a major, if futile trend.

Financial media and IT growth only reflected the huge expansion from the 1970s of audit firms, data collection and credibility assessment agencies. From modest local versions, accountancy and consultancy firms amalgamated incessantly: the 'big Five' seemed unassailable until Andersen's demise (in 2002). The credit-rating agencies Moody's and Standard & Poor's (S&P) also became global. Despite major miscalls about the 'credible commitments' (in Williamson's terms) of firms and governments, Moody's and S&P's influence remains high.

Commercial and investment banks have forecasting divisions collecting every quantifiable aspect of the economy. Past data is released daily by government statistical agencies and central banks, on prices and rates of inflation, employment, interest, trade, deficits and growth ('fundamentals'). Stock Exchanges release round-the-clock computerised data and 'monitors' list the daily futures, money, and bond market activities through to gold, warrants and derivatives prices. Confidence surveys come out regularly; companies must publish 'accurate' information continuously. Global agencies like the OECD, IMF, World Bank, WTO, Bank for International Settlements also weigh in with comparative success and failure stories on GDP, trade, exchange rates and CADs. The financial world is awash with competing information, as Henry Dale puts it:

Dale: Of course the fundamentals are regurgitated and gurgitated *ad nauseam* by each investment bank. Each investment management house has economists, chief economists, strategists, and the Americans have them in spades. At one level, I suspect that people want to hear something reasonably convincing rather than watch monkeys sticking in pins . . . But of course there is another school of thought who are not interested in fundamentals at all. They are looking at movements of markets and they're finding all sorts of patterns . . . Then you get into the whole complicated debate . . . about what is performance. And so you have benchmarks: everyone is trying to perform in line with their peers and better, and they're trying to perform in line with the benchmarks. And . . . a return which is much, much less than the benchmarks is effectively to track the Index. And that's why you have tracker funds. (5 October 2000)

Given catastrophic banking failures (such as BCCI in 1991, Barings in 1995, and losses at AIB in 2002 and NAB in 2004), assertions that firms are superb calculating machines seem off the mark. Maybe organisations conduct 'quasi-scientific procedures' on competing information, on accounts, forecasts and models, as emotional rituals. Focusing attention on a common object is a ritual that enhances solidarity and arouses implicit emotions (Collins 1975: 58), a practice of all organisations. Rituals allay decision-makers' anxieties about completely unpredictable if not chaotically unfolding events (see Gabriel 1998: 305). Chaos theory, like the Keynesians, stresses the inherent unknowability of any economic future except the very short term (Parker & Stacey 1995: 75). Attempts to meet competitive criteria (calculation with guile) can spiral dangerously into doubling bets by banks. Cause–effect models of market prices or fundamentals are run exhaustively, and ritually filtered for signs *ad nauseam*. A cult of CEOs who must be 'credible' to investment banks has led to rapid turnover of CEOs and a consequent headhunting industry. The well-known Jack Welch of General Electric said he thrills to the disorder, passion and fragmentation of his daily time: 'It's nuts!' CEOs turn over a new subject every ten minutes (Haigh 2003: 17). CEOs of investment banks (Chapters 4 and 6) have no better intellectual talents to manage this data either, despite past performance records quantified by headhunting data.

In order to understand this avalanche of financial information to specific audiences, dressed in danger-seeking or mind-numbing jargon, we need to point briefly to the social contexts in which it is produced and given meaning. Quantification in the language of mathematics is today taken for granted. As Theodore Porter argues in *Trust in Numbers* (1995), quantification is a 'technology of distance'. By the 20th century it imposed a certain standardisation across the world: its promise of control had enormous appeal to business and governments. Numbers are a form of communication, a message that attempts to exclude judgement and subjectivity. Quantification is never true to the natural or social world: even hard physics discovered long ago that atoms 'behave' relative to the observer's questions. Quantification's only objectivity is as a discourse independent of specific local people producing the knowledge (Porter 1995: ix). This is not independent either, because a specific datum is created in one context to serve as a proxy for or to indicate more complex phenomena. GDP is a debatable indicator of economic wealth. In counteracting its over-simplification, new, allegedly measurable indicators of human capital and social capital appeared – as if human creativity and trust relations are quantifiable, as if money neutrally represents 'real' production rather than something created from promises and credit relations.

Even so, numbers, categories and public statistics may help describe reality if they can partly define it. In Porter's important argument, quantitative methods provide *relative predictability* only if the objects so described are changed to fit the description and therefore produce that information. Quantification is an accurate description when assessing results of planned intervention. Thus cost accounting gives a fairly reliable prediction of factory costs, provided planning the future in quantifiable categories *creates* standardised goods and assembly-line workers (Porter 1995: 43). Qualitative service work or CEO's activities, for that matter, cannot be measured, despite today's avalanche of audits.

Decision-making by numbers and rules appears to be fair, neutral and impersonal. It is like not 'seeming to decide' (Porter 1995: 8), another of its attractions:

'The transition from expert judgement to explicit decision criteria did not grow out of the attempts of powerful insiders to make better decisions, but rather emerged as a strategy of impersonality in response to their exposure to pressures from outside' (1995: xi).

Porter (1995: 89) shows how discretionary, professional or subjective expert 'judgement', say by actuaries or accountants (or by civil servants in treasuries and central banks), is continuously disputed because powerful outsiders were suspicious. Objectivity in the sense of public standards and objective rules is an adaptation to these suspicions. A different, complementary story on Taylorism is how management may create forms of uncertainty (beyond genuine ones) to further their own ends (Weitz & Shenhav 2000). The uncertainty defined by engineer-type management and the degree to which it is dealt with successfully legitimises and promotes their agenda to suspicious outsiders. Uncertainty claimed from 'rogue traders' and other deficiencies of subordinates is a CEO tactic to deflect blame by outsiders or redefine the demands for certainty. In contrast, banker Werner Frey wanted strong advice from 'one-armed' economists because he knew that outcomes could turn out wrong. His responsibility for decisions fostered frank views.

Dilemmas for investment decisions are generally about true uncertainty, summarised by Paul Chan:

Chan: I think certainly, the history is that we now have less time for making decisions and therefore we place more trust in experts. People who carry the label 'I'm an expert' are trusted. When we have some uncertainty we bring in someone called an independent expert. We don't trust you, but we trust Moody's. You can also have distrust. All you are doing is really just shifting the trust from a direct trust to an indirect trust. (5 April 2002)

ACCOUNTING FOR FUTURE COST

Accounting is at the measuring core of capitalist economic life. There is nothing neutral or technical about accounting, given the elusive nature of estimating cost (Shackle 1972; Porter 1995: 94). A rhetorical, persuasive aspect of accounting plays a symbolic role to this day in shifting frameworks of meanings about certain business innovations which initially aroused public suspicion, such as LBOs, hostile takeovers or booking 'goodwill'. Double-entry bookkeeping (first offered with thanks to God) helped to legitimate merchant practices like usury. A rising status and prestige of numeracy fostered confidence in seemingly technical solutions – third party documentation – for 'critically ambiguous' values such as lending to strangers (Carruthers & Espeland 1991: 62–3).

Accounts answer certain questions to specific audiences: earliest practices answered whether a landowner or merchant had been cheated through embezzlement or error by stewards or distant traders (Pollard 1965: 209). Answers cannot predict future cheating, of course. In contrast, permanent ongoing capitalist enterprises are completely different from merchant trading or seasonal farming. These give an 'accounting' finality after the cargo and boat were sold off or the harvest brought in, since accounts only recorded past transactions. In contrast, company or firm accounts have no finality but must involve projections. Accounts must distinguish between profits and capital, as dividends can only be paid from profits. Double-entry accounting enabled this distinction (as when the permanent East India Company meant a continuity of personnel, boats, wharves and so on: Carruthers & Espeland 1991: 45). This fundamental distinction remains doubtful even when accountants and corporations are totally honest, because capital is future-oriented. Accounts must conjecture what capital *will* be needed to survive, but to audiences of stock-holders, the amount may seem suspiciously luxurious.

Greater problems arise with ongoing industrial firms. How can fixed investment such as factory equipment be valued? Continuous fixed capital has no periodicity or end-point, making calculations of profit or capital far more difficult in any given year. Calculating depreciation of fixed investment with no obvious end had no precedents (Carruthers & Espeland 1991: 46). Costs can vary with output and involve social choices. Why is workers' pay a 'cost', or are wages (the only means of productivity) more honestly counted as adding value? Adam Smith pointed to the double standards of recipients of profits who only complained about wage 'costs' but said nothing of their own dividends in unearned income, that is, costs (Collison 2002: 60). Those CEO stock options were not counted as an 'expense' or cost in company accounts. Standards (Chapter 6) were clearly a product of political and social processes which exclude a range of alternatives (Young 2003).

Measuring whether technical innovations do improve profitability is equally hazardous (Pollard 1965: 214). Rational accounting was not a pre-existent tool to solve contested definitions or future-oriented costs – if such things are solvable. It undermines Max Weber's idea that rational bookkeeping was a precondition for the rise of capitalism, as uncertainty is never settled by bookkeeping, only allayed or repressed. With Internet Technology, for example, the same productivity debates raged at least until 2000. If Alan Greenspan could claim the technology was responsible for a productivity miracle in the USA, a 'paradigm shift' which fostered 'productivity-enhancing capital investment' (Testimony to US Senate, July 1998, cited Brenner 2002: 177; Peston 2002) how could mere accountants disagree with the executive directors of, say, a WorldCom? Back in 2000, the respected *Grant's Interest Rate Observer* compared 'aggressive' US accounting about improvements in information-processing technology with a more conservative German approach. Applying US accounting methods to German IT investment, German growth numbers would have increased from 6 per cent (annually from 1991) to 27.5 per cent (Grant 2000). German education – a skilled workforce – is also superior to the US system. Accountants cannot claim to measure future productivity because the significance of uncertainties is not quantifiable:

Ingham: If you don't know anything about history you can't possibly know whether what's happening now is unusual, is worse than usual, [or] better . . . I don't think you can measure contemporaneously. If you look at the example of electricity, it took about twenty years or more before factories were redesigned to make the best use of electricity because they were built vertically rather than horizontally . . . Of course, the problem with historical data on productivity is that it all depends on the period you choose, because you can prove almost anything . . . If you looked at 1951 to 1973 you'd get a completely different picture than if you looked at 1961 to 1973, for example. (15 March 2002)

Accountants' multiple audiences produced specific practices, shown in the way bookkeeping within early industrial firms was more a tool of management than a tool of reckoning for future investment decisions. Weekly accounts at least gave some regularity in an era of immense change, 'overwhelming detail' and chronic uncertainty (Pollard 1965: 216–17). As usual the greatest difficulties lay in estimating likely future costs and returns of a proposed investment, and how to calculate the total profits and value of an enterprise. Partial cost analyses were highly sophisticated quite early on, but estimates of likely mineral reserves or future turnover were 'wild guesses', childishly unrealistic and crudely naive. Pollard (1965: 220) notes an unreality not only in promotional literature designed to attract investors to Britain's railway and canal-building ventures (where, like today's spin for IPOs, exaggeration is likely), but also in 'calculations for internal consumption'. Firms here not only deceived a share-buying public but engaged in self-deception. But is self-deception dishonesty or merely deluded optimism?

Accountancy only minimally guided business decisions before the 20th century and where used, 'guidance was often unreliable' (Pollard 1965: 245). Bookkeeping was demonstrably 'sloppy' (Carruthers & Espeland 1991: 61). Pollard (1965: 223) doubts whether a 'satisfactory overall cost-and-revenue statement' has ever been found. Internal cost measurements are often contestable within an enterprise. Accounts may be used to justify decisions and to excuse mistakes. Artificial smoothing can give a retrospective enhancement of management decisions (Carruthers & Espeland 1991: 48).

Clearly this is not exclusively an accountancy problem. As I emphasise throughout, the financial sector's colloquial terms for information – and 'risk' – far too often assume or imply future knowledge, but in this banker's usage, risk means uncertainty, and manipulation, a major structural problem:

Shepheard-Walwyn: Fundamentally, a management information system is actually a risk information system. Otherwise why do I want the data? I want it because it tells me what could go wrong. I want it to tell me how I'm managing into the future. So the whole question of how the data is organised and structured in an organisation is a key part of it. I need to know that the data is well designed and has integrity, and that there are people who are not captured, if you like, by management.

On whether capture was a separate issue, or related to the quality of the information, he said:

It is related, because information is power. What you often find is that information gets captured in the organisation, and what you're looking for is a process where information cannot be captured. It should flow through the organisation, so that someone sitting at the centre of the organisation can see through the organisation for the data they need, in a way where it hasn't been manipulated, it hasn't been transformed or fiddled, a gloss hasn't been put on it. (22 March 2002)

Information must have 'integrity' from the 'centre' out, rather than being defined by the top or by a branch that controls it through 'capture'. Whole corporate structures develop towards the areas of most relevant knowledge and greatest uncertainty, creating branches with distinct social locations (Stinchcombe 1990: 342). Those branches or organisations that control information about regions of certainty (e.g. *today's* decision) classically gain control over others (Collins 1975: 310). Internal accounts and information systems are enhanced by suspicions and hopes of the powerful. Quantitative methods need to answer, persuasively, whether an audience is being cheated (Carruthers & Espeland 1991: 39). As further audiences emerge, suspicions are treated variably. Company law expanded the audience to the state, which wanted to know if capital was being maintained or investors cheated by management misinformation. Tax laws ask whether the state is being cheated. Contested questions expose accountancy firms to providing contradictory answers, especially in today's era of shareholder value.

A 'true and fair' view, or 'full and fair' as defined in Britain's 1844 Act, combined ethical professionalism with discretionary judgement (Clarke et al. 2003: 319–21). Judgement about what can fairly be conjectured has constantly been overruled by distrust. Objectivity for accountants became further defined as rigorous mechanical quantification and standardisation (Porter 1995: 90). However honest, objectivity cannot, for accountants, solve what is meant by 'cost'. It depends above all on what the time is when cost is measured. Unfortunately, the future is by far the best time: 'valuation is expectation', a 'conjecture of what the valued object or system *will be able* to do' (Shackle 1972: 8; his emphasis). The 1933 standardised SEC rules insisted that the only way to avert cost manipulation by firms was to base corporate book value on the *original cost* of assets, not on replacement costs (Porter 1995: 94). This left out inflation, technical innovation, depreciation or other current impacts on values. Today's standards are just as fictional in requiring a book value of anticipatory (imaginary) cash inflows and outflows of fixed assets (Clarke et al. 2003: 37)

Failures from the 1950s onward further limited discretionary judgement, as a former chief accountant of the SEC explains. US standards (required by the Financial Accounting Standards Board or FASB) are now 'a veritable mountain of impenetrable rules'. The vast majority of certified public accountants in the USA do not understand FASB's definition of an asset – even a simple truck. Under FASB, the truck is not the 'asset'; rather the asset is 'the economic benefit . . . that *will* arise from using the truck to haul lumber etc.' This benefit, of course, cannot be known, as the same person said well before the Enron syndrome:

We have seen many situations where corporations have been reporting earnings and an excess of assets over liabilities using our current generally accepted accounting principles just before going bust . . . Historical cost of assets and representations as assets of FASB-approved junk such as goodwill, deferred income taxes and tax benefits of operating loss carry forwards, and capitalized direct-response advertising costs have misled investors for years. (Schuetze 2001: 4)

Schuetze cites the case of US airlines teetering on bankruptcy after 11 September 2001, but the lack of passengers did not appear on their balance sheets because, under FASB rules, 'looking to the undiscounted future cash flows from the aircraft, the carrying amount of the aircraft is not impaired' (2001: 4).

Strict rule-following to eliminate personal bias and alleged 'emotive considerations' (Porter 1995: 95) removes the discretionary, ethical 'true and fair' principle. The rules require 'creative' accounting which, because complying with standards has led to so many unexpected collapses, professionals now distinguish from 'feral' accounting, which has the intention to deceive (Clarke et al. 2003: 32). One solution is said to be mark-to-market accounting, which states the current cash equivalents of assets (2003: 278). Even if every firm were to be valued hourly, with every asset marked to market continuously, the conservative accounting principle would allow only a decrease in any asset to be recognised by the hour, not any increase until the asset is sold. During the late 1990s bull market, a popularity in mark-to-market practices saw instances of booking asset price increases as revenue (Haigh 2003: 62).

Value is future-oriented. If accountants stuck firmly to making statements about the past, they could not value fixed capital (into future survival) except by projecting the past profit-capital mix through emotions and creativity. They are also vulnerable to powerful third parties like mutual funds, who want to hear 'the future'. Accountancy firms blame management deceit and remain silent on uncertainty. So too, core audiences, suspicious of 'flexibility' and discretionary professional judgement, reject a revival of the 'fair and true' view. Imposed quantification and multiplying standards barely enable them to retain professional authority (Porter 1995: 98; Clarke et al. 2003). Of course, it never helped that in the USA the Big Five resolutely proclaimed their right to run management consultant operations in clear conflict of interest, and lobbied strenuously with corporations for a 'soft' SEC commissioner installed with the 2001 Bush election. The sorry saga only demonstrates, *contra* Oliver Williamson, that firms rarely understand that their future interests are not always the present ones, however opportunistically they pursue interests. Yet the Big Four revive again, in light of further corporate fiascos (like the Italian giant firm Parmalat in 2004), not because accountants can give a fair view.

CALCULATING RISK: ACTUARIES VERSUS ECONOMISTS

Actuarial statistics in insurance is very different. Although insurance is assumed to be the peak of probabilistic thought, ironically accountancy has none of the insurance industry's discretionary powers. Historians of insurance show that 'objectivity' presumed in 'life tables' – numbers of insured likely to die in any year – mattered less for profitability, even solvency, than stringent rules to minimise payouts, and 'the skilful selection of lives'. Banks similarly screen borrowers, and as Mark Twain complained, lend all the umbrellas on sunny days, only to call them back at the onset of rain. The insurance business cycle moves between alleged 'litigation crises' of 'frivolous' claims, and lax screening by insurers (van Fossen 2002).

Screening with life tables emerged when insurers took on too many dissolute aristocrats (Porter 1995: 39). A popular practice of third party gambling on lives in England is a less obscure link between gambling and insurance than often thought. Government regulation tried to demarcate life insurance – requiring 'a capacity for financial loss' – from speculative life insurance wagers. But legal and statistical boundaries produced between 'speculative' and 'prudential', business and play are no more objective than distinctions between prudence and speculation in financial markets. Economic (psychological) distinctions between risk-averse and risk-loving behaviour are only apparent in outcomes (Clark 2002: 84–5). Motives for either are not easily untangled and are impossible to predict. When does hedging become wild leveraged speculation?

Insurance categories produced from demographic calculation gradually gained respect or credibility, but none are natural, objectively true (Clark 2002: 80–1). Profitability is primarily safeguarded by subjective discretion to exclude powerless groups. Today insurance uses three distinctions, first the ordinary hazards of likely chances of loss (e.g. flammability of material), second moral hazard, and third 'morale' hazard. Actuaries screen against moral hazards by trying to detect shady motives and 'bad character'. 'Morale' hazard – when insurance fosters 'carelessness' – is motivational to the policy and is met by careful design of contracts with incentives for honesty and loss prevention (Heimer 2002: 136). All this discretion is unavailable in the profitability of accountancy firms doing audits, as they are mere go-betweens.

Yet insurance companies are themselves subject to the morale hazard of being uninterested in repaying losses. Competitive insurers are prone to speculation, because the industry has its own business cycle. 'Soft markets' are characterised by easy insurance with low underwriting standards, low prices and profits. High interest rates attract new insurance firms that underwrite risky policies at high premiums, invested at high returns. High returns see premiums stabilise or decrease despite poor underwriting outcomes. 'Hard markets' in contrast are characterised by restrictive underwriting conditions, cancelled policies, reduced coverage and high profits. Insurance firms raise huge 'liability crises', caused by abrupt increases in prices. The insurance market 'softens' as interest rates (and premiums) rise, with new entrants again accepting bad risks in order to attract market share (van Fossen 2002). Insurance firms make their own mistakes, as a London banker points out:

Lazar: They see their job as protecting the capital reserves of their institutions so that they can ensure cash flow which will meet obligations over a range of policy maturity dates, from tomorrow to fifty years out. It's a fine balancing act and they have to employ a lot of extremely, supposedly able mathematicians who have, in the past, done a pretty good job. It all started with Equitable Life, which was the first company to employ mathematicians in order to work out obligations, life expectancies and things like this. They did it very successfully and invented the actuarial profession. But then, look again at what has happened to Equitable Life in the past few years and you see the problem for organisations like this. Equitable stopped following the prudential practices that their own predecessors laid down, and joined in commercial competition for investors' funds, and took their eye off the ball. They stopped taking a proper concern for risk and opened up a dangerously exposed position. Their chickens came home to roost, disastrously for them and their policy-holders. The problem is that if you've got more than one assumption, if you've got two assumptions, your chance of being right goes down to 50 per cent, and if you've got seven assumptions you might as well give up. (4 June 2001)

After 2000, another round of collapses occurred among insurance and reinsurance companies around the world, some for lack of proficient selection of candidates from competitive under-pricing (most enticingly cheap in Australia's HIH collapse, which is to cost taxpayers millions). Many failed to take precautions against over-extended positions on the stock market and other obvious changes. In the case of Equitable Life in the UK:

Ziegler: What the managers of Equitable did, and also the policy-holders, was to assume the world in the future would carry on as it had done in the recent past. I was away at the time, but what struck me was the speed with which assumptions changed just because there'd been one or two bad years in the stock market. So yes, clearly the actuaries hadn't been making much more conservative assumptions about future returns. (14 March 2002)

Their promises of the 1970s were based on assuming high inflation with high interest (to 'cure' the former, of course) which Equitable 'forgot' to revise over a whole thirty years of low inflation, according to *The Spectator* (Trefgarne 2001). New assumptions, new hopes piled up. Unlike Williamson's claim that firms can continuously renegotiate contracts, the Law Lords decided Equitable Life could not break its promise, its fiduciary duty to meet its obligations and to act in its members' interests. Annuity-holders with less wherewithal to cut their losses took out a members' action group suit, to embarrass the industry's penchant to redistribute costs and uncertainties to the most vulnerable.

RISK OR UNCERTAINTY?

'Risk' is a dominant term in economics. The sense in which the insurance industry uses the word is not comparable to the economic sense. Probability calculations are similar in extrapolating into the future; purposes and outcomes are not. An insurance policy against risk does not prevent unknown dangers from occurring. It merely *spreads the possibility of gaining recompense* from the chance occurrence of specified dangers of accident or calamity or fire around to larger, selected, obedient 'types' (e.g. non-smoking or burglar alarms). Insurance provides compensation to those who suffer.

Assumptions about measurable components mount up (often disastrously) in both finance and insurance. The purpose in finance is not to spread costs of unchosen dangers which may befall some but not others. Economic risk is measured in order *to prevent risks* which are freely chosen for gain. Economic 'risks' are imagined as specifiable (extrapolation of past data, new theoretical 'assumptions') and not defined as unknown and unknowable dangers or broken promises to pay. They constitute a punt without known parameters, but orthodox economics misrepresents potential losses as probabilistic risk. Firms also take out insurance, proving the impossibility of posing risk as probability because this action implicitly admits that the future is uncertain and contingent. With 'trust in numbers', we have the 'gesture of accessing the Future via risk calculation' (Gumbrecht 2001: 55), but it remains contingent:

> Paying insurance is our favorite way of adapting in the Present to the 'reality' of a (future) failure. Paying insurance is a sacrifice that we would definitely not incur if we knew for sure that our goal would necessarily be fulfilled in the future. Paying insurance means that we take the possibility of failure very seriously – the proof being that this expenditure will look unnecessary in retrospect if we actually manage to realize our goal in the Future . . . [and because of that, perhaps] we only take the Future *partly* for real . . . [but] it also remains true that buying insurance is damage control for a damage that has not yet happened – *as if* a damage that is still but a future possibility was already present and real. (Gumbrecht 2001: 56)

Insurance against fire is no goal in itself; it only supports actual goals negatively, prudentially. Precaution for prevention is a very different principle from the insurance principle (Chapter 8). But the economic concept of risk, in greater contrast, revolves around an active, freely chosen goal. Here risk is a dignified form of gambling, or is tamed by the comforting notion that 'hedging one's bets' will control unmeasurable, unknowable chances of making money. In the principle of portfolio insurance, for example, the idea of 'risk management' muddled various conceptions of risk and insurance. Harry Markowitz said:

> The objective of portfolio *insurance* is to reduce risk, in some sense, perhaps at the expense of return on the average. This sounds very much like the objectives of portfolio *theory's* mean-variance analysis. The objective of the latter is to present the investor with 'efficient' combinations of risk and return from which the investor picks an efficient combination according to her or his risk aversion, perhaps sacrificing return on the average in order to reduce risk. (Markowitz in Jacobs 1999: xiv; his emphasis)

Bruce Jacobs' *Capital Ideas and Market Realities* (1999) looks at outcomes of the problem Fischer Black, Myron S. Scholes and Robert C. Merton (now infamous from LTCM) apparently 'solved', of how to value an option. They formulated 'the essentially risk-free nature of a hedged option position. An option plus some continuously adjusted offsetting position in the risky asset underlying the option will yield a riskless rate of return . . . a solution independent . . . of the underlying asset's expected value' (Jacobs 1999: 15). Jacobs recounts the disasters from the marketing promises of 'option pricing theory' – packaged as 'insurance' or hedging strategies in numerous versions – in the lead-up to the 1987 stock market crash and later to the collapse of LTCM (of Scholes and Merton inspiration). His summary is concise:

> Purveyors of the strategies asserted that they could insure equity portfolio against market declines while allowing participation in any market advances over the insurance horizon. The strategies thus appealed to the two most basic human instincts of investors – both greed and fear . . . But could synthetic portfolio insurance provide true insurance?
>
> Synthetic portfolio insurance differs from traditional insurance, where numerous insured parties each pay an explicit, predetermined premium to an insurance company, which accepts the independent risks of such unforeseeable events as theft or fire. The traditional insurer pools the risks of many participants and is obligated, and in general able, to draw on these premiums and accumulated reserves, as necessary, to reimburse losses. Synthetic portfolio insurance also differs critically from real options, where the option seller, for a premium, takes on the risk of market moves.
>
> Synthetic portfolio insurance is essentially a form of self-insurance; it is the investors who 'buy' the insurance who take on the risk. They give up some degree of portfolio return in exchange for the theoretical assurance of receiving no less than the chosen minimum return. They are not able to draw upon the premiums of many thousands or millions of other investors in the event of catastrophe. Instead, they are reliant upon the ability to get into or out of the market as needed, hence upon the willingness of other investors to take the offsetting sides of required trades.
>
> Furthermore, synthetic portfolio insurance, in attempting to replicate the behaviour of a long put option, must buy as markets rise and sell as they fall. This trend-following dynamic is inherently destabilizing to markets. It has the potential to create volatility. (Jacobs 1999: 16)

Jacobs argues that Wall Street's 1987 crash was led by synthetic insurance. Other investors, mistakenly believing that the 'mechanistic and information-less trades' contained 'fundamental' information, followed suit, amplifying both rise and fall (1999: 297). Yet it resembles every other crash in one sense. At the moment when selling prevails, regardless how complex the financial instrument, everyone tries to get out of the door at the same time. Jacobs describes how huge investment firms peddled the economic concept of risk. Sellers claimed it would *reduce* losses and enhance gains, yet it did not share the costs of losses from unforeseen events. It is more uncertain than gambling.

Banks take a precautionary, actuarial approach to risk (the aim in principle), and use similar probability calculations as insurance in the granting of loans. They screen potential borrowers – the money market is unlike goods markets because banks allocate credit according to trust or distrust. Administrative discretion applies. Contemporary bankers use a specific parlance, where risk is uncertainty.

Chan: For us risk *means* uncertainty. There's a very exact mathematical relationship between the two. Risk is defined to us as the uncertainty of losing some money. That is a quantifiable effect. So to suggest that we do risk management or risk control without taking into account uncertainty is just not correct. It's so embedded – if you talk to people who are involved in risk management they know they are dealing with uncertainty all the time. They know that they might not get their money back. They know that if they buy something they might not be able to sell it for the same price they bought it at. (5 April 2002; his emphasis)

Discernment, screening and careful, prudential management are the keys here. Keynes's and Frank Knight's distinction between risk in which probability distributions can be set only on measurable 'known chances', and uncertainty where they cannot, remains as relevant as ever. Economists with strong views on uncertainty argue that it is impossible to quantify the probability in the tails of the distribution where the 'central limit theorem' doesn't apply, as with extreme events. Confusion prevails about 'risk'. As we've seen, the term is used differently in insurance and banking from finance economics and stock market speculation. The global banks such as the US Citigroup and Goldman Sachs, the Swiss UBS, Deutsche Bank and ING are the dominant banks engaging in analysis of market risk of price movements of international flows of capital – made possible by the collapse of Bretton Woods. Whether Barings' collapse through to LTCM was a sufficiently cautionary tale, the disaster at Allied Irish Bank was mitigated by having enough reserves to continue: others did not. Does this show that excessive confidence in 'risk management' – the promise of control over nature and the future – is declining? In a 2004 case (National Australia Bank), the 'risk managers' still seemed over-reliant on quantitative value-at-risk tools which give misleading aggregates of traders' excellent records elsewhere. Trading using the doubling tactic (Barings, AIB and NAB) is a loser's gamble, very like LTCM's which engaged in unhedged short volatility transactions, similar to doubling (Brown 2004). Nearly all the global banks mentioned above lent to LTCM. It had used $4 billion 'starting' capital as security for borrowing $120 billion, then used that to borrow a further $1 trillion from investment banks which later professed not to know the extent of LTCM's leverage, even while accepting non-negotiable terms. LTCM considered questions of its exposure impertinent, whereas Chase and UBS were 'awed' by LTCM, 'dazzled' and too 'greedy' (Lowenstein 2000: 81, 233; FOMC 1998).

Kaufman: I would say even the efficient supervisors have questions next to them, because you ask in 1998 when LTCM got into trouble, how come the bank examiners of these major institutions, which had relationships with LTCM, did not detect the magnitude of the leverage that was going on. So [the institutions] had a high degree of sanctity, which has now diminished in some ways. (29 May 2001)

Today in insurance, the former broad pool structure ensuring against dangers is diminishing and even being removed. Some policies give the promise of greater returns if they 'embrace risk'. Thus individuals and business now retain 'risk'. It is a case of insuring more while ensuring less (Heimer 2002). Robert Shiller still believes in a financial world of mere risk, a world insured against loss. It is a near relative of individuals self-insuring, as regional self-insurance cannot hedge against declining values of nationwide or worldwide decline in values – say in real estate (Jacobs 1999: 202).

CREDIT-RATING AGENCIES

Another uncertainty is over promises to pay back loans. In assessing creditworthiness, credit-rating agencies, like everyone, deal with the unknowable. However, they focus on one sole issue, credit, and possibly have only one potential conflict, not exactly of 'interest'. There is no advantage to these few agencies from any particular rating, and they neither lend nor borrow. Raters emerged in the 19th century when commercial dealings became distant and impersonal. Credit-reporting agencies, such as R. G. Dun Company and Bradstreet's Commercial Agency in New York, competed for informants and customers to supply 'impartial' reports on the integrity and creditworthiness of Boston and Chicago merchants.

Today Moody's Investor Services (owned by Dun & Bradstreet) and Standard & Poor's (a subsidiary of McGraw-Hill Companies) are the main credit-raters in the world (Sinclair 1994: 138). These agencies became a near oligopoly in the USA when, in 1975, the SEC introduced criteria to prevent unscrupulous companies from selling triple-A ratings to the highest bidder, a factor associated in the default of Penn Central Corporation (Wayne 2002). The SEC designated Moody's and S&P among a select few as 'Nationally Recognized Statistical Rating Organisations'. Fitch Ratings is in the second tier in America, and similar domestically focused rating agencies operate elsewhere. These private regulators gained global influence in the 1980s when junk or low-rated bond markets emerged (Sinclair 2003: 148). Across the world, corporate and government issuers of securities 'shudder at the effect on investing publics of even a hint that one of these agencies might qualify their credit rating' (Braithwaite & Drahos 2000: 160). 'Don't Mess with Moody's', ran a *New York Times* headline during the 1994 Mexican financial crisis (cited in Cohen 1996: 282). Moody's has had a 50 per cent profit margin, and the SEC criteria mean that a limited number of raters have no pecuniary interest in selling favours and an entire reputation and profit stream to lose if they do so. Compared to accountancy firms, they are a source of fear.

Raters' service to investors, banks or other entities lending to firms or governments is to rate the creditworthiness of borrowers: the borrower pays for the designated rating service. S&P deals with debt-ratings and, separately, equity analysis. Moody's looks only at debt, because its parent firm, Dun & Bradstreet, conducts equity research. Moody's bond-raters claim to judge the 'future ability and willingness of an issuer to make timely payments of the principal and interest on a security over the life of the instrument' (cited in Sinclair 1994: 138). Their main evidence consists in audited financial statements, media reports and information from the bond-issuer, even 'disgruntled former employees' (Sinclair 1994: 139–40).

Debt-ratings give no advice to clients (compared to equity analysis, which gives buy or sell recommendations). Ratings are published investment grades derived from their own vote in a rating committee. S&P have four investment categories from AAA to BBB and speculative grades from BB to D, for Default. Here, 'trust in numbers' is radically simplified – no lengthy reports are required for a quick assessment. Ratings, according to a Moody's analyst, are a 'strong factor in the market' because they reduce all aspects of a debt obligation 'to a letter symbol which is easily understood' (cited in Sinclair 1994: 144). Rating agencies, therefore, neither lend nor borrow, nor put up any finance when they issue a rating. They only risk their credibility and so, many argue, they are rarely subject to conflicts of interest.

One problem, however, is that they are often wrong, particularly in assessing macroeconomic situations, like the Southeast Asian financial crisis. Raters have also miscalled areas said to be their strength, such as corporations like Enron. After Enron, some called for the SEC to permit more agencies to compete for business. Another criticism by the financial sector is that raters only 'look at creditworthiness in historical terms' (cited in Sinclair 1994: 149). 'As though there was any other data', responded John Flemming (13 March 2002).

Historians of financial crashes, like Charles Kindleberger, take little comfort from contemporary views for neglecting the issue of fraud and defalcation among banks. Tellingly, 19th-century texts dwelt on the long history showing that not one bank fraud had occurred where 'the perpetrator was not honest yesterday'. Indeed a 'peculiar feature' is noted about the whole former system, which is *the apprehension of fraud*' (Gibbons, cited Kindleberger: 1989: 104; his emphasis). Historical data indeed demonstrates the unpredictability of fraud.

Even so, some former central bankers have a dim view of credit-raters' applications of rules (BoE and RBA included), as Flemming moved on to explain:

Flemming: I have sat in [on meetings], although I thought it was a complete waste, when I was in the EBRD [European Bank of Reconstruction and Development]. The EBRD borrowed quite a lot in the market, and was anxious to maintain a very high rating. The reason we deserved a triple A rating was that, like the World Bank, we had a capital, most of which was not called ... What we were borrowing against was our ability to call on our shareholders, all of which were sovereign states. Ninety per cent of them were triple A rated in their own markets. So our paper deserved a triple A rating even if all our investments were absolutely lousy. It struck me as a waste of time. I would have brought them in and told them that in ten minutes, and said if you give us anything other than triple A rating I will expose you as incompetent twits. (13 March 2002)

Credit-raters apply rigid or uniform criteria, sometimes misapplying US standards to completely different financial situations (e.g. to small Australian banks like Advance Bank in a highly concentrated banking sector, unlike the USA: Pixley 1999a). The IMF, however, has been far more rigid: Indonesia may take decades to recover from IMF mishandling of the 1997 crisis (Stiglitz 2002). One IMF adviser said some years ago, 'I do regret my advice to Sweden' in applying US financial rules to an utterly different banking situation in 1994. In recounting her time working for *Dow Jones Wire*, a finance journalist compares the IMF and found Moody's better informed:

Schiffrin: I think a lot of it is just laziness. For instance, the way the IMF always give everybody the same formula. I think it is intellectual laziness and . . . it's physical laziness. When I covered banking in Vietnam, I was the only person who used to go to all these little banks in Chinatown in Saigon, and no one from the IMF or the World Bank did that. They just went to the Central Bank and heard what the spokespeople said. Those people were chosen by the government to tell the foreigners whatever they wanted to hear. (19 September 2000)

The credibility of the credit-raters, others argue, is undermined not so much by their miscalls as by who pays for their ratings:

Frey: Rating agencies are undergoing seasonal ups and downs after having missed, in this country, Swissair and in the US, Enron. They are now accused, and with some reason, of an opposite behaviour of down-ratings in multiple steps within a very short period of time just in order to avoid missing another Enron, but that doesn't contribute to their credibility either. Giving them the benefit of the doubt, if they learned the lessons and are successful in embedding this experience into their analytical work, that's fine. Or it would be fine. The credibility of the rating agencies has one major structural handicap: the companies they rate are at the same time their customers. (4 April 2002).

This 'structural problem' is not really conflict of interest but induces behaviour in the borrower, as journalist Trevor Sykes explains:

Sykes: The reason Moody's exist really is because of the financial institutions. A lot of big institutions, fund managers, will not touch any investment which does not have a certain grade, it might be B+, double B, it might be an A or whatever. Anything above that is OK. You might have a quite handcuffed manager who might think that Advance Bank is quite a terrific investment, but if it doesn't get an A or whatever magic grade, forget it, you can't touch it. So a lot of people spend a lot of time trying to boost their liquidity. You widen your market and so forth to try to get the magic grade and so the system becomes a little bastardised. To their credit I think that Moody's are usually awake to that sort of thing. (19 January 2000)

Others suggest that the rating agencies in some respects operate as private regulators. Dominic Ziegler put it this way, describing the structural problem in similarly broad terms:

Ziegler: More powers have accrued to them, yes, as private or quasi-private regulators. They're not entirely happy with these. Part of the reason for that happening is that bank regulators around the world are struggling to come up with a new regime that more accurately assesses risks at banks. Regulators have called on rating agencies to look at banks more closely than any other outside agencies. Credit-ratings and findings agencies are put into the mix to give a sense of what stresses a bank may be under. The trouble is that rating agencies tend to be quite slow reacting . . . They don't tend to adjust their ratings very fast, and although they do look closely at the bank's books, they don't have perfect knowledge about what's going on at the bank.

But that's one problem. Another problem is that what is making banks more risky as a proposition are all the off-balance sheets, derivatives – complicated financial instruments – that they're creating and selling. Here there's a direct conflict of interest for credit-rating agencies, because the more complex these instruments get, and the more that risk is packaged and chopped and diced and resold, the more the banks need credit-rating agencies to rate these products. So the rating agencies are now involved, in a sense, as advisers to the banks. Banks will go to rating agencies and say, 'We're thinking of taking this bunch of loans, securitising them and chopping them up and selling them off. And could you rate these triple A, this bit of it, and what would you rate this bit as?' And the rating agencies become advisers and say, 'Well, if you do this to it, if you do x to it, we'll give you a higher rating.'

So the credit-rating agencies are in that sense the representative agents of the banks *and* of investors. It may be inherent in the way credit-rating agencies are paid. They are paid by the banks to protect investors. As I say, the rating agencies don't always want these potential conflicts of interest. They are not happy about being used as part of the new quasi-regulatory framework. I think they have successfully lobbied to have a lesser role in this whole process of assessing how much capital the banks should carry.

Increasing the number of raters competing would detract from the credibility of those being rated:

This is the problem. It's the same with auditors. There's no upside with taking an unknown rating agency, just as there's no upside for a company to choose an unknown auditor. So in that sense there are high barriers to entry to both these businesses. (14 March 2002)

Auditors and raters are likely to remain oligopolies. The argument, of course, is that both should reject advisory roles, but the very real risks and uncertainties of banks require greater government regulation. Raters are honest, though rigidly conservative. Their problem in financial eyes remains they will never know the future.

FORECASTING

Many economists insist – as this book does – that the future is inherently unknow-able. Forecasting techniques can only be 'informed guesses' or speculations (Pryor

2000: 81). Sceptics who forecast with Keynesian econometric macro models are highly critical of neo-classical models, because Keynesians assume that the 'real world' is inherently messy. Their jargon includes metaphors of shallow water, and sounding ropes with 'degrees' of uncertainty reducing as the future comes closer to the present. When the ship scrapes the rocks, it is too late. Millions and millions of dollars, yen and euros are spent on the business of micro-econometrics and macro-econometrics in constructing and updating models. Forecasts are well known to be often wrong, and 'wrong' together. Economists debate tirelessly how forecasts cluster or herd (around average past forecasts, not, as is usual, like human cattle herds). They find, not surprisingly, that greater unpredictability in the time-series or more volatility leads to higher errors. Some even introduce emotions. Thus forecasters are frightened of taking a lone 'independent' forecast, because the greatest damage to their reputation is being 'alone and wrong' (Bewley & Fiebig 2002). Government forecasts are rarely gloomy, for political reasons, as Duncan Ironmonger recounts of a dispute with the Australian Treasury in 2000:

Ironmonger: The real disagreement happened in November a year ago, when I was the first one to say it looks as though we could be having a recession, and we nearly got into one. It was when Treasury upped its forecast from 4 per cent, and put even a bit more gloss on the expectation of the growth rate for the financial year. So when that happened, I got awful words from Costello [then Australian Treasurer] saying that Dr Ironmonger or Dun & Bradstreet – I'm not sure which – forecasts recession every year so they're going to get it right sooner or later. It was nice to hear [someone] defending me at a journalists' luncheon in Melbourne . . . I then came out a couple of times saying 'wouldn't Treasury ever forecast a recession?' It wouldn't and it never has, and it will only grudgingly recognise it after the Bureau says we've had one. (8 December 2001)

Inherently, forecasting can only use quantities, because trend statements cannot be made about qualitative changes like new policies. Forecasts are really prophecies. Some defend 'predictions' of a narrow type 'if A, then B' – for example *if* there is an exchange rate target, *then* there cannot be discretion in monetary policy – whereas a prophecy tells us what will happen (Baert 2000: 67). Predictions 'if A, then B', are conditional, or they are logical contradictions, not predictions. Forecasts take a run of numbers or static preferences. Assumptions are freely admitted as unrealistic; a model explains only what can be derived from the chosen assumptions. Extrapolating that past trends will continue is always qualified by *ceteris paribus caveat*, assuming other 'things' remain the same or equal. Models reduce complexity, however complex the models.

Mathematical chaos theory denies that macroeconomic forecasting has much point. Even the use of past company data to forecast future costs, consumer demand relations or results of advertising campaigns offers little. A chaotic 'dynamic', being unpredictable, would require an economic model including every seemingly insignificant relationship. None can be known to be relevant, if at all, until after the event. For a reliable prediction, econometric modelling, containing thousands of parameters, each liable to error, must be provided with the future in advance. Parker & Stacey only suggest that 'management may take comfort' from using quantitative forecasts, but firms still fail, despite sophisticated models, at fairly similar rates as when using simpler models (1995: 61).

In talking to those who *must* use forecasts, the issue is not whether there is much trust or confidence in them. Alan Blinder, on his experience as deputy chair at the Fed, argued that forecasts could only be used as guesses:

Blinder: Confidence really depends on the issue. When you're talking about macroeconomic forecasting in monetary policy . . . Everybody knows these forecasts are inaccurate. Even the best forecast is inaccurate, so nobody really has that much confidence. You're making the best judgement that you can on the modes of probability distributions that you *know* are dispersed. What's the best you can do? Go for the mean or the median and act on that basis. But I wouldn't use the word 'confidence'. Everybody knows their forecasts could be quite wrong, but you have to make the best guess that you can. (22 February 2002)

As Arthur Stinchcombe (2000: 53) says, 'the problem with projections of time series is that they can only be *about* those things the series is about'. Every trend, whether the value of the US dollar or the decline of farming employment, occurred through previous institutionalised changes. Economic institutions do not remain the same: they are changed by policymakers and can be altered by intentional choices. Forecasts reduce the extraordinary complexity of the world to trends but, even with *ceteris paribus*, 'trends do not make themselves' (2000: 54).

CONFIDENCE SURVEYS

Much the same applies to confidence surveys, an industry nothing like the size of the forecasting industry. The US Conference Board started in the 1920s, Dun & Bradstreet began business surveys in the 1940s, and the University of Michigan introduced the Index of Consumer Sentiment in 1952 (Roberts & Simon 2001). They ask fairly similar questions: some explicitly ask job questions, and leave out economy-wide questions. Consumers are asked whether they are better or worse off than a year ago, what they expect their finances to be next year, whether the economy will be better or worse in a year and in five years, and whether now is a good time to buy household items. For business confidence, questions are profit expectations, employment (hire more/lay off), whether sales will go up, conditions of their own industry and/or the whole economy now, compared to the past quarter and the next quarter.

Duncan Ironmonger, analyst of Dun & Bradstreet expectation surveys in Australia, says their small business surveys nearly always show an over-estimate of expectations of future profits. As he explains:

Ironmonger: Employment tends to overshoot in a boom; they more than fulfil expectations. You think you'll put on more, and that's one reason why your profits aren't fulfilled as you've hired more people . . . There's always more people who expect their profits to rise than actually do. I felt this was a reflection of the general attitude of people who are in business. They go into business to increase their profits, they're not just sitting there – *that's the whole point*. One would expect people in business are going to be on the optimistic side with high expectations. Our surveys reflect the attitude of smaller businesses. (8 December 2001)

In other words, no capitalism without confidence and optimism. Central bankers gave mixed views about confidence surveys. The RBA examined surveys, filtering out backward-looking data already available elsewhere. Their research shows that confidence surveys explain little more than news and current experiences of the previous months (except employment prospects to a degree), which are available from other economic data. Neither professional forecasters nor lay consumers/business people are any good at 'developing extended forecasts' (Roberts & Simon 2001: 21), hardly a staggering conclusion. Central bankers interviewed were ambivalent about confidence surveys and forecasting:

Flemming: I have a link with the IFO Institute in Munich which does these things in a big way. There used to be quite a lot of excitement about economic forecasts, that they were liable to be self-fulfilling. I think now there are so many of them that is no longer true. I suspect the same is true of confidence surveys. In the case of the economic forecasts, the argument was that whatever the economic forecasters said would come true. If a forecaster started with some credibility, even if not earned [or deserved], if he said the economy was going to go into recession, that would be so damaging to confidence that there would be a recession. The argument about confidence indicators is essentially the same. The early economic forecasts were based on certain data, but also on models. The models might have been rubbish; they probably were. You could have had a forecast of a recession that was essentially an aberration, but it might have been self-fulfilling if enough people read the relevant report. It seems to me that that story is more tenuous in relation to business confidence surveys, because there is no black box associated with an economic model. You simply go out and ask people. The question is why would a whole lot of respondents suddenly say the economy is going into recession when they do not really mean it? It might be self-validating, but it is harder to see why they might do it. I can see why a very small group of people producing an economic forecast could produce one that is aberrant, but that would not happen with a confidence survey. (13 March 2002)

On what is meant by 'confidence', those in the industry tend not to use the term, despite overt titles of their surveys: 'We can't test what's on people's minds', says Goldstein. 'We can ascertain with some specificity, not people's attitudes but changes in attitudes' (25 February 2002). Most journalists are aware the surveys do not tell them very much and certainly nothing about the meaning of 'confidence', as Kadlec says about receiving their press releases: 'Well, I only look at one thing. I look at the new number versus the old number and whether it goes up or down' (26 February 2002).

Again, like the credit-rating data A+ or D, the confidence surveys radically simplify to a sole number, which becomes in itself an attraction in coping with the skyscrapers of information. Quality of information is clearly a problem, but as we saw with credit-raters' semi-regulatory role, context is far more significant. Effects from gathering particular information in an interdependent system can rapidly multiply. What is meant is illustrated in cases where central bankers are trying to maintain prudential stability in commercial bank lending. Such 'information' can raise commercial interbank suspicions. This occurred in stable times, like the 1960s and later, and it is about the shared exposure among the banks. The following is a long but important passage from the former chief economist of the Bank of England:

Flemming: The Bank of England still employs a number of people to go and chat to people in the markets . . . The arrangements in the City of London [then] encouraged most banks to have two-way borrowing transactions with most other banks. This built a dense network. We could find out whether many banks were cutting their lines of credit to a particular institution . . . a certain amount of information could be elicited from the market. You could discover on what terms bank A would lend to bank B and so on. If that changed you knew that something was going on, you could talk to people. I also had a theory that, while a good device for eliciting information, it had the consequence that the information became extremely hard to use. Not quite like the standard military espionage, in that when you use the information you reveal that you have it. The particular problem was many banks were encouraged to have exposure to so many other banks . . . any bank that failed would involve an impact on a large number of banks. Therefore, the distinction between institution and the system was blurred. It is a system which elicits information very well, but only at the cost of converting what might have been an individual institutional risk into a systemic risk. It is more difficult to handle. If you design the system to elicit the information not through statistical returns but through real decisions, which is the thing that is attractive, you discover that bank A thinks that the Bank of England has learnt something about bank B's book. The attitude of other people to bank B's book is that they are reluctant to lend them as much this time. The way you learn that means that if you allow bank B to fail, bank A still has an exposure to it, and is damaged. If you put each into a watertight box then you only have your statistical returns; you do not have any information from relative experts on evaluating each other's books, which is far more useful and reliable . . . If you asked bank A what they thought of bank B, with whom they do not have a business relationship, they might say that they seem to be perfectly competent people. If they have a business relationship they may draw in their horns and let them rest. (13 March 2002)

CONCLUSION

In an entry for a magazine competition in 2001, a company manager apparently sent out the following directive: 'What I need is a list of specific unknown problems we will encounter'. This is the great positivist hope that reached a high peak during the last thirty years. Risk management, forecasting, information searches and transparency are all said to be the answer to this hope. Although hiding information is often intentionally deceptive, openly given information can spiral out to 'system' effects among banks and organisations in trust relationships. Openness may involve, as well, giving advantages to certain parties over others. Small nations are wary of 'transparency' to the IMF, which might publish information for use by investment banks (IMF official, interview, 5 August 1998). Most important here, failures in transparency or 'risk information' easily merges into the unknowability of future outcomes.

Chase, Merrills – all the banks – were presumably armed with (or used) a mass of data on LTCM (as were pension funds with Enron), except the most relevant (its 'exposure' of $1 trillion of debt). We have looked at the skyscrapers of data to conclude that the only mitigating feature is that forecasts, trend statements, risk information and surveys are so conflicting, so multitudinous that they cancel each other out. Yet this does not lessen the search. The more data, the more it must be savagely reduced to the simplicity of a number, or its direction (up/down). Since trust is required for the actual decision, it is invariably backed by volumes of personal and impersonal interrelations. As we saw, accountants are positioned in opposite contexts to actuaries or banks, the latter of which simply screen out, refuse to lend or charge exaggerated premiums to turn red statements into black. Accountants 'know' the most but cannot predict cost: conceding to incessant demands for prescience has cost their professionalism. Different uses of risk, confusing in itself, obscures uncertainty and allows more danger. Informed sceptics spoke of likely or 'probable' future developments as short-term 'soundings', but never as foresight. British Prime Minister Harold Macmillan, being either precautionary or fatalistic, said policies by firms or governments always founder on 'events, dear boy, events', however close the depth sounding. Why, then, so much data allegedly about the future on such hope for risk-free gain? What brought this avalanche into being and how is hope maintained?

8 | The Time Utopia in Finance

Here we look at the morale behind the financial world's expectations. How else is it possible to explain institutional memory loss? Criticisms which reduce the financialisation of life to an ideological triumph of libertarianism are an oversimplification. These days, democracies are openly divided by suspicions, public conflicts and social movements. What orthodoxy presents as an aggregate of individuals, bargaining anonymously – independently – in financial markets, is in fact a social field of mighty organisations struggling over internal credibility. Other fields contend too. Images of herds with amorphous mood-states (during alleged financial instability) are as ideological as rational actor assumptions. Consider the Jubilee debt relief movement led by the established world religions, or the legal and governmental challenges and waves of protests against the excesses of global policies. 'Stop the MAI' movement triumphed after a mooted Multilateral Agreement on Investment (MAI) was leaked from the OECD in 1997 and hastily withdrawn. MAI sneaked back, with a new label, again to fail at a divisive Cancun meeting of the WTO in 2003. The European and Canadian-led ATTAC movement proposes a Tobin tax on currency speculation (named after an economist, James Tobin). Less dramatic, as perhaps prosaically interest-based, are shareholders' revolts and their unseemly behaviour at annual general meetings of banks and corporations in the 'core'. Such a sample of recent activity provides ample evidence that millions of people around the world are not duped by the financial sector's self-rationalisations. Often, however, populations forget how many ignominious bankruptcies, defaults and so on have occurred. Ideology is not an adequate explanation and, this chapter argues, there is a specific utopianism which conditions actions and outbursts within the financial social field. Corporate raids and the cult of personality are only symptoms of hopes for certainty, trust in 'the opportunity'. This utopia takes on social movement proportions, which are necessary to contest the democratic institutions, silence opponents and above all, maintain internal conviction.

IDEOLOGY OR SOCIAL MOVEMENTS?

The framework of my argument is this: short-term emotions now entrenched in the financialisation of life are better explained as emanating from their social movement base. Free-market ideology was not dumbly accepted by electorates. Britain is a case in point: Blair's Labour Government has hardly restrained the City of London's global interdependencies, even given a great public opportunity:

Ingham: Let me take the UK first . . . When interest rates in 1989 went up to 15 per cent, the housing market just fell off the cliff. And I remember talking to people who were suddenly homeless. I'm not exaggerating, I remember very vividly in about 1991 going to visit a family who lived in a detached house just outside London, who were about to go into a homeless bed and breakfast because they had just borrowed and borrowed and they couldn't repay the debts. Property prices actually contracted in the UK, particularly in the south-east and one or two other boom areas for the first time in a very long time, and nobody ever thought they could. The most people thought that could happen was that the pace of appreciation would slow. In fact, prices fell – sometimes quite precipitously and sometimes I think almost to an unrecoverable degree. So this was a major problem, and it was an obsession for news editors for several years. (15 March 2002)

The South is by far the wealthiest region of England and Tory voters predominate. Or rather, they formerly voted Tory. Michael Lazar explains the debacle, in organisational terms, of the Thatcher Government, the Bank of England and (starting with) the commercial banks:

Lazar: [Banks] are in competition to lend, and money is just a commodity. It is something you sell and you've got to sell it because you've got too much of it on your hands. And therefore you've got to price your money so that the customers out there will buy your money rather than anybody else's money. So you get this appalling state where banks lend out at five times people's salaries at ludicrously low interest rates and then there's a credit crunch. And everybody loses their house, and everybody is surprised. That's what central banks are for, and Ministries of Finance are for, but unfortunately you get periods like the late 1980s when neither the central bank nor Ministry of Finance in this country took their responsibilities seriously [and the housing crisis] . . . brought down the Tory Government and has destroyed the Tory Party, maybe for good and certainly for some time. (4 June 2001).

Banks 'forgot' that money is not a commodity but a chain of promises. In the fall-out of this stupendous blunder came greater independence of the Central Bank (the Monetary Policy Committee in 1997), which was opposed by the Tory Party on the grounds of its former cosy governmental relation to the City. Many thought at the time that the Tory Party might never rise again, and indeed its imminent demise just before the 1914–18 War was only stopped by the Tories' electoral craftiness on Irish Home Rule, as George Dangerfield's *The Strange Death of Liberal England* recounts. But in the 1990s, Tories lost electoral loyalty from their own creation – a globalised City – to the Blair Government, which has defended global markets ever since, although not before time introduced a separate regulatory body, the FSA, in 2000. In the USA and elsewhere, housing speculation in 2003–04 hardly heeded this British story.

So, this chapter will argue, the dominant ideology thesis is less plausible on its own than viewing the contemporary era as a conflicting field, shattered by the rise of a present-oriented utopianism in the Anglo-American financial heartland. To say (like Will Hutton 2002 or John Gray 1998) that the interests of the USA as a military and financial hegemon are served by this ideology presumes that the US Administration can predict its interests and that intentional schemes rarely backfire. Consider, however, how the democratic social movements of the 1960s and 1970s managed to achieve significant institutional reforms in legislative and state bureaucratic organisations, even corporations. In my view, this libertarian utopianism needed, and was able, to inspire a new social movement which also institutionalised reforms.

Moreover, the following analysis does not impute motives, or unmask and exaggerate rank ideological interests, as it only cites openly claimed hopes and aspirations for change. I have repeatedly argued, as well, that greed is merely a by-product of the trust (through distrust) necessary to imagine a controllable future. Utopian demands are implicit in key libertarian texts and public declarations which were, and still are, treated with public derision as a dystopia (of distrust) from diverse political viewpoints. Ruth Levitas (1986: 80) was a lone figure in showing the early rise of the New Right in Britain during the 1980s – both 'neo-liberal economics and social authoritarianism' – to be a phenomenon of two conflicting utopias of 'competition and compliance'. Levitas, whose expertise is in utopian thought (1990), has never dismissed utopia as a pipedream; usually, she says, utopian hope is mistakenly reserved for the Left or 'progressive', 'radical' 'reform'. Looking at these declared libertarian and conservative utopian projects for the 'good society', she compared the confident libertarian assertions in Britain of Friedrich Hayek and the Adam Smith Institute with Roger Scruton's conservative utopian challenge (1986: 80–91). She drew on Karl Mannheim's *Ideology and Utopia* (1936) to explain Scruton's conservative aspirations, then enjoying huge publicity (Levitas 1986: 91–7). But a financial utopia was perhaps too fantastic to contemplate at the time: 'competitiveness' and 'inflation first' were the 1980s terms. At that time, too, both utopian projects devoted huge resources to attacking social policy, the unions and the welfare state, with remarkable success. Very few critics then heeded Milton Friedman's main declared aim, which was to restore shareholder control over firms in markets (Chapter 2). Only a handful (like economists) then guessed how financial short-term dominance might later speed up: now it is taken for granted as a public view, whether for good or ill. Twenty years later, the Anglo-American business world is inspired by this utopia most of all. With the financialisation of life – and not despite crises but because of them – the present-time orientation, ecstatic outbursts, corporate collapses and unseemly frenzies are a source of profits for the daily news media. As an anti-state utopia of the present, this world has a scandalously wealthy social base in global financial centres, from CEOs to orthodox economists. It is a utopia led by self-styled 'oppressed' and, as I argue, in farcical contrast to a similar utopia centuries ago of poor and brutally oppressed peasants forming one of the first modern social movements to reject fatalism. Today's version faces much opposition but, unlike those former European peasants, no oppression whatsoever.

'RISKLESS' GREED?

Many of my informants see the past as only a rough and ready guide to the present. They do not say, like active cult personalities, that 'history tells us'. None of their experiences is 'extrapolated' to today. Many hold long cyclical views where euphoria and disillusion alternate, in a similar manner to Albert Hirschman (2002), who describes waves of profound disillusion for long-term views and public policies, with euphoria for short-term privatism.

Alan Abelson speaks of 'intoxication', partly waning in 2000: 'I don't think it's possible to really grasp how pervasive this stock fever is; it's really like an epidemic that's invaded almost every part of this society'. Starting with the overconfidence in the finance world then:

Abelson: What we have had is eighteen years of uninterrupted bull market, which is the longest time ever, and it's encompassed both the stock market and the bond market. The irony is that commodity markets, enormously strong in the '70s, have absolutely collapsed. They have collapsed in gold, oil, and so on . . . Today the equity market is valued at $2 trillion, which represents an exponential rise for a variety of reasons. One of the reasons, as Oscar Wilde said, is that 'nothing succeeds like excess' and the excess has bred enormous interest in the stock market . . . unprecedented.

Also, until the 1980s, he says, 'most pension plans used to be administered by a company or, at best, a company and a union together, and they were very conservative', putting most of the money into fixed income. But now half of American households have money invested in the stock market; it used to be a mere 3 per cent.

They have an exposure to it which have implications that are not entirely salubrious if something happens obviously . . . You know, it used to be that people, if they looked on Wall Street, certainly after the experience of 1929 and for many years, they looked on Wall Street as kind of an alternative casino. Now, the problem is, it isn't play money, this is retirement money, this is education money, it's really, you know, the guts of their lives tied up in the stock market. (21 September 2000)

Stock and bond markets are more intertwined in economic activity than ever before. Far from euphoria for today's financialisation, the greater the wisdom brought to the interviews, the more gloomy they are. These are the eras when no one worries about levels of debt: confidence seems to continue, even after events like Enron. Henry Kaufman mentions the 'extreme period' in the 1920s when 'a variety of ingenious financing activities and investment activities, the lack of supervision', led to restrictive legislation. Official policy, monetary and fiscal policy, is better now, yet he argues that 'the world is still creating more marginal debt' and that its quality since the postwar period has been declining. Events since Enron are 'not extreme enough to push the system into an extreme conservatism', not yet. (27 February 2002)

Ingenious financing strategies are not produced by 'herds' but by investment banks that lack government supervision. The quality of debt is not a large topic of debate, not because it is too difficult to understand, but because there has been no depression since the 1930s that might prevent memory-loss and preserve cautious policies. Therefore Kaufman had 'no doubt that in a year or two there will be new financing techniques and new ways of loosening the relationship between the creditor and the debtor' (27 February 2002).

These conservative financiers worry that only a truly deep recession can shake the rich world out of its short-term money absorption. Greed oversimplifies the phenomenon, so does ideology. What inspires finance firms to create more leverage instruments? What inspires euphoria? The argument that emotional volatility occurs only in the 'periphery' (mums and dads), or as psychological traits of individuals, is at best a rationalisation. Journalists tend to interpret interests too mechanically as greed and fear, in aggregation or in tarnished cult figures – rarely do they write about the 'guts of people's lives' tied up investing for the long term. Others say that speculation and debt are a cultural trend, even a 'fervour' for risk (Baker & Simon 2002: 5–6). But consider the evidence. Opposing trends of risk refusal or precaution are also prevalent: environmental concern takes on the proportions of major social movements. Only one-third of OECD populations, though half in English-speaking countries, hold financial assets (Korpi & Palmer 2003). Indirectly, millions are affected by financial markets: results cannot be 'salubrious' for modest income groups; the poorest have suffered most. Social relations of money between creditors and debtors have greater structural importance today than those between labour and capital. Greed is too simple and not provable, and cynical electorates (and informed sceptics) suggest that the euphoria of certainty – miscast as 'risk' – is most evident in the core of finance.

UTOPIA OR IDEOLOGY?

It is hard to refute arguments about a dominant intellectual fashion, or a hegemonic ideology of the market. Yet there is something missing. Most quoted is a Washington–Wall Street consensus between high finance and politicians (comprised of social strata typically seen as bearers of specific interests). Less quoted are the monetary problems of the late 1960s, when many Europeans saw the USA deriving an unfair advantage as the main international reserve currency. The USA seemed to be financing its deficit internationally by selling dollars that were depreciating in value (Ferguson 2004: 1). Regardless of these debates, new policies, miscast as 'reform', were based on the libertarian ideology of figures from Ayn Rand to Milton Friedman. Starting with Nixon's floating of the dollar, then Thatcher's Big Bang, all the English-speaking countries reversed the postwar policy framework. According to some, it served as a 'revenge of the rentiers' (investors and speculators) against the high inflation of the mid-1970s (Smithin 1996), or the reversal was effected through finance 'class' alliances and 'market developments' (Grahl 2001b). More convincing accounts include organisational actors, the global financial firms that redeveloped out of the Eurodollar markets, and the huge financial stimulus from corporate raiding. From this, 'alliances' of investment banks, accountancy firms, institutional share-owners and CEOs, economic liberal think-tanks, legal firms' new mergers and acquisitions (M&A) divisions and business colleges played a role in forcing policy changes on US administrations first, then others (e.g. Stretton 1999: 372; Ingham 2002).

None of these explanations is satisfactory alone. Christopher Hood's *Explaining Economic Policy Reversals* (1994) argues that 'right-wing ideology' hardly explains Democratic President Carter's turn to monetarism in the USA, nor Labor Prime Minister Hawke's embrace of financial reform in Australia and the New Zealand Labour Government's total policy reversal under 'Rogernomics' (Gray 1998: 39). Moreover, some governments, for example New Zealand, have since tried to temper this ideology (after electoral outcry) but with much difficulty; hence the British Labour Government has not tried. President Clinton swore about how the success of his health program and his re-election hinged on the Federal Reserve and 'a bunch of f—ing bond traders' (cited in Woodward 2000: 126). With institutional milestones for the financialisation of life so entrenched, with larger segments of populations in specific financial positions, whether desired or *not*, governments' powers have been heavily qualified (Pauly 1997). No one disputes the 'ideological' influence on policy, as more institutional inducements to take a punt become fixed policy and more populations are subject to acting as rentiers than as savers and pensioners. Criticisms are not only from the periphery:

Fraser: I think the ideology that we see here of selling everything off, privatising everything, relying on the markets – more and more people are going to question that and will want to see some more responsible governments than we have been seeing recently. (28 June 2002)

Although relations of money are inherently trust problems, old cautious strategies like reducing vulnerability to loss were overwhelmed by investment banks taking another strategy, of trying to reduce uncertainty. Not so successfully, in various bank collapses:

Elliott: The problem with the free marketeers was that they thought you could trust the markets. They thought you could invest large amounts of trust in markets, because markets would clear, and they would come to equilibrium, and they are perfectible. Whereas post-Keynesians like me think that is rubbish. Markets are very volatile, very dangerous, very unpredictable places . . . The whole basis of

Keynesian thought was to give people some security, by saying we will surround these markets with protection, controls. That is a Keynesian approach, that it is a very unpredictable world, so try and take some of the danger out of the situation. (5 October 2000)

One problem for economic libertarian ideology is in sustaining it within the heartland. Over twenty years of financial crises and oscillations to mistrust demonstrate that the issue is not markets per se but the opportunistic organisations operating in them. Markets operate in speculative ways because banks and funds use complex multiples of loans, assets and transactions, often investing largely borrowed sums for small margins. Leverage mounts, then libertarian prescriptions are torn up, failures are no longer ascribed to volatile, silly herds, but to 'systemic' threats needing pragmatic 'intervention' (bail-outs or jail terms). Suddenly the vista of 'free marketeers' – a vista free of structural interconnections of big actors – cannot be trusted. Yet failures seem, strangely, to reinspire trust in new distrust strategies. Not quite memory loss, each new (rational) strategy and policy demand is a reaction to the last disastrous incident. Cult figures rise and fall among CEOs, financial analysts and Nobel Prize-winning economists. Attributions of institutional credibility (financial supervision more or less) move from Moody's to the IMF, on to central banks (e.g. G5 CBs) and back to Moody's or a weaker SEC (see Chapters 5, 6 and 7).

ORGANISATIONAL MORALE-BOOSTING

The wonder is how the 'money power' sustains the 'morale of expectation' (Shackle's term: 1972: 447) and internally resurrects it after each unpredicted horrible event, each theory found wanting. Morale is built from *collective emotional influences* on shared future outlooks, from disputes over uncertainties faced daily in attempts to guess the future with some modicum of rationality. Any financial outlook is made up of various conjectures (e.g. 'fundamental' versus 'technical' analysis) about 'trends' which, Shackle says (1972), bear little relation to others and are always intensely focused on 'the News' of the most latest profit changes, rate moves or any clue to a future entirely *internal to finance*.

This outlook of financial expectations rapidly becomes a new one, just as patternless and laden with superstitions ('dead cats bouncing' is merely one; recycled ideas of how a dead market may 'bounce' up once, or of 'limits' to how low or high asset prices can go, are mere superstitions, since valuations are conjecture: when prices move cannot be predicted). Outlooks twist like kaleidoscopes (Shackle's ingenious metaphor for 1930s financial markets), or fish in the sea, lacking even the intellectual understanding brought to sport or gambling, as my interviews emphasise. A complete and radical change to the future imagined picture of investment possibilities needs only a slight shock to former expectations – based on evidence that is suddenly passé. As investment values are so kaleidoscopic, consequences are also 'formidable and far-reaching' (Shackle 1972: 183). Armies of prognosticators and interpreters of asset values respond to 'the News' by abrupt reaction to unheralded announcements. Reactions today arise among the vast mass of banks, funds and analysts, all 'acutely aware of each other's existence' not as anonymous sellers and buyers but in insider 'seller–critic' relationships (Zuckerman 1999: 1430). There is never analysis of fully known problems because relationships between data are a mere surmise, 'fictional elaboration' as Shackle calls it. As Keynesians describe it (Chapters 2–3), conjectures are about 'the conjectures being made by others' (Shackle 1972: 184–5). All search for the opinion of the majority, about what their opinion will be tomorrow, yet crucially, the majority are those with more power and wealth (the big banks). Once the eddies of the surging movement appear purposive, that 'will in fact shortly become the Direction of general, "conventional" movement' (Shackle 1972: 225). As for modest investors in today's large and remote world of organisations, Bogle is clear:

Bogle: [They are] suckered in by the advertisements, by the heat of the day, the markets, the manias. The mutual fund industry helped a lot by creating the new funds, by hawking performance, and by turning over their portfolios in a way that comports not at all for the long-term investors. (7 March 2002)

Sustaining and renewing such a morale is a constant problem for economic and political elites, obviously to rationalise excesses and blowbacks from their promises and to hawk for new entrants. More inspired by the short term than the rest of us, efforts must convince their own sphere, let alone those whose long-term savings have vanished. *How Do Central Bankers Talk?* gravely acknowledges how the public dislikes volatility. Not so 'the market'. Rapid mood-swings foster abrupt moves into different speculative markets, increasingly marketed by the big organisations.

Bogle: In Wall Street, we've probably got the most efficient, driven, sales machine in the recorded history of the human race! *But that's not the right system . . .* We should be sought for our [professional] expertise in helping people to achieve a financial security for their retirement years or to send their children to college. (7 March 2002)

Securities are not security. Kaufman is not only concerned about corporate debt, but like Bogle, stresses organisations rather than modest investors:

Kaufman: It's just that the Enron situation really encompasses, it illustrates, all of the excesses of the past decade or so and involves a broad spectrum of participants, starting with the senior management, the board of directors, the auditors, the security analysts and the lenders, as well as the absence of good official supervision. (27 February 2002)

'PRESENT-NESS': MANNHEIM AND 'UTOPIAN MENTALITIES'

Kaufman sees little end to interlocking chains of organisational excesses unless the worst occurs, a great depression. The machine can find new ways to entice 'suckers' and boost morale within peak organisations. When nostrums of the 'golden strait-jacket' (Friedman 1999) are found wanting, morale in the 'selling machine' is set back, humiliated, after every unforeseen event, each ruthless struggle lost. Consider Andersen's demise. Other interpretive techniques for valuation revive (Zuckerman 1999: 1431; Ormerod 1998). One sector's or competitor's demise from uncertainties – which unravel any valuation – is another's source for rebuilding a tarnished reputation. Whole industries indulge in *schadenfreude*, another emotion concept as enlightening as *entscheidungsfreudig* – joy at others' harm fosters joy in new decisions (Chapter 4). Libertarian ideology (as institutionalised in policy) is itself discarded as soon as tax-free bail-outs or fines become necessary, at great public cost, symbolic violence and cost to modest investors. Ideology cannot sustain the morale internal to high finance. Morale must have a content, a force for bravely pressing on against constant criticisms: a collective force inspired by utopian energies, emotions and outlooks.

These days, utopia as wish and hope is usually used openly by environmental, feminist and conservative (communitarian) movements against reducing all social life to 'the economy'. Liberation theology in South America is driven by hope for equality with freedom. Vague, postmodern utopias, perhaps regretting their celebration of individualism, speak of 'hope' entirely without content. All utopias (with specific visions and aspirations) are disputed in an ideological field. Utopia is always offered as 'something missing' but Mannheim's *Ideology and Utopia* (1936) shows how to locate the missing drive in the 'money power' because he dissects utopian impulses mainly by their time-orientation. A 1930s intellectual and refugee, Mannheim saw Marxism and socialism as no more scientific or 'true' than liberalism and conservatism: none escape sectional interests: all are ideological *and* utopian. Although he denied that any 'knowing' could be non-ideological, so no one can reveal 'the truth', he tried mistakenly to exempt intellectuals. Class-consciousness (we now add gender, ethnicity, or investment bank milieux and so on) shape every worldview.

Yet modern worldviews are also utopias; everyone intuitively knows that ideological thinking defends and preserves the status quo, which is too backward-looking to be utopian. Mannheim (1936: 173) describes a utopian state of mind as future-oriented – it is a hope – which appears to be incongruous with 'the state of reality in which it occurs'. So no one believed that speculative individualism defined the status quo in the 1970s; yet intriguingly (against Mannheim's distinction), an ideology of free markets can hardly defend today's dismal status quo of market failures and collapse of opportunistic firms with their accompanying impoverishment of former employees. Libertarianism, incessant reform, seems perpetually utopian.

Mannheim's classic study makes sense of emotions in finance; it shows *how* these emotions matter. First, modern utopias exist, he says, in a social field of conflicting, antagonistic utopias or ideologies which are socially effective (or utopian elements may be). Second, and also relevant to finance, modern utopias are inspired by their emotional yearnings about time, whatever the historical period or social base urging a specific doctrine. All utopias are hopes – modern time-utopias are projections of past, future or present times, even though their hopes and goals must be a future. As is well known, the conservative utopian·*hopes* through nostalgia to resurrect some previous era. Hardly discussed today, but far more relevant, is a present-oriented utopia. Also, Mannheim's inconsistent division – utopian ideas deviating from 'reality' but ideological beliefs defending 'reality' – is interesting. If all understandings of reality are socially situated, no unmasking of other ideological defences can reveal the true reality. (For example, Mandy Rice-Davies, a declared working-class prostitute, famously said 'Well he *would,* wouldn't he' when unmasking Lord Astor's ideological claim during the British Tory Minister John Profumo's 'sex-spy' scandal that rocked the UK in 1963. She also said 'My life has been one long descent into respectability' [*Oxford Dictionary of Quotations* 1999]. Her own point, therefore, is that truth is socially situated, whereas intentional lies are different.) In contrast, utopia is openly declared: no one who dislikes a particular utopia is pretending to be scientifically above, or free from, ideological thinking and its inevitable biases. But utopias can be criticised.

Utopias face hostility by ideological defenders of the status quo who dismiss them as unrealisable pipedreams (Mannheim 1936: 177): Utopians can cast themselves as victims of abuse, particularly when undemocratic procedures are used to silence utopian or dystopian visions. Mannheim selected four utopias of modernity: the obscure chiliastic-anarchist; the well-known 'humanitarian-liberal'; the conservative; and the 'socialist-communist' utopian mentalities. Given that liberal, conservative and communist utopias have all been institutionalised, for better and for worse, none is a pipedream. Neither are democratic or environmental utopias mere wishful thinking. Utopia is in principle realisable for, while it shatters the existing order, it is 'always in the process of being realized' (Ricoeur 1986: 273). Ideology tends to legitimate the existing social order because 'ideas which later turned out to have been only distorted representations of a past or potential social order were ideological, while those which were adequately realized in the succeeding social order were relative utopias' (Mannheim 1936: 184). Consider too, given advertising industries' pretensions to utopia (manipulation of hope), how 'wishful thinking' is not utopian. Fairytale retirements on one's pension fund or 'travel romances' are merely 'continually changing expressions of that which was lacking in actual life. They were more nearly complementary colours in the picture . . . existing at the time [as supporting wishes] than utopias working in opposition to the status quo and disintegrating it' (Mannheim 1936: 184).

The utopian element or 'the nature of the dominant wish' is 'the organizing principle' which 'moulds the way in which we experience time'. The heart of Mannheim's originality, his emphasis on time, seems so apt: 'The innermost structure of the mentality of a group can never be as clearly grasped as when we attempt to understand its conception of time in the light of its hopes, yearnings, and purposes. On the basis of these purposes and expectations, a given mentality orders not merely future events, but also the past' (Mannheim 1936: 189).

No mentality has one specific history. All time-mentalities order utopias and dystopias in a contested field, their attitudes are present in 'forms of thought and experience' in various social movements then and now. Chiliasm (a form of anarchism, inspiring the Peasant Revolutions of 1524–25) is fixated on the present, the 'chance moment' (Mannheim 1936: 192–3, 212), whereas humanitarian liberalism wishes for gradual evolutionary progress towards an ever better future (through education and merit, or the Whig view of history, still obvious in technological determinism). The first 'modern' conservatism (as a response to 18th-century revolutionary liberalism, hence 'reactionary'), idealises the past as folk, community or national traditions and aristocratic hierarchy, whereas a socialist-communist mentality is a synthesis of the near and the remote future.

If the wish is the present, past horrors must be expunged from memory; the future must not be thought of because it holds not merely daring risks but unthinkable dangers. This sociological approach to 'concrete thinking, acting, and feeling' tries to understand their 'inner connections in concrete types' and groups (Mannheim 1936: 189). The emotional element is crucial to identifying a specific utopianism, not the ideas that inspired the utopias, their earlier history or their social bases. So 19th-century anarchism is similar to 16th-century chiliasm but it included aristocratic social bases, particularly in Russia. Anarchism is anti-state and present-oriented like the collective consciousness of chiliastic optimism, yet it is quite misleading to view either through a history of ideas. Emotions are far more important. An anarchist approach to time is embedded in the dominant wish, an 'absolute presentness' which is an 'ecstatic substance' continually whipped up in the here and now (Mannheim 1936: 194). No delay is contemplated between idea and reality, even though a lack of congruence between the wish and reality is greatest in anarchism and chiliasm: '"Ideas" did not drive these men to revolutionary deeds. Their actual outburst was conditioned by ecstatic-orgiastic energies. The reality-transcending elements in consciousness which here were aroused to an active utopian function were not "ideas" . . . This eruption had its roots in much deeper-lying vital and elemental levels of the psyche' (Mannheim 1936: 192). With anarchism too, future dangers must equally be unthinkable, so bravery was required for the many futile attempts to assassinate Tsarist Chiefs of Police.

When corporate 'hostile' raids (in the 1970s) became normalised as 'mergers' (in the 1980s) by 'dark knights' bravely defending shareholder value, it was a triumph of a present-oriented finance utopia which shattered the former corporate sector. Not ideology alone but metaphors of brutal courtship ('preferred suitors', 'takeover by rape') and macho warfare ('cyanide pills', 'shoot-outs') (Hirsch 1986: 816–17) typified that battle and the ascendant utopian cultural frames. It was no longer the 'criminal devils' in *The Pride of Lucifer*, on Guinness's 1986 takeover bid for Distillers, driven, as the critic had it, by the City's 'public school bully boys' at Morgan Grenfell (cited in Walsh 1990). By the 1990s, industries of 'hired guns' and 'headhunters' were as established as M&A divisions of investment banks and legal firms. In 2000, 'the News' was focused on highly charged drives towards 'the deal' as an end in itself, when 'old economy' 'dinosaurs' were terrified of the 'new economy'. The Time/Warner Bros CEO, in a televised merger with AOL, spoke of his ecstatic experience in concluding the deal, but by the end of 2000 the deal was in tatters, IBM's boss (with hindsight) intoning that there was no 'new economy' (Hale 2000b).

As before, however, crises and *schadenfreude* had no lasting impact, as Michael Lewis rightly argued after the collapse of Drexel Burnham Lambert and the 1987 crash. At that time, mainstream editorials (*Time, Business Week*) all predicted the end of 'greed, excess and bravado'. They were wrong, he said, as there was 'no sign that anyone on Wall Street was chastened by Drexel's ordeal'. Nor did Tom Wolfe's book *Bonfire of the Vanities* or the movie *Wall Street* achieve a sense of shame; rather, Wall Street took them as signs of flattery, according to Lewis. Similarly in the City and other finance centres (as after 2000 etc.), Lewis's own book *Liar's Poker* included in the batteries of criticism that there was no predicted 'abrupt end' to the two words of the 1970–80s – 'me' and 'money' – said to be 'the driving forces in Anglo-Saxon economies' (Walsh 1990; Lewis 1991: 58–9).

The utopian function as identified by Mannheim are the striking analogous elements of today's finance. The gap between wish and 'reality' is truly infinite: the reality of uncertainty and the existence of huge reckless organisations are denied, the cautious silenced. Beliefs in the neutrality of money – a time-space of today where financial crises cannot happen – continue, although the dominant wish always meets disappointment. Then 'the pontifical tone' of prophecy is often replaced by 'uncertain vacillation'. Suddenly indecision and 'quietism' prevail, which can allow 'activist' conservatism to overrule and try to control 'the concept of "inner freedom"' (Mannheim 1936: 214). Here lies today's link to neo-conservatism.

Karl Polanyi's accusation is often raised today: that a 'fanatic utopian faith in the market' drove 19th-century economic liberals to engineer *The Great Transformation* (Polanyi 1957) in Britain, the first fully capitalist country. His thesis is popularly expressed in hopes for a similar countervailing force that will rise against today's fanaticism. Many criticisms of financial instability, conservative, liberal and socialist, argue that today's libertarians are 'irrational'. John Gray's *False Dawn: The Delusions of Global Capitalism* (1998), Joseph Stiglitz' *Globalization and Its Discontents* (2002) and Susan Strange's *Mad Money* (1998) are a small sample of *rational* criticisms. British conservative John Gray sees global laissez-faire as an American 'utopian project' made possible by the US Enlightenment remaining a 'living political faith' (1998: 100–1). Rationality is used to criticise a deluded, emotional fanaticism. Polanyi is cited by Gray to argue that the present is a similar grim experiment whose outcome – breakdown – we can know in advance (1998: 16); both Right as well as Left predict collapse. Nevertheless, Gray's use of Polanyi (1998: 16–21) gives too much intentionality to the 'fanatics', and his analogy to an undemocratic 19th-century era is less relevant today. Democratic electorates cannot be persuaded by that former grim fanaticism alone. Utopianism in today's economic libertarian form is more plausible in Mannheim's sense of a 'dominant wish' for the 'god of opportunity'. For a significant elite in high finance, utopian short-termism is posed against a dour long-term cautionary utopia. The latter dourness is not the fanatic commodification of land, labour and money imposed by elite 19th-century politicians and economists when few had the vote, but some of Keynes's cautionary policies when many more peoples of the world did. In the present ecstatic utopianism, rational goals are reached in short-term distrust strategies, but the movement must keep attracting new conviction and new converts to the faith in unlimited securities. Critics are, in effect, posing other utopias inspired by other emotions (e.g. caution, or hope for a future generation of children welcomed into a more peaceful world) and other modes of rationality (e.g. precautionary strategies for some modest security against an unknowable future; see Chapter 9).

Analogies to earlier financial 'exuberance' also miss the 21st-century organisational form. Economic historians describe typical patterns of international financial crises accurately in one respect (e.g. Kindleberger 1989: 24, after Minsky 1985). A crisis starts with a move of profit opportunities into a particular sector (railways, land speculation, dot.coms). This leads to euphoria and excessive optimism, which prompts overtrading or speculation, monetary expansion and excessive bank credit. A rise in asset prices then leads to a mania. 'Financial institutions accept liability structures that decrease liquidity, and that in more sober climate they would have rejected' (Kindleberger 1989: 33). This is followed by a sharp fall, possible discredit, a panic and a rush into money (1989: 24, 33). And yet Kindleberger's 'mob psychology or hysteria' (1989: 32) is inadvertently about firms and banks:

> A fall in prices reduces the value of collateral and induces banks to call loans or refuse new ones, causing merchant houses to sell commodities, households to sell securities, industry to postpone borrowing and prices to fall still further . . . If firms fail, bank loans go bad, and then banks fail . . . Merchant houses, industrial firms, investors, banks in need of ready cash – all sell off their worst securities if they can, their best if they have to. Firms, corporations and households known to be in trouble may be carried on the books for a time, in the expectation or hope that prices will pick up again and float the frail bark of credit off the bottom. (Kindleberger 1989: 127)

Kindleberger is hardly describing individuals. A more adequate view is an inter-organisational emotional phenomenon: a fragile and dynamic set of relations of trust and distrust in a global network of corporate entities. I do not point out this utopianism, with its cycles of trust to distrust, to argue that emotions distort normal operations in the financial world and leave it fragile. Rather, there is no avoidance of emotions in the everyday, complicated world of corporate entities engaged in competitive struggles for dominance. To recall one interview, banks have 'an infinite capacity to lose money' in decisions which take 'bravery' (another emotion) and a longer-term horizon to resist. If routine decisions are based on expectations, then current interlocking chains between organisations can provide confidence, for a time. Hence the interviews included an array from banks proper to all the outlying and supporting sectors. Few are excluded, as an informed sceptic notes:

Abelson: The law firms are very heavily involved in the process. They are the ones who are the handmaidens of the investment bankers; they are the ones who make the whole thing possible in the end. Without law firms you can't get anywhere. Law firms are paid to see what is possible, not to tell people what not to do. Basically law firms are really part of the apparatus that feeds this whole capital system. (21 May 2001)

That form of legal mendacity supports the system, on the one hand, but on the other, law firms are also used for radical opposition against mendacity:

Birt: Companies are now paranoid about not telling the truth because of the fear of class action suits – perhaps being too cautious. You can almost mislead by being too pessimistic, which trashes your stock price and depresses your investors. There is now a massive industry of firms running class action suits. This is an increasing cause of concern for business, so that makes them cautious about what they say. Analysts at the moment have a very bad reputation . . . Enron had analysts all over it and they didn't do a very good job on that. (22 March 2002)

Lone speculators and retired fund-holders do fight back, but only collectively in class actions run by legal firms, in institutional settings with shareholder activist groups, or action by their fund firms.

PRESENTNESS: SEARCHING FOR TODAY'S OPPORTUNISM

All utopias foster emotional energies that inspire action. This present-oriented utopia, in today's financial form, expresses no worry about the distant future (unlike today's environmental and feminist movements). Likewise it fosters absolutely no nostalgia about any previous golden age (like old Keynesians with their passé attachment to full employment and modest security for all). It cannot dare to remember the bleak, gloomy history of the Great Crash. There is no relationship to 'historical existence' such as financial history, however relevant, since history could introduce fear. Instead, the attitude is one of 'tense expectation' for a 'propitious moment' in the here and now (Mannheim 1936: 195). The mythology of the 'God of Opportunity', Kairos, forever searches for 'the genius of the decisive moment' (1936: 198).

Opportunity, it seems to me, is the dominant wish of 'present-ness'. It is seen in the search for each new financial guru or CEO who has triumphed over the market with conviction. Once that guru, CEO or economic theory fails, a new *entscheidungsfreudig* figure is found. The opportunism and the unseemly, blind haste to more 'reforms' is what most disgusts many of the sceptics I interviewed. Equally, the bitterness of CEOs sacked after a corporate raid is not always mitigated by a golden parachute, as Paul Hirsch's interviews attest (1986). As with anarchism, the political cousin of market libertarianism, this utopia dismisses 'constitutions and laws'; it is greatly attached to 'storm and vitality', and a 'new lawless and consequently free world' (Bakunin, cited in Mannheim 1936: 196). As Mannheim suggests, the only creative principle is 'ecstatic presentness'. But while sceptics know about the City – 'if you're dealing with money, if you're close to it, some of it sticks to your palms' (Ziegler, cited in Chapter 5) – the lawless debacles are breathtaking (to my sceptics and us laypeople alike). Freedom from all official supervision is demanded by finance.

Tellingly, when this 'spirit ebbs' or their demanded freedom backfires, the result is 'a naked mass-frenzy and a despiritualised fury' (Mannheim 1936: 196). *Schadenfreude* infests multiple other publics and financial firms over each cycle of frenzied blame and anger, like the months following the US Savings & Loans crisis, Barings' collapse, the Mexican debt crises, the Southeast Asian financial crisis and LTCM, the spate of corporate Enrons to Parmalats. When trust collapses, fear of failure gives rise to hypocritical blame. Scapegoating is typical. This cannot be characterised as a panic of a crazy crowd but rather a panic generated at inter-organisational levels of huge and powerful organisations which, when the disaster occurs, gives rise to more general panic.

Recall Oliver Williamson's claims, even during debt crises in the 1980s, that the world can be reduced to transaction costs, the future information about which can be known by organisations in advance, or that economics could 'design control systems with reference to all consequences', even unintended ones (Williamson 1993: 460). The wonder is that he had such influence. Instead of widespread ridicule, such views only met polite, restrained critique, as this utopia, as described in Williamson's fervour for 'opportunism with guile', had infused the major organisations and core state bureaucracies. Williamson spoke to this, because if the future can be collapsed into the present so effortlessly by reducing uncertainty to risk, long-term issues and 'anxieties' of regeneration, conservation and stability are possibly avoidable.

THE CULT OF PERSONALITY

The cult process in gaining status makes heroes by personalising business people and other figures in finance's epistemic community whose status rests on correct predictions or a new theory, which rarely last. Once a theory becomes a source of competitive advantage, firms and banks are pressured to join the bandwagon. The movement must focus on Kairos, a new opportunity, for each trust strategy employed. The story of stock options fits this pattern: beginning as a distrust strategy, it gave rise to a different trust in the future, but when it failed by the time of Enron, further methods are sought:

Bogle: And I'm not so sure that we'll get there through stock buybacks. Forty per cent of all stock buybacks are used simply to avoid the dilution that would come from the exercise of executive stock options, which have gotten completely out of hand. Stock options are one of the great disgraces of our current system. (7 March 2002)

How does each disgrace, such as stock options, or theories like portfolio insurance, get so 'completely out of hand'? Stock buybacks became the alleged saviour after billions of losses. The time-frame is very short for financial innovations, and the epistemic field provides a more limited attention space than do other intellectual fields. In struggles to win attention space, the financial 'genius' is created out of the dense network of contemporaries and former teachers. As in all intellectual fields, according to Randall Collins, eminent teachers bestow status – but usually through cognitive and emotional effects on star pupils, who elicit higher emotional energy and concentration: success is created in feedback loops. It propels the lonely, isolated desk worker, tapping out his or her latest theory, out into a public intellectual life of conferences and world forums. The lone intellectual emerges to a contrasting heroism, able to present 'fresh' ideas at intense gatherings where a quasi-religious aura can inspire followers. But whereas, in aesthetic and academic fields, the rare few who gain recognition propose new problems (Collins 1998, 1990), in the financial field the search is for answers to the same old problem, how to make money by controlling the future. Although the emotional energy percolating any network is stratified – a few recognised, the rest embittered – the time-frame for a finance genius is very short.

Warren Buffett, an American fundamental or value investor, is not really an exception as his long-term success is partly because his huge investment fund's stock selections now tend to influence the market (Paulos 2003: 65). As a mathematician puts it, most financial gurus are merely so due to the luck of being on the up-side rather than the down-side (Paulos 2003: 64). 'Outperforming the market requires that one remain on the cusp of our collective complexity horizon . . . If this is possible for anyone or any group to achieve, it's not likely to remain so for long' (Paulos 2003: 196). The interviews on finance television shows and business pages dwindle, as do the investor seminars and salary bonuses. Abelson highlights this oddity: 'When somebody has had great success as a predictor or forecaster, that often is the time to be most suspicious, because they invariably fail to repeat this success, it is almost a one-night-stand act' (21 September 2000).

During the dot.com boom, as Michael Lazar said, 'every professional investor knew it was a bubble' because they had seen too many in their lifetimes. As to why the boom still continued, he said:

Lazar: The thing is that there are always these 'gurus'. People started to be called gurus by journalists who are illiterate . . . The problem is that journalists and customers, because they're ignorant, are always looking for people who they can regard as a touchstone, and say this guy or this woman knows everything. 'We don't have to worry any more, relax, we can just do what they tell us to do.' What happened was, as technology stocks went up and up and up, the bulls of technology stocks were seen to be right. 'Of course they were right, look at this, these people must be geniuses, these people must be gurus!' . . . Everybody whom an investment market perceives as having that little bit of knowledge which can transform dross into gold, is called a guru. (4 June 2001)

As he said, Henry Kaufman was the original guru – of the 1980s – and 'everybody believed that everything he said was right, until it wasn't'. As we saw (Chapter 3), untrained journalists are forced to trust these analysts. Kaufman said of his final years as executive of Salomons' research that he had to defend 'honest' independent research through 'stonewalling', partly because his Dr Gloom tag of expressing concern about 'excesses', over-leverage, inflation, and lack of supervision was falling out of favour with analysts and, more seriously, with investment banks (2000: 182). As underwriting and merger activity grew, bank–client relations became more impersonal. Investment bank research was directed to selling bank products, not to independent advice. Salomons' highly publicised 'problems' after his retirement in 1989 confirmed his earlier stand (Kaufman 2000: 179).

PROPAGANDA

Propaganda is 'that branch of the art of lying which consists in very nearly deceiving your friends without quite deceiving your enemies' (Cornford 1949: 4). Lies intentionally aim to deceive and may succeed, though not 'to all of the people, all of the time' (Abraham Lincoln), whereas an inescapable worldview or ideology does not deceive. During the dot.com boom the formerly banished term 'capitalism' came to be used defiantly, as billboards in Manhattan proclaimed: 'Proliferate capitalism'.

Even so, propaganda about shareholding presumes a classless social base. New York investment bank economist Stephen Roach at Morgan Stanley is an interesting example. With a limited freedom to present unpopular views (independently, as defended by Kaufman, to no avail, in Salomons) Roach defies the climate of Wall Street's propaganda and censorship. Since 2002, the forecasting business has been blindly cheerleading a 'perfect recovery' in America. Informed sceptics are not merely ridiculed but ostracised, according to Paul Krugman. Defying 'orthodoxy', Roach now signs his e-mails 'From the wilderness' (Krugman 2003: 75). During the dot.com collapse, Roach was indeed brutally honest about the forces behind the boom, and the problems facing any recovery: 'There are times when the balance of power shifts in favor of labor or capital, and usually those shifts go to extremes . . . This has been a period when economic power has shifted enormously in favor of capital', argued Roach to the *New York Times* (Steinberger 2001). Open admission of winners and losers in class terms is rare on Wall Street.

A classless ideology of individual consumers and free markets cannot cope with crisis. Emotions of distrust and resentment among broader publics are perceived with force. In discussing financial regulators, during another crisis (Andersen's collapse), this was said:

Ingham: Financial regulators . . . are very important and often have a role that's not totally understood by the outside world. Every time there's a bank failure or an investment scandal, the media in particular tends to whip up an hysteria implying that regulators are there to eliminate risk, and they're not. There's a fundamental problem about the perception of risk in a lot of media coverage that goes way beyond financial matters. There's an increasing tendency, which is tabloid media driven, to encourage people to think that life in general should be risk-free. (15, 18 March 2002)

Even so, many people are taking on more risks, as Roach's class analysis implies, in casual under-employment and imposed unemployment. It is difficult to agree that only the tabloid press and commercial finance television programs have driven

An advertisement on a Manhattan building opposite the famous Flatiron Building, on the corner of Fifth Avenue where Broadway crosses at West 23rd Street. Photograph taken by the author during her investigations, when the dot.com boom was actually subsiding; 14 September 2000.

the opposing tendency to believe that money is neutral and risk-free, that creditors and debtors are not totally reliant on huge banking organisations. Bankers Trust advertisements asked 'How future-proofed is your portfolio?' but that was nothing to the shock therapy imposed on the Russian population, let alone the later LTCM investment failure in Russia. Among those implicated in each debacle, a few extracted themselves with evidence of shame. Some MIT economists who prescribed shock therapy for Russia (Gray 1998: 144–5) have retreated to studies of world poverty and the AIDS crisis. Paul Krugman, when on the advisory board of Enron in 1999, thought its lack of vertical integration illustrated how the 'change in ideology, the shift to pro-market policies' had made 'freewheeling markets possible', closer to 'Adam Smith's vision' than the corporatist future predicted by generations of pundits (cited in Blackburn 2002: 26). Having believed Enron, Krugman is now the harshest and most influential critic in the *New York Times*.

Maintaining morale at impersonal levels in contemporary finance cannot be done from ideological conviction. Propaganda does play a role – deceiving friends. Of note, Robert Heilbroner wrote in 1953 of the 'strange injustice' that Adam Smith, 'more avowedly hostile to the *motives* of businessmen than most New Deal economists', came to be regarded as business's patron saint (1967: 64, his emphasis). But the question is whether the propaganda in the pro-market Adam Smith think-tanks which edited out Smith's views about 'the mean rapacity' of merchants and grasping industrialists, who 'neither are, nor ought to be the rulers of mankind' (cited Heilbroner 1967: 62), deceived themselves.

Many would say that these scandals – the techniques for mounting Ponzi schemes and secret dealing with other people's money (embezzlement) by the mutual funds and Wall Street forex traders (in 2003) – would prompt more than a few class actions and government inquiries. The question arises why governments remain so weakened that intervention is ad hoc. Central banks can do nothing much about deflation. President Bush's tax cuts on capital gains augment the existing structure of incentives within banks. Being Labour, the Blair Government is more obviously under question, particularly from the conservative press but equally from *The Guardian*. Ideology cannot explain either the corporate deceit, and government inactivity towards it, or what now seems self-deception ('delusion' according to critics) in the face of public opposition. (In 2003, a World Economic Forum survey of trust in public institutions found that corporations were rated as the least trustworthy, even less than governments; see Rose 2003). In today's situation, short-termism prevails. It is difficult to imagine reconstruction, as right and left-wing critics agree. At the peaks of finance, energy in trust strategies ebb and flow at different paces, over diverse geographic regions. Yet was and is this mere ideology?

SOCIAL MOVEMENTS

The utopian aims ('individuals' free to act in markets) could not be achieved without action of the social movement type, that is, transformative action. Although high finance had already gained new ground in the 1970s, only activity on the scale of a movement could contest solidly democratic Western governments and the extraordinary gains achieved by the democracy movements of the 1960s to 1970s, culminating in anti-Vietnam and the welfare, feminist and civil rights reforms. But in what respects is this utopian project regarded as a social movement? It consists not merely of elites but well before the 1970s was highly institutionalised, with financial firms and lobbies working at that aim. Social movements are not defined by street marching but by their aim for transformation. A necessary but not sufficient condition for change in liberal democracies is to 'capture' the state or at least gain legislative changes. Changing the corporate sector was also important. Equally, mobilisations are not possible without emotions.

Emotions may help to change the sense of futility or danger perceived in attempting to change the situation. (Why would electorates accept great insecurity? Derision was meted out to Milton Friedman's early efforts and the extreme individualist views propounded by the growing Adam Smith think-tanks). Optimistic emotions can overcome apathy or turn fatalism into perceptions of potential opportunities and success (Goodwin et al. 2000). A key 'opportunity' here was inflation in the late 1970s. It could be cast not merely as bad but as an evil that only mass unemployment could cure. More groups recognise this optimism and convert. Social movements also act rationally; strategic action and use of resources for mobilisation and cognitive deliberation is well researched. 'Resource mobilisation' approaches argued that social movements act rationally and deploy resources to mobilise and achieve their goals (Pixley 1998). Optimistic emotions are also important to inspire movements to face uncertain outcomes. The future can only be dealt with by emotions. As on the streets, so too in the boardrooms and among financial institutions, specific emotions infuse and drive a global financial movement.

Let us explore the emotional side first, before briefly touching on the well-discussed use of resources, rationally deployed in mobilising a public onslaught, and then in maintaining it. 'Rational' critics touch on this emotional element. 'Reaganite activists' were not trimmers but radicals bringing an avowed revolution, according to the conservative Gray. 'Its goals demand large-scale social engineering, not reverence for the inheritances of history. Its rhetoric does not invoke prudence or imperfectability. It is a ranting eulogy of technology, a demonisation of government and a militant assertion that all social evils are problems soluble by market forces' (Gray 1998: 107).

The contradiction in demonising governments always lies in the urgent need to capture the state. The UK, Canadian, NZ and Australian governments were probably more difficult than the USA, with parties of labour of over a hundred years old, full employment and/or serious welfare state commitments and, by and large, democratic systems superior to that of the USA. When the libertarian utopian drive began in earnest, emotions were heightened in ritual shaming and ridiculing of 'wet' conservatives, as Thatcher called them. As a battle inside the elite political and economic classes, it was crucial. In 1985 the *Sunday Times* joined in the hilarity, dismissing Tories who rebelled against Thatcher's policies as 'the grouse brigade'. They were only 'distinguished for their wealth, wetness and country pursuits' (cited Levitas 1986: 9). So too all those cautious industrialists (loyalty to 'the firm') and financiers were shamed about their restrictive practices (old school tie), their rigidities and hierarchical principles in workplaces and professions. The

Henry Kaufmans were merely 'Dr Gloom'. Thatcher was an icon to transform conservative parties, like Australia's later Prime Minister Howard of 1996 onwards, who had 'credentials' for victimhood dealt out by old snobby elites. A petrol station manager's son, John Howard shared a petit-bourgeois background with Thatcher, a grocer's daughter. As is well known, both straddle the two utopias, foremost as libertarians, but at ease with divisive – often racist – reactionary rhetoric and deep authoritarianism.

In general, rise by seniority (with its potential managerial or professional expertise, craft skills and institutional memories) was alleged to stultify initiative and exciting competition. Every organisation was stifled by 'dead wood' which must be chopped out. 'Upstart' corporate 'raiders' were not 'raping' decent corporations using 'funny money' – now 'mergers' were 'corporate cockfights' and target firms were managed by 'self-interested posturers' (Hirsch 1986: 819). Likewise bureaucrats and bankers were shamed for their paternalism, their formal application of rules. Only self-interest could motivate anyone: the answer was to sell, to let self-interest, the consumer and opportunism rule. Who could defend rigidity and paternalism in public? Many Keynesian bureaucrats had, like the rising pro-market public servants, falsely assumed that political problems could be reduced to neutral technical administration. Perhaps, for some elites, antagonistic political decisions could be quietly buried in 'market' decisions. Central bankers facing problems of treasuries, debts and inflation, and the earlier offshore euro-currency markets, seemed to be caught. Hidebound unionists, rent-seeking industrialists and social democrats were allegedly too patronising, too elitist and above all, denied choice. The working class could be 'incentivised' or made 'aspirational' if they became mini-capitalists. 'Perfection' could be reached (as Gray rightly says) but mainly because there was no interdependency in this utopia, no vast corporations, only consumers and investors.

In my view, shame played a role in hounding 'wet' elites from office in the public and private sectors. Old elites defended a cosy existence – the old mixed economy, price-fixing oligopolies and the classic 'ten – twelve – two' banking as they called it: 'borrow at 10 per cent, lend at 12 per cent and be on the golf course by two' (Shepheard-Walwyn, 22 March 2002). Only whistleblowing developed as evidence of remaining 'wets' inside lean corporations and privatised government agencies. As the financialisation of corporations, universities, health systems, international bodies and so on progressed, as concentration and innovation occurred among hedge funds, banks and consultancy firms, these trends became further documented. My point here is to stress the utopian emotional energy and the social movement scale of activity. The development of libertarian think-tanks to mobilise opinion used massive resources for research, large staffs and salaries, to counter multiple theoretical perspectives used by university research centres. Of relevance too, limitations on university funding except via the corporate and financial sector saw the destruction of economic history departments across Anglo-America and the rise of business and finance faculties.

Capture by social movements is not domination but, as argued in Chapter 4, emotions in all organisations make dissent difficult, particularly in the face of 'excessive' confidence. Social movements with long-term concerns are also visible, and the numbers of defectors with ability to publicise their opposition, like George Soros, are growing. The WTO has modified its agenda considerably and the World Bank is not as aggressively pro-market as formerly.

In Thatcher's program to establish 'worker capitalism', the expressed hope of a 1986 report for the Centre for Policy Studies was that once every adult was a shareholder, it would be an antidote to the alleged 'passivity and lassitude that overcome dependants of a welfare state'. Personal pension schemes entail more 'risk', as final payment depends on performance of the 'pension products' (cited O'Malley 2002: 110–11). A World Bank report of 1994, *Averting the Old Age Crisis*, consists in a long attack on public pensions: 'resistance is likely to be strong', the report says. 'The groundwork must be laid by an extensive public information campaign' (cited Therborn 2003: 140).

The reason *Fortune* said the fallout from Enron was 'wide but not deep' (cited Blackburn 2002: 31) was because the possible $60 billion losses (compared to LTCM's $3.6 billion bail-out) were not faced by banks (even some central banks had apparently used LTCM to hedge their positions). Instead, losses were born by millions of US workers: employees in the 401(ks) retirement plans and pension-holders in the Californian Public Employees' Retirement System (Calpers), Florida and Ohio state employees and University of California pension schemes, which had invested in Enron shares, credit derivatives or 'special purpose entities'. Many pension schemes are now taking class action suits. Changes in pensions from defined benefits to contributory benefits were not the only problem in general for old-age schemes, since defined benefits were used also to pass on risks, such as to US steelworkers in the 1980s, when companies facing difficulties were allowed to 'delay or skip contributions' to the defined fund. As an 'implicit industrial policy' it left many funds seriously low, and in the USA and Australia, bankruptcy cases led to loss of benefit to workers and retirees. Contributory schemes (401(k)s) only further this tendency of the employers imperilling the retirement funds of their workers. In Britain, huge shortfalls were left in pension funds when corporations took 'contribution holidays' during the stock market boom (Blackburn 2002: 42–3). As Blackburn notes, although Bush's plans to fully privatise public pensions are meeting far greater public criticism, in Britain, recent accounting rules require that firms show the costs of a company's commitment to funding their pensions by revealing the value of fund assets on current prices and with the liabilities discounted by the corporate bond yields. Required shortfalls must be registered which, since pension funds are often so huge, can heavily detract from a company's bottom line. ICI closed its British pension scheme in 2002 having successfully claimed 'legal custody' (Blackburn 2002: 44–7). With the 'future collapsed into the present' by using the current valuations and discounting rules (and not what the future may unfold, if employers were cautious), other routes to privatising are just as possible.

Expansion of markets fostered utopian claims about certainty that cannot be met, least of all those promises to pensioners (who are now blamed for corporate excesses such as Enron's abuse of its pension scheme). Although Hayek's doctrine actually stressed uncertainty, he used this obvious point against state involvement in economic management, against democracy (Berman 2003). What the market 'sold' was not exactly certainty but products alleged to be risk-free or, if somewhat risky, said to be an individual preference, not a function of extent of wealth (which provides a cushion for risky ventures) or of government supervision. Criticisms were never lacking in this whole period. Strong convictions play a large part in antagonisms between elites, institutions and social movements to the present, because utopias are mutually antagonistic. Looking at the whole range of utopias in any period gives a sense of the major conflicts between them (Ricoeur 1986: 274). In today's contested field, the short-term utopia and 'dominant wish' of its dense social movement is, quite literally, hated by other utopias that inspire opposition in areas as diverse as jubilee debt relief led by religious movements or environmentalists.

Yet having captured major social democratic states at inter-organisation levels of global reach, these social fields of regulation and governments are of course transformed. Short-term market sovereignty was a substitute for further democratising of governments, but now there is little public trust either in governments, with their civil services or regulatory bodies, or in corporate finance. Governments thus accede to further demands for control over uncertainties, to revive confidence in a new opportunity.

Take the case of the 'Golden Straitjacket'. Governments that failed to aim for low inflation, chronic unemployment, flexible, non-unionised workers, budget surpluses, rigidly imposed competition rules, easy exit of capital and minimal corporate taxation were said to diminish investor confidence. But when expectations collapse, various 'fundamentals' are abandoned. Without blinking at previous inconsistencies, budget deficits loom large (in the USA) and are not directed to economic revival but to 'confidence'. In 2003 Wall Street noted lay-offs and the 3 million job losses in the USA with some alarm, though only brave loners like Roach say the distribution of wages and profits has gone too far towards capital. These revisions highlight how the 'fundamentals' depend on context. The utopian energy of hopes to collapse the future into the present continually endures failed strategies. Then vacillation prevails until the next outburst, while neo-conservatism steps in. Most time-utopias look either to the long-term future or, in conservatism, to the past. Instead of fears mounted by conservatism, in the 'present' utopia, today is supreme. It is cavalier in gesturing towards how today's 'shock therapy' or sacrifices will work out 'in the long run'.

IMPARTIAL MENTALITY OF THE CENTRAL BANKS

Having argued that emotions are necessary for facing the future, the time-frame matters for the type of rationality entailed. For long-term, future-oriented utopias, lack of trust and fear of today's governments and corporations are perfectly rational, but they are irrational for short-termism (profits today, or opinion polls). Central banks are in an invidious position: their long-term institutional reputation matters but their regulatory roles are now minimal, and they face short-term markets and short-term mentalities in governments and politicised civil services. Central banks are caught, structurally, in independence. For the bureaucratic view, administration and technocratic decisions take over from politics, but this is not possible, as administration cannot 'reduce' decisions about winners and losers to bureaucratic rules (Mannheim 1936: 104).

All central banks contain inescapable ideological elements, yet interviews and transcripts of FOMC meetings showed some awareness of social inequalities and also of evaluative judgements in facing the future. The argument that central bank independence frees them to act in the interests of their constituency, financial in-stitutions and bond-holders (Smithin 1996: 133) restates the dominant ideology thesis. It misses their official responsibility to act 'without fear or favour'. It led irate US builders to abandon a study they commissioned during Volcker's high-interest regime, as it only found a pattern of technocrats with small town and small university, even lower-class, backgrounds (Greider 1987: 7–1). Although Greenspan's Federal Reserve presents its discourse framed around narrow, tech-nical issues, and has often claimed that tough supervision is not necessary, it has demonstrated concern about unemployment. There are two keys to central bankers' self-understanding. One, which applies to any bureaucracy, is that central bank officials sincerely believe their functions are 'vital to the nation's well-being' (Greider 1987: 6–8). We saw this in the inordinate self-reputation of the Bundesbank for inflation fighting (more excessive than Volcker's, whose credit squeeze was to save the dollar flight: Grahl 2001b: 152). Their personal reputations are connected to the reputation of the institution they serve. The second key to self-understanding applies particularly to the public management of money – that it is undemocratic. Transparency in effect *regulates* central banks and governments, so investors know every detail of government activities (Patomaki 2001: 15–16). Banks are 'timid'. Abelson argues that an 'inordinate complacency' among investors was encouraged by 'Dr Greenspan & Co's crafty construction of a new bubble – housing – while striving frantically to contain the damage done by the destruction of the old one – equities – which they should have popped early on, but lacked the courage to do so' (Abelson 2002: 38). Even so, independent central banks enabled elected politicians to evade their responsibility, even to cast them as scapegoats (Greider 1987: 304–6, 752).

Since 2002, with the worst bear market since 1929–32, central banks suffer extreme embarrassment in switching after 'fighting inflation' for thirty years. This shows that the entire burden of economic management cannot lie with central banks (as it now does) but with the democratic process and with more responsible politicians.

EMOTIONAL 'CLIMATE'

At any one time, the specific configuration of utopias gives the sense of their mutual antagonisms. In the Anglo-American world today, although a short-term mentality is only one of many, it shattered much of the caution behind the order and regulation of the postwar era. It was presented as an openly declared utopian vision. However, other contemporary Western visions are open to democratic debate and are not 'total' utopias (total as in Marxism-Leninism). The financial short-term utopia is also 'total' in ushering in the financialisation of life, and was presented dogmatically: when Margaret Thatcher said 'There is no alternative', it had all the pontifical tones of early chiliastic prophecy. The God of Opportunity could be found today and the next day: too much caution or anxiety about the future was said to be stultifying. Action by individuals is the key, financial utopians proclaimed, ignoring how the world is more interdependent than ever before. As with the anarchists, libertarians' sensibility towards time is 'eruptive' and reckless (Mannheim 1936: 219). Big Bang expresses this unseemly haste.

Outside this utopia, Raymond Williams saw, in the late 1980s, how more general 'structures of feeling' had dramatically changed to 'a widespread loss of the future'. In the 1960s this 'structure of feeling' was of protest, warnings and an official mood of 'managed affluence; managed consensus; managed and profitable transitions from colonialism'. But the dominant mood changed rapidly to rhythms where a more terrifying balance of terror brings dominant cultural messages of danger and conflict, and dominant cultural forms of shock and loss. Here feelings overlap in today's 'curiously decentred culture'. Williams spoke of a 'deliberate constitutional authoritarianism' to manage this loss politically. This dominant message of conflict and danger emerged as the capitalist economic order defaulted on its brief contract to provide full employment and high social expenditure as 'conditions for a political consensus of support'. Apart from the 'human costs of that default', Williams argues that a graver sound than recklessness or calculations of temporary advantage is 'the loss of hope; the slowly settling loss of any acceptable future' (1989: 96–7).

For many financial organisations, hope lies in today; the main chance is now, not any democratically decided 'acceptable future'. It is worth remembering that 'the American middle classes can move a lot of money' (Grahl 2001b: 152), but they mainly do this through the huge funds and banks, and as the world's most indebted consumers. Even Britain, old finance capital, cannot match the depth of US money movements – one day into equity, the next into housing speculation. Asian banks, even European, have attempted to retain caution. But perhaps the dominant message is more like Franz Kafka's dark comedy, before Williams' diagnosis of today: There is, he said, 'plenty of hope, an infinite amount of hope – but not for us'. Infinite because only locked in an infinity of 'presents', this hope is held out not to mums and dads or, more seriously, to a troubled world but to Kafka's cast of strange assistants. Figures in the twilight like his confidence man, either rising or falling in status – Kafka says hope is for these, the unfinished and the bunglers (cited in Benjamin 1969: 116–17). The dominant message is, in this sense, therefore, not merely an ideology of making more money, but a utopia of recklessness, a fool's paradise.

CONCLUSION

My conclusion is directed to both the defenders and the opponents of libertarian views. Defenders are not promoting a crude, self-interested ideology alone, as no one is 'above' worldviews nor is libertarianism without a serious vision for the 'good society'. Libertarianism is an anti-democratic social movement, which prefers to see markets, not mighty organisations. Its utopianism lies in today. Only today is predictable, only today can be extrapolated into the future. Utopian hopes and inter-organisational emotions within the world of finance gain meanings not usually articulated as emotions, but which arise from conflicting if quite rational *emotional* behavioural responses to the social relations in which they are enmeshed (Burkitt 2002: 152–3). This is not imputing beliefs to actors but is derived from reported statements and actions of financial elites and the organisations they represent; it is an emotional climate, sometimes a 'contagion' among elites, or a social structure of feeling, though rarely described in this way. The process is not describing the fallacy of composition (or not only), namely that what is rational for individuals is irrational for the collective. This is partly because a collectivity means an ascribed emotion, a belief held in common, imputed to a class or status group, in the aggregate. Contagion arises from all the interactions among the office-bearers in the heartland of finance, and from the mediated and impersonal hopes for each guru or elite group proposing a serious breakthrough in the futile attempt to control the future. This utopia infuses the main financial institutions and still primarily Anglo–American policies, and helps to maintain morale despite the mess and bungles, to the implications of which we now turn.

9 | Implications: Emotions and Rationality

NO ONE CAN reduce uncertainty, but in the attempt to do so, financial institutions have undermined trust in trust itself. Their decisions are guesses about the credibility of their latest parcelled promises. Any firm selling assets is bound to defend its product but, being a mere claim on future wealth, the temptation to minimise inevitable uncertainties always exists. As soon as 'too many' organisations sell or buy through 'clustering' – the typical process of competition – the product becomes unbelievable. Exactly when the Ponzis of mutual leverage and the stream of customers slow down or stop is least predictable of all. In treating money as an alienable asset when it consists of fragile promises, the idea of risk-free money is a chimera.

What follows from the evidence of this book are three basic propositions:
1. The finance world can never find certainty (internally or externally).
2. Emotions are not removable.
3. Therefore, caution is the requisite emotion for relations of promises. Caution acknowledges the limitations of rationality towards the unknown.

IMPERSONAL EMOTIONS IN A WORLD OF ORGANISATIONS

As we have seen, the 'money-power' seeks external certainty and sells it under various banners of risk. Certainty of events is never attained, and that is sometimes acknowledged, far more behind closed doors than in public. Rather, it is certainty of the convention (as Keynesians put it), namely that past *expectations* will be validated in the future. This certainty is newly necessary for each stalled low point. Reassurance is needed that the present emotionally shaped expectations about chosen parameters will continue into the future. Whichever entities are involved in attempting to validate past decisions, be they central banks, international accounting standards or the IMF, they must provide the correct policy. They must guarantee the certainty of the convention (not, of course, the certainty of 'events') (Negri 1988: 24). Each new expectation for selling a new 'sure thing' must be validated by actually selling the thing. Depending on the models' chosen parameters and the fundamental need of sellers for buyers, decision-makers must trust these selected elements that *may* produce a predictable, risk-free environment. Charles Goodhart (1984: 96) showed that any assumed predictability of selected parameters collapsed under the pressure of assigning a control function to them. In the attempt to gain control today, the moment when action is taken, that parameter becomes uncontrollable by tomorrow. In this way, fundamentals are never fixed: they explode or implode (sooner or later), whether guarantees were given or not.

The effects of guaranteeing financial expectations – squeezing uncertainty from some parameter – have destabilised many regions. Governments have secured low inflation by mass unemployment and (attempted) destruction of the civil services that provide social security and the organised union movements that aim for employment security. Impoverishment (and imprisonment) grew for those segments not financially implicated in promise-selling. Yet because they are context-dependent, fundamentals keep changing. Self-deception about uncertainty is evident when sectors 'forget' decades of low inflation (one part of the insurance industry's slump) and try to tear up promises based on rising inflation (or assets etc.).

In contrast, a mixed economy of social and public property alongside private property was a long-term attempt to make money – being a promise – less fragile. It cannot fuel the great Ponzi schemes of moving so-called risks to higher levels of abstraction. Worse, from the view of financial acceptability for private banks, the genuine mutual funds and not-for-profit friendly societies undercut private investment. This is because social security schemes, and public goods, are produced far more cheaply than financial goods in the private sector. Modest yet dependable, they offered some collective security; they were not an individual, private product sold competitively as a 'security' to make a profit for the producers. Moreover, newly privatised public goods and funds are usually still guaranteed by government, in secret, confidential contracts. Thus, however badly run, another way to guarantee expectations from mass privatisations is to pass all the risks onto governments and populations.

As we have focused more on the money-power than its widespread lack of legitimacy, the more damning conclusion of this book is that finance cannot generate its own internal certainties, even in the short term. The sector has diced and packaged social relations of debts and mortgages, of future promises into future securities, futures, and derivatives of futures, into reinsuring assurances of insurance – in a phrase, into every possible 'new, new thing' (Lewis 1999). These 'things' are social relations of trust that many would presume are not alienable and, perhaps, ultimately they are not alienable. Money is a claim on society, yet internal uncertainties also build up: Minsky's paradox that stability gives way to instability (Chapter 2), to firms taking on unacceptable debts, is one aspect of internally generated uncertainty. Inflation is no longer an economic 'fundamental', when debt-deflation is likely. Institutionally, it is an unbearable predicament for the whole financial sector to admit humiliation in public after decades of distrust strategies proclaiming a controllable future.

Although many sceptics these days cannot avoid extrapolating the 1930s into the future, that focuses too narrowly on finance. Internal problems, too, are different in today's financialisation of life. The worrying context of billions depending on this flimsy trust could even be turned around before too late, if learning from the past was more profound, if emotions under uncertainty could be recognised over the strict rules of the libertarian utopian game: solidarity and no public doubts.

Peak financial firms have attempted to remove discretion from the major institutions of the mixed economy: democratically elected governments, trust-worthy central banks and non-financial corporations. Fuelled through distrust, this utopian movement has deployed 'markets' for various investment requirements – threatening to pull out or exit for non-compliance in raising shareholder value – whether with mergers or imposed management consultants. Non-financial and public corporations are now consumed with forex dealings and transparent 'management' – all with fees, audits, compliance lists and risks and insecurities passed on to outlying departments (whether hospital wards or college faculties). There is a pervasive sense that this game is unsustainable when (in Abelson's words, Chapter 6) corporations are now 'running a stock, not a firm', let alone a hospital. While fees and potential Ponzis flow in from privatising or outsourcing child-care centres and prisons, perhaps it is sustainable for financial firms. But how far can investment banks play the capital markets, leveraged to every other bank, when so many lose? Claims on society have limits, yet it is anyone's guess when these unimaginable limits will be reached.

My argument centres on how endemic crises and low ebbs render the heartland publicly untrustworthy, mainly because of its own self-deception in clinging irra-tionally to fantasies of a predictable future. Inside the money-power, the temptation in low and hence more competitive times is to use insider knowledge for today's 'certainty', to grab the next opportunity before rivals can. Doubling bets requires more funds, more so-called greed, higher levels of leverage to hedge the latest bet. Contributions 'holidays' have left firms owing on their pension funds, often the largest debt component: scandals are increasingly regular; competition forces out the honest; insurance firms are, again, making fabulous profits, now even on our fears of walking, uninsured, in a public park.

Rather than wait, the challenge is to start debating incremental reverses towards prevention. According to my argument, if some precautionary principles were put in place they would be based on caution as the essential emotion.

ACCEPTING RATIONALITY'S LIMITATIONS

The main difficulty for rethinking emotions in finance is people's insistence that emotions are distinct from rationality. Many Keynesians acknowledge 'animal spir-its' but assume that emotions are a 'virus'. Rationality restored in order to quell these emotions, they argue, would lead to a more equitable, in the sense of a more rationally determined, path.

Although Keynesians are responsible for introducing the notion of radical uncertainty, Keynesian policies historically involved governments: in vouchsafing a sense of confidence to business expectations, governments would restore rationality: they would help industry and maintain full employment (1950s). Today governments do so (detrimentally to citizens) in providing confidence to finance. This confidence might set aside 'animal spirits'. The term was used in Descartes' question of how to relate mind to body, a question hardly solved by his suggestion that the thinking mind is linked to our bodies by the movements of tiny particles, 'les esprits animaux'. These little 'spirits', he thought, race around the bloodstream and connect to the soul, which he located in a 'little gland in the brain' (cited Robertson 2001: 44). Aside from philosophical debates against Descartes' circular mind/body distinction, his defence of the mind is an old Western and Enlightenment hope for superior humans who can rule through rational control over the world. Returning to conventional economics, it is the basis of Rational Economic Man with a dismissive self-deceptive gesture to the vile body, the 'gut feelings' when things go wrong or, more revealing of its worldview, when 'uncertainty is running rampant', as a Wall Street trader had it just after September 11 (Hale 2001). The distinction leads to hopes for superior 'models' or better data to overcome emotions (ironically including the emotion of confidence, given uncertainty). The insistence of neo-classical economics on 'first principles' (a theoretical assumption about selfish utility maximisers to conquer Keynesian policy) is about cognitive control.

In the Western tradition, romantic irrationalism (such as dubious distinctions between authentic and non-authentic emotions) and postmodern playfulness are the opposing poles to rationalism. Ironically, when positivist hopes for predictability fail, a similar irrationalism is in fallback positions – a *deus ex machina* – evident in the technological determinism of the 'new economy', or the heroic entrepreneur, the 'authentic' CEO or 'guru' who allays our fears, obfuscates with domineering conviction. Let us beware not only false prophets but prophets of any sort.

Rationality per se is not the problem, but rather the failure to recognise its deep limitations in facing uncertainty. While I am as opposed to romantic irrationality and postmodern variants as any rational choice theorist, I take issue with Rational Economic Man's strenuous and irrational opposition to emotions. Emotions arise internally to this highly future-oriented world (in the jargon, endogenously). Finance generates its own problems, which include denying radical uncertainty.

Consider evidence of how reputations are made on the strength of a run of successful predictions, typically ascribed to an individual financial guru. But because this social field is so large and remote, it relies on the cult of personality. The guru must fail, but the search continues for a prescient chief central banker or a CEO said to have a reputation for 'tough' decisions or who is 'decision-joyful' (Chapter 4). The role of information, as we saw, plays an extravagant part in reconvincing the positivists that better data will predict the future. We recognised how forecasting is not peculiar to the financial sector, since in many aspects of life prescience has its attractions and its bitter temptations. Yet for most jobs, a 'trust in the future' is not an important focus compared to the task at hand.

In contrast, any financial work is necessarily itself a task of guessing the future. Anticipations of trust, confidence and fear are the only ways of coping with the future. However much the *past* may be assessed rationally (endlessly or thrillingly), the future-orientation is guessing unknowable outcomes.

Another difficulty in our commonsense view is how impersonal and organised are these relations of trust and distrust within finance. Our taken-for-granted experience is in making individual, rational calculations about our trust or lack of trust in *somebody* or in a corporation, where we must project the past into a future. Yet recall former regulations like the American SEC and the Glass-Steagall Act (1933), which aimed to remove conflicts of interest and potential abuses from personal trust by substituting impersonal trust in agent–principal relations. External accountancy firms henceforward acted as independent agents for the principals (shareholders) in scrutinising corporate accounts. We noted that these regulations assume that firms *know* their future interests, but today it is the short term that dominates. Glass-Steagall – systematised earlier in other countries – separated investment from commercial banking to prevent bankers from investing depositors' funds in anything from safe to wildcat ventures. Such practices returned with a vengeance: if the Regents of the University of California invested their pension fund in Enron, if nearly every corporation must hedge against exchange fluctuations by playing the global forex market, even central banks apparently invested in LTCM (see Chapter 8). Although Glass-Steagall is everywhere repealed, the impersonal forms remain in all these financial institutions, each under intense pressure to outperform each other. There is no turning back to a world of small-scale firms which get by through face-to-face trust relations: the question is, can we hope to face a reasonable world?

Considering the evidence as a whole, it is fair to say that any aim to reduce emotional elements from decisions in this large and remote world is irrational and unreasonable. None of these impersonal organisations can predict the future, but that brute fact remains unlearned as the imposed asset trading becomes more furious, more inventive, more difficult to keep track of or even slow down. Re-generative processes of hoping for new risk management and distrust strategies continue. Impersonal anticipations and the art of judgement are not removable. Given populations' exposure to finance, since we can never reduce uncertainty, the important thing is to reduce vulnerability, over-exposure, over-borrowing, in order to promote long-term cautious investment.

LONG-TERM AND SHORT-TERM

Although traditionally the world of finance was associated with dubious ethics, tulip manias or casinos, this book has explained the emotional underpinnings of this sector. Uncertainty, redefined as risk or even daring bravery, gives rise to many mistakes, which encourages brazen, dishonest dealings. Informed sceptics above all criticise short-term horizons, not the social relations of money per se. Symbolic and moral evaluations of money are often thought to have gained positive moral connotations only with the rise of capitalism. Among sociology's classics, Simmel extolled the modern individualism, independence and anonymity he thought came from the freedom promised by money, and the trust arising from impersonal exchanges among strangers (Parry & Bloch 1989: 5). A whole symbolic system (modernity) is often said to be suffused with private, individualistic money-seeking. This is plain exaggeration, since modernity is not defined solely by a capitalist economy. Even behaviour with, and beliefs about, money are not so clearly positive or negative, either in today's or in pre-modern cultures.

In many cultures which exchange with money or money-substitutes, even rank opportunism is not necessarily a moral problem. For Max Weber (1976: 17), 'unlimited greed for gain' has existed in all countries, among all types of people and at all times. Weber, among so many, ambiguously assumed that only capitalist profit-seeking was purely 'rational' because 'predictable' interest struggles could free calculations from emotions. But if meanings of money differ widely across cultures, many provide a space for exchanges which appear to exhibit similar 'modern' relations to those of contemporary monetary relationships. Many are analogous to all the private vices of rabid self-seeking assumed of modern capitalism (Parry & Bloch 1989: 28–30). These exchanges promise a degree of impersonality, freedom and self-gratification usually associated only with 'modern' money. Thus money transactions are represented by many different symbolic systems, but Jonathan Parry and Maurice Bloch (1989) see deeper regularities. A key issue is their distinction between short-term and long-term cycles. The short-term cycles may be concerned with calculative, even puritanical amassing of money, for status and massive expenditure for competitive conspicuous consumption. Long-term cycles are about regeneration of the whole order over many generations, which may involve money but usually does not.

Long-term cycles which prevail over short-term private property (money as asset more than public good) were involved in the public provisions and social property (such as state pensions and public education for our future, children) that have been institutionalised in most Western countries. Economic activity was usually mixed, some more socialist, such as Sweden, Australia and New Zealand by the early 20th century. Bismarck's administration of public reproduction in Germany was the most paternalistic. The major democratic effort was the Keynesian financial system of the postwar era. Although high finance favoured parliamentary sovereignty, with international financial 'threads' to pull to ensure 'credible' government debts (only small trade wars, only poll taxes, etc.), the world wars severed those strings, as we saw. Thus Bretton Woods was more inadvertently a sovereignty of 'the people' over money than many thought (except, for example, Polanyi 1957: 14–19; Braithwaite & Drahos 2000: 602–6; and see Chapters 1 and 2) The fledgling US welfare of the New Deal and on to Lyndon Johnson's 'war on poverty' never matched the northern European welfare states. Cultural landmarks of that US era when money and labour were less commodities than today are still seen in semi-cult Kapra movies of the postwar era, particularly *It's a Wonderful Life* starring Jimmy Stewart or critiques such as *Blade Runner*.

In this historical sense, former state regulations over the free market seem less imaginable, and likewise there were paternalistic forms that are better forgotten, though not by today's neo-conservatism, which wants to revive all the former hierarchies (e.g. tax the poor, send mum home to breed) and render our democratic rights even more fragile. Long-term control of the short-term money order is maintained by policies radically divorced from apparently more egalitarian, even gender-neutral, short-term rules: under neo-liberalism anyone apparently can get a mortgage, anyone can be a day trader, but millions cannot get jobs. Free markets need strong states. A safety-net marriage between conservative and libertarian policies catches the fallout of treating money as a fictional commodity, via the national debt in small wars and longer peaces, as Polanyi emphasised of the 19th century. Economically 'irrational' outcomes of state warfare and housing tax-breaks build up deficits and speculation elsewhere, perhaps damaging the prospects of any long-term return on the debtor's promises: in 2004, tax cuts keep Wall Street afloat while unproductive state expenditure diminishes international buyer trust in US bonds and the hegemonic dollar. US consumption is a global duty, at present supported by Japan's and China's purchase of declining dollars. Rigid cultural conservatism, religious fundamentalism among all faiths, and periodic warfare state activity (an undeclared form of Keynesian fiscal policy and job creation of the past thirty years), may seem unrelated to controlling short-termism, but fewer are fooled these days. If the slogans 'There Is No Alternative' (Thatcher) or 'It's the economy, stupid' (Clinton) reduce all social relations to economic ones, others, from anti-war protests to 'family-friendly workplaces', attempt to build new democratic links to the long term.

Yet in so far as conflicts between short-term and long-term horizons are dependent on abstract democratic processes – so long filled with mind-numbing neo-classical propaganda, to the extent that competition among financial firms goes far beyond individual avarice – an ethical critique is indirectly derived from my evidence. As caution is inherently an emotion of the long-term view, it leans to ethical justice. So, is caution needed *inside* the impersonal financial heartland, as well as externally? In this book's introduction, we saw Wall Street or Renaissance Florence revelling in public fear and moral opprobrium, but their practices are and were mundane. A childlike innocence of naive cynicism is embedded in financial institutions: these Chuzzlewits want validation of the convention that never really eventuates: or 'there is infinite hope' for these bunglers, but not for us (Kafka, cited in Benjamin 1969: 116). Credit-money is the driver of capitalism while billions are willingly (or not) enmeshed in credit–debt relationships. So informed sceptics are correct: caution and humble acknowledgement of organisational (human) frailties is desirable and not impossible, however unpredictable.

NOT 'MARKET' SOLUTIONS

Global and national financial regulations are directed to markets or corporations. Reduced supervision and reduced caution are by no means the same as 'deregulation': there are thousands of 'rules', but few for caution. The 1980s banking crises – a fallout from new competitive rules like Big Bang – in Europe, the USA, Japan and Australia saw various global capital adequacy requirements placed on banks. Yet some financial institutions operating like banks, but not required to hold reserves, benefit from a 'competition of laxity' among governments or 'regulatory arbitrage' (Schaberg 1998: 197). The weakest global financial regulations are corporate tax, speculation and that now quaint term 'unearned income'. Indeed, that term's obsolescence illustrates how conflicts between capital and labour have been superseded – given the drastic reduction of freedom for labour – by conflicts between creditors (global money free to roam) and debtors (governments, citizens and corporations; non-citizens are not, in harsher regimes, *counted* beyond their detention debts). Many experts in this new regulatory field argue that coordinated international taxation is needed to prevent tax evasion and tax competition among countries trying to attract corporations in a race to the bottom (Braithwaite & Drahos 2000: 117, 142).

Financial and corporate regulations today are, by and large, reactions to the previous disaster, often imposing further competitive or transparency rules and new ways of 'aligning interests', all based on distrust. One result of competition and privatisation is increased state regulation in the far greater volume and complexity of rules imposed on corporations (Parker 2002: 12) at greater cost to governments (taxpayers). In no longer owning and gaining revenue from public utilities like airports, governments must still ensure air traffic safety and therefore public trust in privatised airlines. Numerous compliance rules tend to shore up a loophole said to lie behind the last unforeseen disaster: they squeeze on that uncertainty just as new loopholes, new 'cookie-jar reserves' or 'legal' evasions are found with equally unpredictable outcomes, leading to more rules and further global guardians of trust. We cited International Accounting Standards in Chapter 7 as now impenetrable and requiring 'creative' accounting rather than a full and fair view (honest discretion about unknowable futures). 'Global finance' texts typically provide glossaries and acronyms of finance products, rules and institutions running to many pages.

In general, some of the main liberal democracies in the world are not fulfilling existing democratic duties and, despite or because of this massive rise in distrust rules, neither corporations nor governments are perceived by world populations as trustworthy. Some pervert international charters for world justice and freedom inscribed in existing global institutions from the UN to the IMF – they even spy on the UN. It is, therefore, on corporations and governments that we should focus our sights. One quite popular proposal illustrates my counter-argument well, namely the Currency Transaction Tax or Tobin Tax which aims to tax foreign exchange transactions for long-term global development funds.

However interesting at first sight for imposing some caution, it seems to me that market solutions to speculation leave out of account the banks and hedge funds that produce the financial products by drawing in more and more societal resources; they also fail to tackle legitimacy deficits of corporations and governments. The Tobin Initiative is for a small tax on every currency transaction, aimed at inducing, *through the market*, slower financial movements: it is an incentive structure reform. The founders declared it could throw 'sand in the wheels' of international finance, because a small tax encourages money to stay put for long-term investment, by making fast and heavy speculative flows much more expensive, hopefully prohibitively so. They also thought a 'modest national autonomy in monetary and macroeconomic policy' could ensue (Eichengreen et al. 1995: 163), while being unlikely to reduce the risks of a massive crisis or excessive volatility. A second-tier Tobin, a prohibitively high tax, is also included to prevent exchange rate runs (Patomaki 2001).

When I began this research, the benefits of taxing financial transactions (for caution) seemed great, but my evidence gives more conclusive support to other approaches. Market taxes appeared appropriate to this emotions approach because it is not possible to reduce emotions. Trust and confidence are unavoidable, but perhaps emotions might be reconfigured. The small tax might foster long-term strategies by slowing the pace of speculative transfers, and the higher, guillotine-type tax on a massive exit imposes a cooling-off period, to reconsult 'gut feelings'. Perhaps rituals in financial decision-making and high-powered trading might be changed in a procedural sense, rendering banks more trustworthy, again by aligning their 'interests', but in this case in preserving their reputations.

Taxation is essential to support long-term measures, although tax (another major debate) is not an issue in this book's main argument. For long-term caution, more important are socially accountable banking corporations and more democratic governments. Given taxes on goods and services, given taxes on gambling but virtually no taxes on financial transactions, the justice argument for taxing specu-lation is compelling. But it is less obvious whether the small Currency Transaction Tax is a way to reconfigure impersonal emotions or to move towards democratic control over the finance sector. A small tax on transactions may not differ from portfolio insurance where the logic was to pay a small premium to 'self-insure'. Financial firms sold hedging 'precautionary' products but failed to prevent financial hyperactivity rising to the 1987 crash (Chapter 7). A small tax may lend a spurious credibility to banks but they might trade currencies differently, to gain returns higher than the tax rate. Financial organisations peddle their inventiveness. This tax is said to gain high revenue, as do gambling taxes in many countries. Instead of reducing the incidence of gambling, which by analogy Tobin should do, we see greater gambling addiction, particularly by governments to install more gambling outlets (however easier gambling taxes may be to impose on the dispossessed). Controlling governments and corporations through more cautious, democratic procedures is surely more necessary: our only elected representatives must be more responsible for managing the economy.

Others want taxes on equity, debt and derivatives as well as currency transac-tions (Schaberg 1998: 195) to stem tax evasion and slow trading. As a market model, however, this assumes atomised individuals who incorporate the future into their investment assessments, however 'slowly', nay 'safely'. Corporate distrust strategies, leverage and counterparty borrowing relations might simply take new forms.

Other difficult questions are the number of governments required and the ap-propriate body to distribute the tax equitably. Proponents of a Tobin tax argue for the UN or World Bank, others for a new international institution. But corporate and government legitimacy needs improving first, because the richest nation-states are undermining the existing international institutions: how could we, the people, control a new one better?

Arguments for a second-tier Tobin scheme – with a prohibitively high-penalty tax to apply automatically on panic or contrived panic runs on exchange rates – suggest prevention, more caution, indeed plain punishment for recklessness (Patomaki 2001: 161–5). Controls can be managed by electorally accountable, individual governments and are far more justified from the emotions perspective. Instead of aiming with a small Tobin to slow the pace, precautionary principles are more obvious here. They try to reduce the generalisation of non-probabilistic risks in finance, the extreme vulnerability where the fallout is imposed on specific populations. Examples involve specific government re-regulation, in Chile, and others:

Elliott: The problem with the Tobin tax is that, at such a small level, it won't really have any impact. You need more direct controls on capital. It is very unfashionable to say, because people who have an interest in having no controls run most of the world financial system . . . Chile has a system of taxing speculative flows. It welcomes direct investments to build factories. But if you want to come in with some hot money, park it there for a week and take it out again, then you pay a 30 per cent tax. It is quite successful. (5 October 2000)

Former central bankers like Bernie Fraser emphasise the role of specific governments, and the fact that offshore banking poses inter-organisational problems in effecting a market tax on large corporate players:

Fraser: The Tobin Initiative is not practicable in my view as it requires more than 160 countries to agree to impose it, and this is very unlikely to happen. Some of the biggest banking systems in the world are in places like the Cayman Islands. I am sceptical that there can ever be an international agreement on taxation, which is one reason why I think we have to focus harder on taxation at the national level. (31 August 2001)

He has often agued that governments should stand up to markets:

Fraser: I still have this broad notion that the globalisation of markets for capital . . . in the absence of international institutions to regulate those markets, means that national governments have to do more by way of regulations, and in fiscal terms for example. I think as more and more of these problems unfold in the US, it will click with a lot of people that while markets do some things pretty well, they do a hell of a lot of things very poorly. (28 June 2002)

And as emotions in finance matter, descriptions of the present state of global markets are partly beside the point, as they imply that the future will stay the same. Each description tries to derive what 'ought to be' from what 'is', and if sights are set on 'markets' rather than the organisations operating in them, market solutions are sought.

MODERNITY IS NOT ONLY MODERNISATION

It is beyond the scope of this book to consider the significant debates on taxation, on seeking progressive economic policies, on whether governments can control fiscal and monetary policy, or whether they could but won't. Major discussions are on whether global bond and foreign exchange markets, for example, actually rule or whether governments refuse to rule them. For some progressive economists, former ways of control cannot work in global markets, therefore we need new controls. But if 'governments will not intervene in finance because they simply will not intervene in markets any more', new policies are no more feasible than old policies, said to be now hopeless for 'technical reasons' (Grabel, in Schaberg 1998: 217).

These critiques, lacking a broader social analysis, are unable to interpret government 'refusal'. Governments guarantee the convention for the financial sector, often uncomprehendingly, and the fallout of imposing risk on populations is managed by heavy-handed state intervention. It not only perverts governments and international institutions but frequently backfires into more distrust of governments (recall the fate of the Tory Party). This is not merely unintended but rather unimagined. 'Exit strategies' are said to rule governments, but these analyses are derived from empiricism and extrapolation. The future is not always like the present. When the investment banks promoting the exit strategies become untrustworthy, that is, when trust vanishes, so too does their exit power. From LTCM, Enron and so on, all the past trends carefully extrapolated in economic analyses fall apart, however honestly constructed. The major nation-states have always had a measure of sovereignty to respond to their own country's conflictual social fields and to their international 'standing': the more democratic countries have proved that their best global bargaining chip is to fall back on sovereignty of the people (national and international human rights) in facing the more unilateral, aggressive nation-states. To see interminable lack of government 'will' is to oversimplify the social world, one more interdependent, conflict-ridden and overly based on impersonal trust and distrust than earlier times.

To take that social view seriously, 'modernity' consists of many more features than 'modernisation'. The latter refers to economic and technical development, mainly capitalist dynamics. Enlightenment values of liberalism and rationality are part of modernity, yet democracy was a separate struggle and a utopian ideal. Tensions between modernisation and democracy are deep-seated, and democratic processes have always been fragile. Rationality survives in the financial sector but cannot serve it, whereas Democratic Enlightenment is so much 'an incomplete project' (Habermas) that democracy as practised today in many major liberal democracies is in ill repute.

The democracy movements arose from largely different social bases to conservatism, liberalism, even some socialism (Chapter 7). It is a different logic: democracy offers no utopian blueprint but a long-term form without content. It is therefore a very different utopia from all others and, by being inherently anti-positivist, it also acknowledges impersonal emotions. First, utopias must vary under majority franchise (a bare minimum). The social field is contested thereafter. Any utopia or dystopia – always inescapably ideological – is in principle open for democratic debate. Second, precautionary principles are allied to democracy and oppose positivism. If the future is inherently unknown, care is required and procedures against tyranny by the winners over the losers. Here are judicial umpires for a sporting game. Open debate is needed to reject positivist technocracies, and democratic processes for throwing out imprudent governments. All organisations are frail entities coping with unpredictable events, but many are failing in the required honesty and hence avoiding caution – above all, to acknowledge the uncertain future.

Ideological aspects of today's economic libertarian utopia, as we saw in Chapter 8, are twofold: most contemporary utopian projects reject 'total' utopias, but finance utopias are totalising and anti-democratic. Like other totalising utopias such as religious fundamentalism, the libertarian utopia offers contemporary, technocratic market 'solutions' in bad faith. A world society founded on vast global organisations and current state capture by the financial sector can never offer free-market individualism, however fervently believed. Therefore these double standards are an ideology of bad faith. As I said, the major governments run the international institutions, so focus is required on governments and, as this book is mainly concerned with English-speaking financial centres, many of these governments are a good start. Significant debates on these vital issues are not, however, of immediate relevance to our concluding theme: seeking caution, democratically. Corporations are *also* capable of transformation because no one owns them, so their democratisation is not impossible.

EMOTIONS WITHIN FINANCIAL ORGANISATIONS

Corporations have short survival rates, but not nation-states: some of the worst catastrophes for major nation-states have resulted in far greater democracy; Germany is exemplary. Yet it is not unimaginable that emotions within financial organisations, as within governments, can be redirected in positive pathways, from self-debilitating quests for control over the future to a more responsible, even reasonable caution. Here we explore broad possibilities, as precise formulas are democratically debatable. There is considerable documentation of corrupt corporations which 'learned' from exposure, through legal sanctions and public shaming, to restructure in positive ways (see Fisse & Braithwaite 1993). Can financial corporations also learn from genuinely accepting uncertainty?

Competition among the money creators drives everyone to selling very similar packages. Inevitable but unpredictable collapses under a glut of similar financial instruments drive some banks to the wall. Survivors of stock market crashes, after mass sackings, hire a new generation of traders who are 'emotionally correct' and have the requisite fearlessness (Chapter 4). For non-survivors, internal mistakes may be exposed to damaging publicity, with reputations shattered, jail terms and former trustworthy brand-names unusable thereafter. *Schadenfreude* from all sides. Remnants of bankruptcies are purchased and rebranded by firms that barely survived except by abandoning and vilifying their rivals, as we saw in highly charged attribution struggles. Whether corporations today primarily aim for survival is debatable. They insure against collapse, and some even insure against their own dishonesty (evident after the insurance industry's survival strategy – high premium charges – in government guarantees in capping insurance payouts and even in reduction of fiduciary duties of firms: Merritt 2003).

Consider insurance (Chapter 6). Precaution is a very different principle from insurance and the abstraction to reinsurance. Precaution admits the uncertain future – all democratically inspired social movements are precautionary. In contrast, prudently insuring against possible loss only monetises likely costs of 'predictable' dangers: death is inevitable but many modern dangers like over-leverage are preventable and will not turn out OK in the long run. In *pre*-caution, the aim is to prevent dangers in the first place, not to prudentially insure against their likelihood, allowing confidence to rise. Recall the lead-up to 1 January 2000. The Fed and other central banks insisted (by providing amply through monetary policy) on governments intervening in the mock-hysteria over computer crashes on the 'Y2K'. While prevention here shows that precaution is easily possible, in hindsight (mostly) Y2K measures were needlessly precautionary, mandatory computer upgrades merely prolonging the Nasdaq inflation.

As a general point, the only way to act on the precautionary principle is prevention, ideally consensual regulation; the Kyoto Agreement at least implies environmental precaution (Ewald 2002: 298). In contrast, insurance and bank screening are precautionary measures against too many payouts on the risks of early death or defaulting a loan; they are preventive for the insurance firm or bank. The economic concept of risk, in contrast, is an active, freely chosen decision to gamble on unmeasurable, unknowable chances of making money. In the principle of portfolio insurance (Chapter 7), risk was to be reduced but buyers were in effect self-insured and ultimately generated dangers.

Starting with this idea of precaution and prevention, then, I will consider the cult of personality in relation to structures of responsibility in financial firms (fiduciary and decision-making lines) and also the structure of rewards.

Prevention issues are put clearly by John Bogle (founder and former chief executive of the Vanguard Group), in opening his widely cited 2003 Statement before the US House of Representatives Sub-Committee on Capital Markets, Insurance and Government Sponsored Enterprises (Committee on Financial Services). In his statement to the US Congress, he notes changes to financial services since World War II:

Bogle: The mutual fund industry that I read about in *Fortune* magazine in 1949 is almost unrecognisable today. Over and over again, the article spoke of 'trustee', 'trusteeship', 'the investment trust industry', words that we rarely see today. Over the half-century-plus that followed, in my considered judgement, the fund industry has moved from what was largely a business of stewardship to a business of salesmanship, a shifting of our primary focus from the management of the assets investors have entrusted to our care to the marketing of our wares so as to build the asset base we manage. (12 March 2003)

As we saw, libertarian utopianism imposed short-term views whereby firms are simply the property of shareholders, or the nexus of private contracts (Parker 2002: 5), to the detriment of fiduciary duties and stewardship notions of the firm that a Keynesian such as Bogle stresses. Moreover, in selling money as a 'fictional commodity', sales divisions rarely flaunt its social fragility in promises, except in fine print (perhaps Williamson's reference to Keynesian myopia finds its referent, although we myopics have excellent short sight). In consequence, each inevitable crisis and outbreak of so-called 'rogue traders' (who, as Mike Lazar said, are 'fish in the sea' only looking for the next mouthful; whether they know money cannot be neutral is not on their job description) leaves the libertarian searching for a god of opportunity. Perhaps central banks will save a failing bank. Emotional energies are expended on blaming previous CEO mistakes, while demanding a new personality with a new technique or a new distrust strategy.

In contrast, precautionary restructuring to full legal fiduciary responsibilities and specified lines of duty of care are not short-term distrust measures of more audits and 'risk management'. After Andersen's audit of the scandalous Enron and public criticisms of the financial services industry, informed sceptics like Bogle implicitly seek precaution. Some discussed 'risk management', not as mere risk tools like derivatives or as compliance, but risk as uncertainty. One London banker queried how audits related to corporate risk management:

Shepheard-Walwyn: Is risk management more than just an audit function, and if so, how does it relate to the audit function? In that model, an audit is often regarded almost as an afterthought to doing the business and usually as something that is mandated for the organisation by external regulators, stock exchange requirements and so on. But that way of thinking says: 'Let's get this over and done with and get on with running the business.' (22 March 2002)

Long after the SEC introduced independent rules for auditors in 1937, we now see new compliance rules set by external regulators designed only to put out the last fire, that is, from CEOs treating audits as mere 'afterthoughts'. CEO responsibilities for grave uncertainties remain unacknowledged, but this is not fair. Such 'rule-making as a firefighting exercise' can never prevent the next unpredicted and slightly different fire (Flanagan 2004). Indeed, incessant compliance rules increase corporate irritation with this imposed and heightened distrust. Professions are bogged down, and governments are further blamed for circumstances not created by their weak responses to sector-wide demands for certainty.

Ever since the competitive regulations brought increased impersonal distrust rules – shareholder value – the results are prominence of corporate raiders, minimising of debt-holders' interests by banks, and a CEO cult of personality and competitive performance rewards, even for extraordinary incompetence. A recent regulatory focus, or global buzzword since the corporate frauds and misstatements of the early 21st century, is 'corporate governance reform'. Given the orthodox views dominating 'reform', which rarely depart from ideas like Williamson's of firms and their directors acting 'opportunistically with guile', most governance debates are heavily influenced by agency theory. Reform has centred on the theory's assumption of the self-interested opportunism of executives (human nature is here universally untrustworthy), which must be countered by strengthening the role of independent non-executives on corporate boards. Thus, in order to reduce this imputed CEO opportunism, reforms have sought to strengthen the 'control' role of non-executives by separating the chair of the board from chief executive roles, and by increasing the number of non-executives, introducing stricter definitions of independence, and by giving non-executives a leading part on audit, remuneration and nominations committees (McNulty et al. 2003).

In the wake of Enron's scandal in 2002, more hearings and royal commissions sprang up, such as the UK Higgs review. It too looked at how non-executive directors could be 'effective' in stemming CEO abuses, but honourably included research on the behavioural dynamics of relationships between executives and non-executives (McNulty et al. 2003). The Higgs review suggested that these economistic 'control' roles may be counterproductive and may indeed encourage the very self-interested behaviours that agency theory is seeking to prevent. This, as John Roberts and colleagues argue (Roberts, McNulty & Stiles forthcoming) might include self-defensiveness and deceit, and therefore non-executive roles might be more effective if accountability within the board were properly designed. It was a bombshell, as that same London banker told me on two occasions:

Shepheard-Walwyn: What I am as clear about now as ever is . . . we still don't have the right sort of debate about the really important issues, which are how you constrain the egos of senior management and how you get the right dynamic and culture within a company. (E-mail, 16 May 2003)

The reaction of senior management to any suggestion that they should be subject to some form of check and balance – as evidenced by the response of some chairmen and CEOs to the recent Higgs Report here in the UK – underlines the importance of this issue. (If 'Good to Great' is right about the psychological profiles of truly successful CEOs, then many of the people who make it to CEO are in the wrong job!) (E-mail, 10 May 2004)

This British banker is alluding to a paradox in the way that big companies operate, because the political and interpersonal skills necessary to get to the top are very often different from the skills required when that official becomes a CEO. In particular, self-confidence and presentational skills are valued highly, for example, but these are precisely the characteristics of people who, on taking top office, do not take kindly to criticism. Boardrooms end up with rituals that simply reinforce what these top people want to hear. These are the problems wrought by *entscheidungs-freudig*, the cult of personality and agency and behavioural psychological theories, which other sceptics mention. And while American and British sceptics joke about how Australia seems to specialise in these companies – and certainly Australian journalists and 'mum and dad' investors have been highly critical about the way that NAB or AMP, for example, have been run over the past decade – all my international sceptics agree that Australia has no monopoly in this regard. Indeed, many of these Australian companies have been run by headhunted American and British executives.

Of course, criticisms of CEOs are mounting, which all points to an inappropriate use of individualistic theories for organisational structures. Distrust assumes greed and imputes opportunism, therefore CEOs and 'independent' directors 'live down' to these selection criteria, which is part of my lesser quarrel with stakeholder models as they imply self-interested opportunism of diversely interested stakeholders (as we will see). Structures of responsibility, legally binding and publicly visible, are highly significant to remove options for blaming and scapegoating, not only for faulty decisions but mostly for lack of caution about the unknown future. Caution is not vacillation but prevention; if a decision is likely to go badly wrong, then borrowing is unwise. Werner Frey referred to two-handed economists being inconclusive and less appropriate for informing decision-making that recognises uncertainty. As the official in charge, his point in recruiting 'one-armed economists' was that he made the decision: 'That's right, but even then I was requiring a clear statement because I know myself that it can go right or wrong. I didn't listen to the economist, therefore, just for that!' But did this imply that the economist should take a formal part in the decision?

Frey: Not necessarily, it's rather in order to broaden the band of views, but of clear views and not of wishy-washy views. I made it clear all the time that although they contributed in the decision-making process, the responsibility for the decision at the end of the day would be with me. This is a very important element and I have seen, more often than not, executives who put the blame on others participating in the decision-making process, while others kept to themselves. (4 April 2002)

We saw time and again diversity of opinion silenced by the chief or chair (Chapter 4) drawing on experience ('Wall Street since 1948', claimed Greenspan at an FOMC meeting), proven prescience, convincing credibility until it goes wrong. A lone independent voice in such an environment risks a whole board or committee structure turning against the dissenter. Chamberlain argued that fear of financial crises was less dominant than fear of regulators. Share options were often without performance criteria (Chapter 6), nor did they encourage directors' interest in the survival of firms. Fraser argues that control of CEOs is not impossible:

Fraser: Only yesterday I was advocating at an Industry Super Fund board meeting . . . that it was time for us to stop talking about corporate governance and actually do something. The particular action I suggested that we could do straight away was to instruct all our fund managers to vote against every share option proposal that comes up . . . It was a bit of a bombshell for some of these people because the board comprises representatives of employers and employees, and the employers weren't so instantly persuaded, but I think I'll be able to persuade a couple of the boards I'm on to take this step. It's just a gesture at this stage but someone has to start somewhere. (28 June 2002)

The structure of incentives matter, but more so how responsibilities and caution are specified from top to bottom. It moves to the political question of control in a firm. Clearly there is a problem if CEOs are rewarded even if they fail:

Shepheard-Walwyn: Absolutely. It goes back to the fundamental question of who sets the standards for the organisation, who determines what the strategic objectives of the organisation are, who determines how much risk the organisation is prepared to assume in achieving those objectives, who determines what the sanctions are. Sanctions are very important in a firm.

A structure that aims for corporate survival which, in banks, focuses on debt-holders over shareholders' short-term interest is to diminish the normalised cult view of the role of a CEO:

I know exactly what you mean. What it is seeking to do is design something which is, in a sense, independent of the people who run it . . . The moral I draw from that is that far too little attention is paid to organisational design and one of the reasons is it's a tough issue to get at. It's about requiring people to give up power, it's about requiring people to change the way they think about things. Now, look at it the other way round. I would say that there is a huge opportunity for firms that strategically choose to manage this as a strategic priority . . . If you look at corporate survival, it's very short. If you look at a thirty-year period, corporate survival rates are very low. If all you are concerned about is maintaining your position as a survivor, you'd have thought it's worth doing something about it. (22 March 2002)

Regimes of incentives and sanctions in financial services vary. Caution and disapproval of bankruptcy still remain in Europe and Asia. We saw Zürich banker Paul Chan comparing general 'punishment systems' in Swiss and German banks with mistakes punished, whereas in America 'if you lose money it's the bank's money; if you make money it's your own bonus' (5 April 2002). The latter fosters recklessness, not caution. Share options, for example, turn CEOs into risk-takers; to raise shareholder value they must take on more risks. Yet CEOs face no downside, only an upside even after taking completely foolish risks. They only get sacked, with their huge payouts. It is low-risk for them, not the firm or its many constituencies, all of which suffer. US mutual funds prohibited profit-based incentives, and in a similar way for investment banks, the 1940s regulators used to assume that profit-based incentives encourage risk-taking and short-term views. These assumptions remain correct. Now, in the City of London as on Wall Street, equipped with 'basic skills' and 'drive' (less than any teacher), brokers earn huge salaries but bonuses are far more, even among commercial bank dealers (Augar 2000: 332; Patomaki 2001: 61–2; Augar calls the pay 'a social and moral disgrace'). A London banker compared the present six-digit and seven-digit salaries to his modest income when he started:

Chamberlain: We were under a Labour Government; it was illegal to have a pay rise. Friends my own age have forgotten . . . Kids today have absolutely no fear of the Labour Government, because they think that could never happen again. (19 March 2002)

A precautionary principle assumes that dealers are not permitted to win personally or to pass losses on to the bank. Bonuses are money for luck, which is completely at odds with the fiduciary purposes of banks. Those former debt-holder rules imposed precautionary principles on directors and CEOs. As well, a punishment system instils a sense of responsibility, the opposite of fund managers requiring 'fearlessness' among young traders. This is not a personality trait but a lack of markers in people's experience of dire events (Chapter 4). Cognitive control over expectations is not possible; for example, when a managed coolness requiring constant recourse to forecasting data gives rise to uncontrollable, below-the-threshold emotions, professionalism suffers. Heightened competition among traders leads to a pace where dealing is too fast. The idea that short cooling-off periods might reconfigure the emotional component was also discussed in interviews. Werner Frey partly agreed:

Frey: Definitely, definitely, and in the banking, or financial industry as a whole, there are instruments in place these days, like the value-at-risk concept, and the value-at-risk limit, which would force such cooling-off periods. That is, when a certain amount of risk is accumulated, the manoeuvring room would get smaller or in the extreme case nil . . . [But] it would be more than an hour, it would typically be more than an hour. If you reach such a limit, for the individual decision-maker, this is an awful event, so you will have to give him time, and this is the cooling-off period, to really get a sober mind again. (4 April 2002)

On Wall Street to Sydney, 'VAR and Raroc' (risk-adjusted return on capital) are said to be 'full of holes', capable of manipulation under the bonus reward systems, as all my evidence shows (Johnson 2004). Potentially more effective if regular cooling-off periods were held for trading, regardless of volatility, it could enable a general reconfiguration of the current emotions, and less fiddling (fed by fear or arrogance, recall) could escape detection. With panic runs, a 30 per cent tax on hot speculative money is clearly effective for countries where it is imposed, and for firms, if they acknowledged long-term interests.

Explicit emotions like fearlessness as standard operating procedures, explicit rituals among decision-makers prohibiting diverse views, and lack of explicit lines of responsibility all detract from professionalism, fiduciary duties and the 'steward-ship' John Bogle defends. The drive to shareholder value has resulted in recklessness among firms where those taking decisions are amply rewarded in a structure of irresponsibility. Experience of a ghastly event in which responsibility is defined, my interviews suggest, is extremely important in changing outlooks towards facing the unknown.

Moreover, education is not irrelevant to encouraging cautious outlooks: an ageism permeates finance where cynical old hands use those inexperienced in crashes, as we saw. In two decades, departments of financial and economic history have dwindled across English-speaking universities. Extensive awareness of cen-turies of financial disasters is a sensible precautionary job criterion for personnel in the financial sector, whereas for neo-classical economics, history is 'anecdotal'. For example, the reputation of the Nobel Prize to economists is now tarnished, only mildly offset by awards to Stiglitz and colleagues (on straightforward work about coping with imperfect information, albeit in a neo-classical framework). By award-ing those claiming to predict a risk-free future like Merton and Scholes (LTCM), the prize enhanced this fantasy. Nobels for caution would be very different.

The issue of journalism is broader again, but obviously, similar training in eco-nomic history for financial journalists could improve their competence in preparing and asking difficult questions of corporate leaders and bankers in this secretive, childlike financial world that seeks certainty. Some newspaper boards are now requiring that level of education, so too a liberal arts degree as far less narrow, even against managerial resistance on grounds of cost. Of course, journalist indepen-dence from proprietors, from news 'values' (inconstancy, short-term focus, selling) may seem as difficult to attain as requiring truly responsible CEOs. Journalists are swamped also by PR although, as I argued, PR is a sign of journalist effectiveness, unlike the rapid downsizing of the current journalist profession. Equally, media proprietors always seek new revenue sources to hang their selling machines. None of this aids the public institutional role of the press to question and expose the fibs and dubious tactics of high finance.

In the public sector of finance, many treasury and IMF officials are as convinced of the neutrality of money as the private sector. In contrast, central bankers are now caught in a straitjacket of institutional memory and dependence on markets.

EMOTIONS BETWEEN ORGANISATIONS: PUBLIC TO PRIVATE

The logic of the public sector is institutional longevity in the core areas of Finance and Treasury, and Foreign Affairs and Defence, whereas few private firms are built to last these days. Libertarians assumed that policy changes would dissipate organi-sations into amorphous markets. In effect, though, corporations and governments became less trustworthy precisely because of distrust strategies aimed against both of them: neo-classical economics, as we saw, accepts the existence of corporate forms only as agents: the world opportunistically seeks profits. Perhaps public sector dependence (handmaiden to 'markets') is only apparent. If governments can reduce corporate fiduciary responsibilities – in effect permitting dishonesty – governments can also increase them.

Nation-states have a proven capacity for democratic reform, and judiciaries are the bulwark in bringing corporate malpractices to public light. We saw how economic libertarianism gained policy strength to undermine major democratic institutions in Chapter 7, yet this often unravels. Many nation-states try to improve their democratic procedures and constitutions, such as European constitutional reforms; others do not. The tragedy in the UK and the USA is how these two great nation-states seem unable or unwilling to reform democratic procedures. For example, first-past-the-post gives so little 'choice' to voters that it is surprising the free marketeers did not demand preferential voting (where Nader votes would have passed on to Gore). The USA retains a system of rotten boroughs. More democratic nation-states have genuinely independent, nationwide electoral commissions to redraw boundaries on a systematic, regular basis to ensure one vote, one value on demographic grounds. These procedures require sharing power, ceding power (as Shepheard-Walwyn said of corporations), but they give fairer results to both winners and losers, greater stability, and often instil greater caution in governments.

Yet inter-organisational distrust strategies remain prevalent in high finance and create exclusive forms of public/private 'trust'. Entrustors can threaten to destroy the reputation of a trustee, to give a sense of control, of trust (Heimer 2001: 54). Threats impose fear of retribution and anger at trust broken. Trustees can only offer evidence of the past; they cannot foretell future claims of profits or national debts. Impersonal distrust relations among corporate and government sectors give rise to further guardians of trust: the problem remains, *quis custodiet ipsos custodes?* (Who guards the guardians?) If the answer is 'trust', the problem is unclear lines of responsibility in existing institutions, undemocratic procedures, diminished possibility of voting out failed technicians or foolish guardians, and greater need for more generalised trust. Having claimed to be trustworthy, this claim foolishly rests on predicting the future – well! Debates are locked in conflicts of interest, not honest, fair and reasonable claims about the future. Once a corporation or government is reduced to asking for trust, it is too late; trust is irretrievable. Once entrustors trust so little, that is the moment when no discretion or professionalism is left. Distrust is a self-defeating prophecy which discourages internal discipline and increases the likelihood of abuse of trust (Shapiro 1987: 647–51).

The options therefore are either to urge precaution and rise above mean, petty, allegedly predictable interests or to wait. Pessimists say only a total collapse will bring change, so wait. Optimists in finance still hope that memories are short, that the market will revive, that another round of distrust strategies will 'cure' failed ones, that the future can be controlled. Proposals for a global currency, for example, mean a global central bank as another technocratic solution, an unaccountable guardian of the guardians of money with no institutional basis except the same old G7, with their own debts and their own economic highs and lows, rarely synchronised. Money is abstract and complex but, as social relations, money rests on institutionalised promises and, at its core organisational level, is entrusted and vouchsafed by the society that guarantees these promises. These guarantees are by democratically elected governments which, in English-speaking countries and in the terms of the ECB, are overly dominated by beliefs about the neutrality of money.

Precaution means focusing on existing bodies, not creating new ones first. Caution is posed against distrust, for the following reasons. First, distrust as organisational strategy is an emotion which implies (and seeks) a controllable and predictable future. Second, distrust gives rise to trust in the certainty of an imagined future being attainable. It is now a form of organisational self-deception, a pathology within firms, banks and treasuries. At the core of the mighty corporate form, this basic deception about future control is a greater dishonesty than the numerous corporate crimes. (Crimes, however, are intentional, and must be punished through legal processes.)

Caution is therefore preferable because the future is unknown: firms and governments do not know it and never will. It is not merely a matter of unintended consequences. Corporate forms do not know their future intentions any better than individuals, though they have vast resources to defer and not 'know' their own intentions. But the cases of winning the battle and losing the war, from empires to corporations, are legion.

Alan Blinder said to me that confidence is probably a supremely capitalist emotion. Certainly he saw optimism as a prerequisite, though adamant that private banks should not be permitted to 'proliferate credit unduly'. Confidence can be also about a 'certain' grim future and gives rise to terms like depression or flight to liquidity instead of long-term investment. But the confidence in a future understood as risk and mere liquidity – not social promises – is a quest for certainty: not all options or preferences can be squeezed at once; uncertainty maddeningly pops up elsewhere. Impersonal distrust strategies in finance seek to reduce uncertainty and reduce vulnerability.

Abelson: The second part is the most important. You can't reduce the uncertainty by definition. One of the things that LTCM showed, which is repeated over and over again, is the danger of leveraging, of borrowing huge sums of money and in a sense leveraging your bets. Now a more conservative approach, which uses a very minimal amount of borrowing, or uses none at all, is obviously a lot safer. (21 September 2000)

But how boring and 'brown cardigan' (jargon for old retail banks) to be safe rather than use other people's money as a commodifiable asset (usually to bet on minuscule CB rate movements, or multiple 'sovereign' and securities movements, hedged against each other). Precaution in reducing vulnerability does not, like hedge funds, attempt to spread the vulnerability by borrowing. That only increases the dangers; only reducing massive borrowing lessens the dangers. Banks require proper supervision and regulation as each is interdependent. One failure affects many. If banks again became the cautious gatekeepers of development for uncertain yet potentially sound projects for increasing productive capacity and for fostering decent, stable arrangements, they would be a far cry from aggressive bank lending for speculation in financial assets. The uncertainty resulting from this only creates greater uncertainty.

Central banks today have lost regulatory powers and are quarantined from elected governments and social responsibilities. Yet as the only 'public' bulwarks against the ill effects of global capital flows, central banks are *de facto* governments over a major social conflict (creditors and debtors, taxpayer-debtors and governments); they are conservative technocracies which are required to reduce political divisions to matters of technical administration and one-way communication to 'markets'. However, in comparison with treasuries:

Budd: There are other differences. The main difference is that central banks are always a lot richer than treasuries. That is true everywhere. Treasuries have holes in the carpets and nothing works. Central banks are lavishly paid, lavishly equipped and lavishly funded. When I speak as a Treasury official, I used to have great contempt for the Bank of England and all its lavish appurtenances. Whenever people said it should be an independent Bank, I always said 'okay, but it mustn't be those people'. It is not that the Bank was cleverer than the Treasury. I would reject that analysis *completely*. It always annoyed me, because it wasn't the problem that Bank of England officials are cleverer or more hard-working than Treasury officials. I do not think that they are. They have more funds. However, the *point* is just that Treasury officials, or the experts, don't take the decisions, that is the problem in the Treasury. (12 March 2002)

In my words, Treasury was no longer to be trusted by high finance. When central banks emerged, the institutionalised deal between the private banks gave CBs control over the short-term interest rates. Massive funds from the central banker's control over private banks enabled central banks to act as lenders of last resort to prevent dire banking collapses. These functions are inconsistent without proper re-regulation of the finance sector (Kaufman 1986), and with many free of that control, it reduces the source of CB funds but raises so-called 'systemic' societal bailouts. Caution is required so that central banks can effectively lend (at a high interest) as the last resort when private banks become too aggressive (foolish). That, in turn, needs brave governments to restore the deal, to refuse to 'help' without regulations that work. Recall Budd's remark about how former British clearing banks were restrained by a public duty, how they were less greedy. My interpretation is that cosy personal ways were less at issue than postwar precautionary principles of relatively decommodified money (before Big Bang and so on).

Today, central bankers, potential heroes or scapegoats of politicians *or* markets, obviously aware they please neither, are locked into public defence of their banks as institutions, and rightly so, from my evidence. But governments have the capacity to require that finance to take a smaller and more responsible role both by control and by refusing to relinquish so many functions to the private sector. Why are governments so fearful of the 'money power'? Privatisation of public utilities only feeds the Ponzi schemes and makes possible the growth of investment banks. Government can reclaim the field of collective security, public services and sound government investment in wealth production that is far more reliable if modest. Government can honestly take responsibility, rather than leaving it to central banks. Is it worth trusting high finance when it is so (secretly) reliant on government? Government retreat from responsible fiscal policy has benefited corporate and un-earned income tax minimisation (but they 'need' it to fuel more asset speculation). As one informed sceptic argued before the situation degenerated further, the idea that monetary policy can fix everything has confused central bankers themselves: 'They think they are running the universe now, whereas their role is still to rescue the system when it collapses.' Central bankers know 'their main problem will be the banking system' (V. J. Carroll, 18 January 2001).

Central banks are the independent, statutory bank of government. Their formal line of accountability is to government, and the Fed is exemplary in its requirements to report regularly to the legislature, not only to the executive behind closed doors. But fiscal means for keeping some stability remain important, despite years of opposition from financial 'pro-market' concerns. Monetary policy is a fragile, uncertain 'string' for sole economic management, whereas fiscal policy is an elected government's proper task. Fraser argues:

Fraser: For my part I've always talked about central bank independence as being a partnership with governments and about pursuing broader objectives. That is not a culture that is shared by most central bankers. Most want to keep the government at arm's length and get on and do what they believe they should do, in their own little area. I think it's much better for central banks to work with governments and simultaneously pursue objectives on lots of fronts . . . Monetary policy and fiscal policy are similar in their economic impacts and should be coordinated. (28 June 2002)

In so far as it is the ideal for all public servants to act professionally, without fear or favour to their executive and legislatures, treasuries do not lack formal powers and never have. Therefore, against a technocratic 'rule', decisions over objectives must rightfully remain with elected representatives in the public political discourse of winners and losers. Politicians are 'responsible'. In contrast, a free-market pro-posal arising from the Enron-Andersen debacle in 2002 – among *The Economist*'s journalists, according to Ziegler – was to nationalise accountancy functions. As we saw, CEOs use accountants as handmaidens for deals, and non-executive directors cannot be 'independent' from major but complicatedly murky constituencies like huge institutional shareholders (profits today from owning voting and exit rights). The idea implies that the state should keep these shareholder 'firms' honest. Worse, the state would be required to predict future profits and prevent executives from bullying 'state accountants' and other pliable public professionals, or from bribing them. We have overwhelming evidence of the City or Wall Street (and its massive links to the non-financial sector including media corporations) keeping secrets from journalists, hence the public, while demanding transparency of CBs and treasuries. Far preferable to return to 'full and fair' views which admit that the future cannot be known.

Much has been written about whether corporate governance would include stakeholders on external reviews and boards. Galbraith preferred shareholders being relegated to debt-holders and, instead of boards of directors, public interest monitoring groups established, on the grounds that the shareholder is without power or function (Galbraith 1977: 278; Dow 2001: 90). We mentioned Parker's *The Open Corporation: Effective Self-Regulation and Democracy* (2002), which argues that commitment could spread from top management to self-regulating professionals (seen as a critical linchpin) and then to all employees. Stakeholder concerns could permeate the corporate shell.

'Exit' and 'loyalty' are no bases for corporate citizenship or corporate survival, as Albert Hirschman said in 1970. Clearly, having a voice is vital to employees, unions, customers (also clients, patients, students – all by definition not customers), professionals and the broader social and political environment in which corporate public reputations ultimately rest, because corporations perform socially important tasks. We all depend on these functions being performed professionally and fairly, but if corporations silence the honest criticisms and constructive proposals, they are often doomed to decline. Our focus, however, is on the money-power and how shareholder value detracts from stable corporations. The whole society is the guarantee of the value of money, so even a wide range of stakeholders could neglect minority voices. Where is the public duty of banks (Budd) or the broader national responsibilities of central banks (Fraser) and international concerns? Only the Fed and RBA are required to juggle employment and inflation objectives. These are political juggling acts but their charters need government support. The range of social conflicts involved in the social relations of money are never solvable and least of all predictable. Instead of burdening the central banks with duties of prescience way beyond rational calculation, economic decisions are better left to democratic process and deliberation over precautionary principles. Creditors and debtors among populations change their positions at different stages of life; for example, after house mortgages are paid off, these generations become creditors (modest rentiers). Although the wealthy have gained secret bonuses in inflationary declines and so on, winners and losers over any decision do not need to be so extreme. Therefore, citizens' advisory boards are interesting, but more important are governments brave enough to make decisions which might go wrong and which will, like an honest sporting game, involve losers. A cautious world aims to prevent some of the dangers arising from selling promises as if money were just a 'thing'.

A FINAL WORD

We have been sold venal rubbish that denies money's intrinsic social nature as *promises*. We know that nothing is certain, therefore promises, so highly institutionalised and so apparently abstract, need safeguarding, not marketing. From this book's perspective, governments can in principle reject further requirements to guarantee the convention for this selling machine unless financial institutions accept limitations and precaution. 'Buyer beware' is insufficient when neo-classical views prevail about money's neutrality: this fiction that promises between creditors and debtors have no long-term effects, or none that 'matter', was demolished by Schumpeter and many of the Right and Left long ago. The ability to discharge a debt and the issuer's promise to take money back in payment of a debt owed is a complex circuit involving governments, taxes, banks and repayment of loans. Caution is required to try to keep these circuits believable and dependable. Hayek preferred 'the market' while, at least more openly, admitting that limitations on democracy were 'necessary'. But for whom? we may ask.

Doing nothing entails more state expenditure on providing Ponzi schemes by privatising remaining public utilities not already contracted out, brought to you by Enron etc., and feeding low-income pension funds to private sector fees (while taxing these minuscule retirement nest-eggs back further). Instead, governments can refuse this and its heavy state expenditure for preventing the worst excesses, unless it gains significant revenue from the private sector and the democratic right to control and open it to public deliberation. Legal requirements of fiduciary trust can be *re-placed* on corporations which can also cede power to broader concerns.

From the market as apparently 'sexy', many see how Market Rules are clearly opposite to further democratisation and public deliberation, or debate on preferred precautionary measures for the unknown future. Uncertainty is unsayable: an Australian Treasurer (Kerin) was forced to resign for admitting he did not know the future. Market Rules were implemented by Anglo-American governments' policy changes. State power, however, is not unchangeable if social movements, 'enlightened' middle classes or frightened retirees and less comfortable groups demand it. The issue is not how to limit state power but how to put this power to democratic purposes and impose precautionary principles. Positive uses of political power (by electorates, from the bottom up) have shaped decent institutions in the past.

In conclusion, this book has presented three major propositions, the first of which is that the finance world can never find certainty (internally or externally). Second, my evidence shows that emotions are never removable; they arise internally to this highly future-oriented world. But the distrust strategies used to generate trust in the future have destroyed a more generalised trust in simply coping with our difficult and dangerous world. Therefore my third proposition is that caution is the requisite emotion for relations of promises, and our financial institutions require that modest caution for facing the future; modest caution acknowledges the limitations of rationality towards the unknown.

Instead of pretending the future is knowable, we know, by and large, as do informed sceptics, that we all rely on a huge framework of institutions that are important in giving us some modicum of security in facing the always unknown. The emotions of distrust driving global financial institutions will never bring certainty, only more foolish decisions. As I said before, honest and humble acknowledgement of organisational (human) frailties is desirable and not impossible. This book shows that all contests for knowledge or information about the future – the meaning of that dubious 'information society' concept so popular during the greatest asset boom since 1929 – are doomed. The quest for control over the future is driven by emotions of distrust which enable opportunistic calculations for very short-term horizons. Even then events, as always, intervene with increasingly surprising effects, mainly because the world of money insists, irrationally, on the rationality of risk. We know the future is never certain: our large world of organisations needs caution in facing it.

References

Abelson, A. 2002, 'Eternal hope of the bulls', *AFR*, 18 October 2002: 38; reprinted from *Barrons*.

Abelson, A. 2004, 'Greenspan's course of inaction' *AFR*, 13 January 2004: 45; reprinted from *Barrons*.

'All too human' 2002, *Economist*, 12 October: 76.

Arrighi, G. 1994, *The Long Twentieth Century*, London: Verso.

Askew, K. 2000, 'Merrill dumping mums and dads', *SMH*, 14 November 2000: 27.

Augar, P. 2000, *The Death of Gentlemanly Capitalism*, London: Penguin Books.

Aylmer, S. 2004, 'Greenspan gives monetary policy credit', *AFR*, 5 January: 8.

Baert, P. 2000, 'The End of Prophecy', *American Journal of Economics and Sociology* 59(1): 65–9.

Bagehot, W. 1962 [1873], *Lombard Street*, Homewood IL: Richard D. Irwin, Inc.

Baker, P. 2003, 'It wasn't our fault', *AFR*, 23 May: 36.

Baker, T., & J. Simon (eds), 2002, *Embracing Risk*, University of Chicago Press.

Baker, W. 1987, 'What is Money'. In M. S. Mizruchi & M. Schwartz (eds), *Intercorporate Relations*, Cambridge University Press.

Barbalet, J. M. 1998, *Emotion, Social Theory and Social Structure*, Cambridge University Press.

Barbalet J. M. (ed.) 2002, *Emotions and Sociology, Sociological Review Monograph*, Oxford: Blackwell Publishing.

Benjamin, W. 1969, *Illuminations*, New York: Schocken Books.

Bell, D. 1976, *The Coming of Post-Industrial Society*, New York: Basic Books.

Berle, A., & G. Means 1932, *The Modern Corporation and Private Property*, New York: Macmillan.

Bernanke, B. 2003, 'Why the world's central banks must become more vigilant about falling prices', *Foreign Policy*, November–December: 74–5.

Berman, S. 2003, 'We didn't start the fire: capitalism and its critics', *Foreign Affairs* 82(4): 176–81.

Bewley, R., & D. G. Fiebig 2002, 'On the the herding instincts of interest rate forecasters', *Empirical Economics*, 27(3): 403–25.

Blackburn, R. 2002, 'The Enron Debacle and the Pension Crisis', *New Left Review*, 14: 26–52.

Blinder, A., C. Goodhart, P. Hildebrand, D. Lipton & C. Wyplosz 2001, *How Do Central Banks Talk? Geneva Reports on the World Economy* 3, Geneva: International Center for Monetary and Banking Studies.

Blitt, B. 2002, 'Saving Face: a Contemporary Folktale', The Back Page, *New Yorker*, 13 May.

Bogle, J. 2003, Statement before the US House of Representatives Sub-Committee on Capital Markets, Insurance and Government Sponsored Enterprises (Committee on Financial Services), 12 March 2003.

Braithwaite, J., & P. Drahos 2000, *Global Business Regulation*, Cambridge University Press.

Brenner, R. 2002, *Boom and Bubble*, London: Verso.

Brown, S. 2004, 'Doubling the risk of damnation', *AFR*, 21 January: 47.

Burkitt, I. 2002, 'Complex Emotions: Relations, Feelings and Images in Emotional Experience'. In J. M. Barbalet (ed.), *Emotions and Sociology*, Oxford: Blackwell.

Burns, T. 1974, 'On the Rationale of the Corporate System'. In R. Marris (ed.), *The Corporate Society*, London: Macmillan.

Burns, T. 1977, 'The Organization of Public Opinion'. In J. Curran, M. Gurevitch & J. Woollacott (eds), *Mass Communication and Society*, London: Edward Arnold.

Calhoun C. 1992, 'The Infrastructure of Modernity'. In N. Smelser & H. Haferkamp (eds), *Social Change and Modernity*, Berkeley CA: University of California Press.

Caporaso, J. A., & D. P. Levine 1992, *Theories of Political Economy*, Cambridge University Press.

Carroll, V. J. 2000, 'Why these men lead from behind', *SMH*, 15 April.

Carruthers, B., & W. N. Espeland 1991, 'Accounting for Rationality', *American Journal of Sociology* 17(1): 31–69.

Cassidy, J. 2002, *Dot.Con: The Greatest Story Ever Sold*, London: Allen Lane.

Cerny, P. G. 1993, 'The Deregulation and Re-regulation of Financial Markets'. In P. G. Cerny (ed.), *Finance and World Politics*, Aldershot: Edward Elgar.

Chick, V. 1983, *Macroeconomics after Keynes*, Oxford: Philip Allan.

Chulov, M. 2002, 'It's more than just a PR stunt', *Australian*, Media section, 22 August: 4.

Clark, G. 2002, 'Embracing Fatality through Life Insurance'. In Baker & Simon, *Embracing Risk*.

Clarke, F., & G. Dean 2004, 'Lapping it up and ignoring the evidence', *AFR*, 13 January: 47.

Clarke, F., G. Dean & K. Oliver 2003, *Corporate Collapse: Accounting, Regulatory and Ethical Failure*, Cambridge University Press.

Cohen, B. J. 1996, 'Phoenix Risen: The Resurrection of Global Finance', *World Politics* 48: 268–96.

Collins, R. 1975, *Conflict Sociology*, New York: Academic Press.

Collins, R. 1990, 'Stratification, Emotional Energy, and the Transient Emotions'. In T. D. Kemper (ed.), *Research Agendas in the Sociology of Emotions*, Albany NY: SUNY Press.

Collins, R. 1998, *The Sociology of Philosophies*, Cambridge MA: Belknap.

Collison, D. 2002, 'Propaganda, Accounting and Finance'. In G. Frankfurter & E. McGoun (eds), *From Individualism to the Individual*, Aldershot: Ashgate.

Cook, K. S. (ed.) 2001, *Trust in Society*, New York: Russell Sage Foundation.

Cornford, F. M. 1949, *Microcosmographia Academica*, Cambridge: Bowes & Bowes.

Curran, J., & J. Seaton 1997, *Power without Responsibility: The Press and Broadcasting in Britain*, 5th edn, London: Routledge.

Damasio, A. R. 1994, *Descartes' Error: Emotions, Reason, and the Human Brain*, New York: G. P. Putnam's Sons.

Dangerfield, G. 1936, *The Strange Death of Liberal England*, London: Constable.

Davidson, P. 1990, 'Shackle and Keynes vs. Rational Expectations Theory and the Role of Time'. In S. F. Frowen (ed.), *Unknowledge and Choice in Economics*, London: Macmillan.

Davidson, P. 1991, 'Is Probability Theory Relevant for Uncertainty?' *Journal of Economic Perspectives* 5(1): 129–43.

Davidson, P. 1996, 'What are the Essential elements of Post Keynesian Monetary Theory?' In G. Deleplace and E. Nell (eds), *Money in Motion*, London: Macmillan.

Davies, G. 1994, *A History of Money*, Cardiff: University of Wales Press.

De Bondt, F., & R. Thaler 1985, 'Does the Stock Market Overreact?', *Journal of Finance* 40(3): 793–805.

Dequech, D. 1999, 'Expectations and Confidence under Uncertainty', *Journal of Post Keynesian Economics* 21(3): 415–30.

Dequech, D. 2000, 'Confidence and action: a comment on Barbalet', *Journal of Socio-Economics* 29(6): 503–15, www.sciencedirect.com/science?_ob=ArticleURL&_udi (downloaded 6 February 2001)

Dexter L. 1970, *Elite and Specialized Interviewing*, Evanston IL: Northwestern University Press.

Donlan, T. G. 2002, 'Same old Wall St, 132 years on', *AFR*, 22 November: 38; reprinted from *Barrons*.

Dow, G. 2001, 'The Legacy of Orthodoxy: Political Causes of Unemployment'. In E. Carlson and W. F. Mitchell (eds), *Economic Labour Relations Review*, Supplement to Volume 12: 83–96.

Dunbar, N. 2000, *Inventing Money: The Story of Long-Term Capital Management and the Legends Behind It*, Chichester: John Wiley.

Dymski G. A. 1996, 'Basic Choices in Keynesian Models of Credit'. In G. Deleplace & E. Nell (eds), *Money in Motion*, London: Macmillan.

Eichengreen, B. 1990, '1929 and 1987: Parallels and Contrasts'. In E. N. White (ed.), *Crashes and Panics: The Lessons from History*, New York: Dow Jones-Irwin and New York University.

Eichengreen, B., J. Tobin & C. Wyplosz 1995, 'Two Cases for Sand in the Wheels of International Finance', *Economic Journal*, 105, January: 162–72.

Elster, J. 1998, 'Emotions and Economic Theory', *Journal of Economic Literature*, 36(1): 47–74.

Elster, J. 1999, *Alchemies of the Mind: Rationality and the Emotions*, Cambridge University Press.

Ewald, F. 2002, 'The Return of Descartes' Malicious Demon'. In Baker & Simon, *Embracing Risk*.

'Fed finds the sweeties in behavioural economics', Reuters in *SMH*, 21–22 June 2003: 55.

Ferguson, N. 2004 'The dollar dilemma', *AFR*, 11 June 2004: 1–2: reprinted from *Prospect*.

Fisse, B., & J. Braithwaite 1993, *Corporations, Crime and Accountability*, Cambridge University Press.

Flam, H. 1990. 'Emotional "Man"', *International Sociology*, 5(1): 39–56.

Flanagan, J. 2004, 'True independence an elusive dream', *AFR*, 9 February: 60.

FOMC transcripts of meetings on pdf. files released by statute five years after each meeting. Meetings of 1994; 3–4 February 1994; 16 August 1994; 24 September 1996 (all downloaded May 2002); Meeting of September 29 1998 (downloaded 17 June 2004) from <www.federalreserve.gov/fomc/#calendars>

FOMC press releases of 18 March and 28 October 2003, <www.federalreserve.gov/boarddocs/press/monetary/2003> (downloaded 12 November 2003).

Fraser, B. W. 1996, *Collected Speeches B. W. Fraser, Governor Reserve Bank of Australia 1989–1996*, 2 vols, Reserve Bank of Australia.

Friedman, B. 1987, 'Capital, Credit and Money Markets'. In J. Eatwell, M. Milgate & P. Newman (eds), *The New Palgrave: Money*, London: Macmillan.

Friedman, T. 1999, *The Lexus and the Olive Tree*, London: HarperCollins.

Fukuyama, F. 1995, *Trust: The Social Virtues and the Creation of Prosperity*, London: Penguin.

Gabriel, Y. 1998, 'Psychoanalytic Contributions to the Study of the Emotional Life of Organizations', *Administration & Society*, 30(3): 291–314.

Galbraith, J. K. 1958, *The Affluent Society*, Harmondsworth: Penguin.

Galbraith, J. K. 1975, *Money: Whence It Came, Where It Went*, Boston MA: Houghton Mifflin.

Galbraith, J. K. 1977, *The Age of Uncertainty*, Boston MA: Houghton Mifflin.

Gittins R. 2002, '"Irrationalism" wins credence', *SMH*, 12–13 October: 44.

Goddard, P. 1998, 'Press Rhetoric and Economic News'. In N. Gavin (ed.), *The Economy, Media and Public Knowledge*, London: Leicester University Press.

Goodhart, C. A. E. 1984, *Monetary Theory and Practice*, London: Macmillan.

Goodwin, J., J. M. Jasper & F. Polletta 2000, 'Return of the Repressed', *Mobilization*, 5(1): 65–82.

Grabel, H. 1998 Commentary in Schaberg, M. 'Globalization and financial systems'.

Grahl, J. 2001a, 'Globalized Finance', *New Left Review*, 8, March–April: 23–48.

Grahl, J., 2001b, 'The Sway of Finance?' *New Left Review*, 9, May–June: 148–53.

Grant, J. 2000, 'Transatlantic pair trade', *Grant's Interest Rate Observer*, 18(17): 1–11.

Gray, John 1998, *False Dawn: The Delusions of Global Capitalism*, London: Granta Books.

Greenspan, A. 2002 'Remarks by chairman Alan Greenspan: economic volatility, at a symposium sponsored by the Federal Reserve Bank of Kansas City, Jackson Hole, Wyoming, August 30, 2002', <www.federalreserve.gov/boarddocs/speeches/2002/20020830/default.htm>

Greider, W. 1987, *Secrets of the Temple: How the Federal Reserve Runs the Country*, New York: Simon & Schuster.

Greider, W. 2002, '*Il Maestro*'s failed magic', *Nation*, March 25: 6–7.

Grimes, K. 2003, 'The chemical key to lust and trust', *AFR*, 16 May.

Gumbrecht, H. U. 2001, 'How is Our Future Contingent?' *Theory, Culture & Society* 18(1): 49–58.

Haigh, G. 2003, 'Bad company: the cult of the CEO', *Quarterly Essay*, 10: 1–97.

Hale, B. 2000a, 'Angels from on high drag market to safer ground', *SMH* 23 October: 27.

Hale, B. 2000b, 'Wall St counts down while Florida recounts', *SMH* 13 November: 39.

Hale, B. 2001, 'Anthrax and dismal housing figures', *SMH*, 19 October 2001: 28.

Hardin R. 2001, 'Conceptions and Explanations of Trust'. In Cook, *Trust in Society*.

Hartcher, P. 2003, 'Atlas Shrugged', *AFR Magazine*, August: 20–4.

Haugen, R. A. 1997 *Modern Investment Theory*, 4th edn, Upper Saddle River NJ: Prentice-Hall.

Heclo, H., & A. Wildavsky 1981, *The Private Government of Public Money*, London: Macmillan.

Heilbroner R. 1967, *The Worldly Philosophers*, New York: Simon & Schuster.

Heimer, C. A. 1985, *Reactive Risk and Rational Action*, Berkeley CA: University of California Press.

Heimer, C. A. 2001, 'Solving the Problem of Trust'. In Cook, *Trust in Society*.

Heimer, C. A. 2002, 'Insuring More, Ensuring Less'. In Baker & Simon, *Embracing Risk*.

Helleiner, E. 1993, 'When Finance was the Servant: International Capital Movements in the Bretton Woods Order'. In P. G. Cerny (ed.), *Finance and World Politics*, Aldershot: Edward Elgar.

Henwood, D. 1998, *Wall Street*, New York: Verso.

Henwood, D. 2003, 'Irresistible Temptations', *Left Business Observer*, 104, April: 4.

Hirsch, P. M. 1986, 'From Ambushes to Golden Parachutes', *American Journal of Sociology* 91(4): 800–37.

Hirschman, A. O. 1970, *Exit, Voice and Loyalty: Responses to Decline in Firms, Organizations and States*, Cambridge MA: Harvard University Press.

Hirschman, A. O. 1997, *The Passions and the Interests*, Princeton University Press.

Hirschman A. O. 2002, *Shifting Involvements*, Princeton University Press.

Hood, C. 1994, *Explaining Economic Policy Reversals*, Buckingham: Open University Press.

Hutton, W. 2002, *The World We're In*, London: Little, Brown.

Ingham, G. 1984, *Capitalism Divided?* Houndmills: Macmillan.

Ingham, G. 1996a, 'Money is a Social Relation', *Review of Social Economy* 54(4): 507–29.

Ingham, G. 1996b, 'Some recent changes in the relationship between economics and sociology', *Cambridge Journal of Economics* 20: 243–75.

Ingham, G. 1998, 'On the Underdevelopment of the "Sociology of Money"', *Acta Sociologica* 41(1): 3–18.

Ingham, G. 2002, 'Shock Therapy in the City', *New Left Review*, 14: 152–8.

Ingham, G. 2004, *The Nature of Money*, Cambridge: Polity Press.

Inglehart, R., M. Basaêz & A. Moreno 1998, *Human Values and Beliefs*, Ann Arbor MI: University of Michigan Press.

Jackson, S. 2001, 'Clue Klutz Clan', *Australian*, 23 March: 34.

Jacobs, B. I. 1999, *Capital Ideas and Market Realities: Option Replication, Investor Behavior, and Stock Market Crashes*, Malden MA: Blackwell.

Jenkins, S. 1999, 'Maxwell's Backroom Boys', *The Australian*, 5 February: 38. Reprinted from *The Times*.

Johnson, P. 2004, 'Banking's back-office weakness', *AFR*, 14 April.

Jones, P. 2000, 'Paradigmatic tensions in the sociology of news', *Journal of Sociology* 36(2): 239–45.

Katona, G. 1957, 'The Function of Survey Research in Economics'. In Komarovsky, *Common Frontiers of the Social Sciences*.

Kaufman, H. 1986, *Interest Rates, the Market and the New Financial World*, New York: Times Books.

Kaufman, H., 2000, *A Wall Street Memoir*, New York: McGraw-Hill.

Kemper, T. D. 1978, *A Social Interactional Theory of Emotions*, New York: John Wiley & Sons.

Kennedy, S. 2004, 'Fed has vital role, even in low-rate environment', *AFR*, 5 January: 9.

Keynes, J. M. 1937, 'The General Theory of Employment', *Quarterly Journal of Economics*, 51, February: 209–33.

Keynes, J. M. 1964, *The General Theory of Employment, Interest, and Money*, New York, Harbinger.

Kindleberger, C. P. 1989, *Manias, Panics and Crashes: A History of Financial Crises*, 2nd edn, London: Macmillan.

Kirman, A. 1993, 'Ants, rationality and recruitment', *Quarterly Journal of Economics*, CVIII(1): 137–56.

Knight, F. H. 1964 [1921], *Risk, Uncertainty and Profit*, New York: A. M. Kelley.

Komarovsky, M. (ed.), *Common Frontiers of the Social Sciences*, Glencoe: Free Press.

Korczynski, M. 1996, 'Trust, Power and the Market', *Centre for Corporate Change Paper 061*, Australian Graduate School of Management, University of New South Wales.

Korpi, W., & J. Palmer 2003, 'New Politics and Class Politics in the Context of Austerity and Globalisation', *American Political Science Review*, 97(1): 425–46.

Kriesler, P., & J. Neville 2003, 'Macroeconomic Impacts of Globalization'. In H. Bloch (ed.), *Growth and Development in the Global Economy*, Cheltenham: Elgar.

Krugman, P. 1997, *The Age of Diminished Expectations*, 3rd edn, Cambridge MA: MIT Press.

Krugman, P. 2003, *The Great Unravelling*, Melbourne: Penguin Books.

Kurtz, H. 2000, *The Fortune Tellers*, New York: Touchstone.

Kurtz, H. 2001, 'Wall Street's Hype Machine', *SMH*, 13 January: 39.

Kynaston, D. 1994, *The City of London* vol. 1, London: Chatto & Windus.

Kynaston, D. 1995, 'The Bank of England and the Government'. In R. Roberts & D. Kynaston (eds), *The Bank of England*, Oxford: Oxford University Press and Clarendon.

Lazar, D. 1990, *Markets and Ideology in the City of London*, London: Macmillan.

Lekachman, R. 1957, 'The Non-Economic Assumptions of John Maynard Keynes'. In Komarovsky, *Common Frontiers of the Social Sciences*.

Levitas, R. 1986, 'Competition and Compliance: The Utopias of the New Right'. In R. Levitas (ed.), *The Ideology of the New Right*, Cambridge: Polity Press.

Levitas, R. 1990, *The Concept of Utopia*, Hemel Hempstead: Philip Allan.

Lewis, M. 1989, *Liar's Poker: Two Cities, True Greed*, London: Hodder & Stoughton.

Lewis, M. 1991, *The Money Culture*, New York: Penguin Books.

Lewis, M. 1999, *The New, New Thing*, London: Hodder & Stoughton.

Lowenstein, R. 2000, *When Genius Failed: The Rise and Fall of Long-Term Capital Management*, New York: Random House.

Luhmann, N. 1979, *Trust and Power*, Chichester: John Wiley & Sons.

Luhmann, N. 1988, 'Familiarity, Confidence, Trust'. In Gambetta, *Trust*.

Macfarlane, I. J. 1999, 'The Stability of the Financial System'. Speech of the Governor, Reserve Bank of Australia, Sydney, 29 July, <rba.gov.au/speech/sp_gov_290799.html> (downloaded 2 August 1999).

McNulty, T., J. Roberts and P. Stiles 2003, 'Creating accountability within the board; the work of the effective non-executive director'. Report for the Department of Trade and Industry/ Treasury [UK] Higgs review of the role and effectiveness of the non-executive director, <http://www.dti.gov.uk/cld/non exec review/pdfs/stilesreport.pdf> (downloaded 17 June 2004).

Mannheim, K. 1936, *Ideology and Utopia*, London: Routledge & Kegan Paul.

Marris, R. 1998, *Managerial Capitalism in Retrospect*, London: Macmillan.

Marris, R. (ed.) 1974, *The Corporate Society*, London: Macmillan.

Mayer, M. 1997, *The Bankers*, New York: Truman Talley Books.

Merrell, C. 2002, 'Incompetent trader relied on bullying to cover traces', *The Times* 15 March: 29.

Merritt, C. 2003, 'Victoria defends exemption clause', *AFR*, 28 November 2003: 55.

Mieg, H. A. 2001, *The Social Psychology of Expertise*, Mahwah NJ: Lawrence Erlbaum Associates.

Miller, D. 2002, 'The Unintended Political Economy'. In P. du Gay & M. Pryke (eds), *Cultural Economy*, London: Sage.

Minsky, H. P. 1985, 'The Financial Instability Hypothesis'. In P. Arestis & T. Skouras (eds), *Post Keynesian Economic Theory*, Sussex: Wheatsheaf Books.

Minsky, H. P. 1996, 'The Essential Characteristics of Post Keynesian Economics'. In G. Deleplace & E. Nell (eds), *Money in Motion*, London: Macmillan.

Misztal, B. A. 1996, *Trust in Modern Societies*, Cambridge: Polity Press.

Mizruchi M., & L. Stearns 1994, 'Money, Banking and Financial Markets'. In N. J. Smelser & R. Swedberg (eds), *The Handbook of Economic Sociology*, Princeton University Press.

Negri, T. 1988, *Revolution Retrieved: Writings on Marx, Keynes, Capitalist Crisis and New Social Subjects*, London: Red Notes.

Oatley, K. 1992, *Best Laid Schemes: The Psychology of Emotions*, Cambridge University Press.

Office of the Attorney General, New York State 2002, 'Merrill Lynch stock rating system found biased by undisclosed conflicts of interest'. <www.oag.state.ny.us/press/2002/apr/apr08b 02.html> (downloaded 29 April 2002).

O'Malley, P. 2002, 'Imagining Insurance'. In Baker & Simon, *Embracing Risk*.

Ormerod, P. 1998, *Butterfly Economics*, New York: Pantheon Books.

Oxford Dictionary of Quotations 1999.

Parguez, A., & M. Seccareccia 2000, 'The Credit Theory of Money: The Monetary Circuit Approach'. In J. Smithin (ed.), *What is Money?* London: Routledge.

Parker, C. 2002, *The Open Corporation*, Cambridge University Press.

Parker, D., & R. Stacey 1995, *Chaos, Management and Economics*, Smithfield, NSW: Centre for Independent Studies.

Parker, J. 2001, 'When nothing makes sense', *AFR*, 19 October: 30.

Parry, J., & M. Bloch (eds), 1989, *Money and the Morality of Exchange*, Cambridge University Press.

Partnoy, F. 1998, *F.I.A.S.C.O.: Blood in the Water on Wall Street*, London: Profile Books.

Patomaki, H., 2001, *Democratising Globalisation: The Leverage of the Tobin Tax*, London: Zed Books.

Paulos, J. A. 2003, *A Mathematician Plays the Stock Market*, New York: Basic Books.

Pauly, L. 1997, *Who Elected the Bankers?* Ithaca: Cornell University Press.

PBS Newshour, 'Full Disclosure: Stock Tips', 27 December 2000, PBS Online: <pbs.org/newshour/bb/media/july-dec00/stocks/12–27> (downloaded 27 December 2000).

PBS TV Newshour/Lehrer Interview with John Bogle in 'Mutual Fund Fraud', 4 November 2003, PBS Online: <pbs.org/newshour/bb/business/july-dec03/mutual_11–04> (downloaded 12 November 2003).

Pennant-Rea, R. 1995, 'The Bank of England'. In R. Roberts & D. Kynaston (eds), *The Bank of England*, Oxford: Oxford University Press and Clarendon.

Perelman, M. 1998, 'The Neglected Economics of Trust', *American Journal of Economics and Sociology*, 57(4): 381–9.

Perkins, M. C., and C. Nunez, 'Why investors don't feel your pain', *Washington Post*, reprinted in *AFR*, 16 March 2001: 58.

Peston, R. 2002, 'Net losses', *The Guardian*, 9 February.

Pixley, J. F. 1993, *Citizenship and Employment: Investigating Post-Industrial Options*, Cambridge University Press.

Pixley, J. F. 1997, 'Employment and Social Identity'. In M. Roche & R. van Berkel (eds), *European Citizenship and Social Exclusion*, Aldershot, Ashgate.

Pixley, J. F. 1998, 'Social Movements, Democracy and Conflicts over Institutional Reform'. In B. Cass & P. Smyth (eds), *Contesting the Australian Way*, Cambridge University Press.

Pixley, J. F. 1999a, 'Impersonal Trust in Global Mediating Organisations', *Sociological Perspectives* 42(4): 647–71.

Pixley, J. F. 1999b, 'Beyond Twin Deficits: Emotions of the Future in the Organizations of Money', *American Journal of Economics and Sociology*, 58(4): 1091–118.

Pixley, J. F. 2002a, 'Expectation, Emotions and Money'. In S. Clegg (ed.), *Management and Organization Paradoxes*, Amsterdam: John Benjamins.

Pixley, J. F. 2002b, 'Emotions and Economics'. In J. Barbalet (ed.), *Emotions and Sociology*, Oxford: Blackwell.

Pixley, J. F. 2002c, 'Finance organizations, decisions and emotions', *British Journal of Sociology*, 53(1): 41–65.

Polanyi, K. 1957, *The Great Transformation*, Boston: Beacon Press.

Pollard, S. 1965, *The Genesis of Modern Management*, London: Edward Arnold.

Porter, T. 1995, *Trust in Numbers: The Pursuit of Objectivity in Science and Public Life*, Princeton University Press.

Pryor, F. L. 2000, 'The Millennium Survey Again', *American Journal of Economics and Sociology*, 59(1): 79–85.

Rabin, M. 1998, 'Psychology and Economics', *Journal of Economic Literature*, 36(1): 11–46.

Raghavan, A. 2002, 'Self-confessed shredder wanted only to please', *AFR*, 17 May: 59.

Reserve Bank of Australia 1999, 'Consumer Credit and Household Finances', RBA Bulletin, June, <www.rba.gov.au>

Ricoeur, P. 1986, *Lectures on Ideology and Utopia*, New York: Columbia University Press.

Roberts, I., & J. Simon 2001 'What do sentiments surveys measure?' *Research Discussion Paper* RDP2001–09, Reserve Bank of Australia, www.rba.gov.au/PublicationsAndResearch/RDP/RDP2001–09 (downloaded 9 July 2003)

Roberts, J., T. McNulty and P. Stiles forthcoming, 'Beyond agency conceptions of the work of the non-executive director: creating accountability in the boardroom', *British Journal of Management*.

Robertson, A. F. 2001, *Greed: Gut Feelings, Growth, and History*, Cambridge: Polity Press.

Rose, J. 2003, 'Ethics means more than just codes of conduct', *AFR*, 13 August: 55.

Rowthorn, R. 1996, 'Ethics and Economics'. In P. Groenewegen (ed.), *Economics and Ethics?* London: Routledge.

Schaberg, M. 1998, 'Globalization and Financial Systems'. In D. Baker, G. Epstein & R. Pollin (eds), *Globalization and Progressive Economic Policy*, Cambridge University Press.

Schuetze, W. P. 2001, 'A Memo to National and International Accounting and Auditing Standard Setters'. R. J. Chambers Research Lecture, 27 November, University of Sydney.

Schumpeter, J. 1954, *History of Economic Analysis*, New York: Oxford University Press.

Seligman, A. B. 1997, *The Problem of Trust*, Princeton University Press.

Shackle, G. L. S. 1967, *The Years of High Theory: Invention and Tradition in Economic Thought 1926–1939*, Cambridge University Press.

Shackle, G. L. S. 1972, *Epistemics and Economics*, Cambridge University Press.

Shapiro, S. 1984, *Wayward Capitalists: Target of the Securities and Exchange Commission*, New Haven CT: Yale University Press.

Shapiro, S. 1987, 'The Social Control of Impersonal Trust', *American Journal of Sociology*, 93(3): 623–58.

Shiller, R. J. 1989, *Market Volatility*, Cambridge MA: MIT Press.

Shiller, R. J. 2000, *Irrational Exuberance*, Princeton University Press.

Simmel, G. 1978, *The Philosophy of Money*, London: Routledge & Kegan Paul.

Sinclair, T. 1994, 'Passing Judgement: Credit Rating Processes as Regulatory Mechanisms of Governance', *Review of International Political Economy*, 1(1): 133–58.

Sinclair, T. J. 2003, 'Bond rating agencies', *New Political Economy*, 8(1): 147–61.

Smart, D., & J. Higley 1977, 'Why not ask them? Interviewing Australian elites about national power structure', *Australian and New Zealand Journal of Sociology*, 13(3): 248–53.

Smithin, J. N. 1994, *Controversies in Monetary Economics*, Aldershot: Edward Elgar.

Smithin, J. N. 1996, *Macroeconomic Policy and the Future of Capitalism: The Revenge of the Rentiers and the Threat to Prosperity*, Cheltenham: Edward Elgar.

Solomon, S. 1995, *The Confidence Game*, New York: Simon & Schuster.

Soros, G. 1998, *The Crisis of Global Capitalism*, London: Little, Brown & Co.

Spotton, B., & R. Rowley 1998, 'Efficient Markets, Fundamentals, and Crashes', *American Journal of Economics and Sociology*, 57(4): 663–90.

Steinberger, M. 2001, 'A Dark View of the Street', *New York Times*, 17 May: C7.

Stevenson, R. 1998, 'Fiscal Stones, Glass Houses: Bailout Points Finger Back Toward the U.S.' *New York Times*, 26 September: 1 & C2.

Stiglitz, J. 2002, *Globalization and its Discontents*, London: Allen Lane.

Stinchcombe, A. L. 1990, *Information and Organizations*, Berkeley CA: University of California Press.

Stinchcombe, A. L. 2000, 'Institutional change and projections', *American Journal of Economics and Sociology*, 59(1): 53–6.

Strange, S. 1998, *Mad Money*, Ann Arbor MI: University of Michigan Press.

Stretton, H. 2000, *Economics: A New Introduction*, Sydney: UNSW Press.

Sztompka, P. 1999, *Trust*, Cambridge University Press.

'The worldly philosopher: interview with Paul Krugman by Barbara Belejack', *Texas Observer*, 10 October 2003. <www.texasobserver.org/showArt.asp?ArticleID=1460>

Therborn, G. 2003, 'Capital's Twilight Zone', *New Left Review*, 22, July–August: 133–42.

Tiffen, R. 1989, *News and Power*, Sydney: Allen & Unwin.

Tobin, J. 1987, 'Financial Intermediaries'. In J. Eatwell, M. Milgate and P. Newman (eds), *The New Palgrave: Money*, London: Macmillan.

Trefgarne, G. 2001, 'Less than Equitable', *Spectator*, 11 August: 18–19.

Van Fossen, A. B. 2002, 'Risk havens: offshore financial centres, insurance cycles', *Social and Legal Studies*, 11(4): 503–21.

Vickrey, W. S. 1957, 'A Note on Micro- and Macroeconomics'. In Komarovsky, *Common Frontiers of the Social Sciences*.

Vina, G. 2004, 'Liquidator sues Bank of England', *AFR*, 13 January: 37, reprinted from *Dow Jones Newswires*.

Walsh, M. 1990, 'Abrupt end to the "me" and "money" decades', *SMH*, 5 March: 13.

Wayne, L. 2002, 'Credit Raters Get Scrutiny and Possibly a Competitor', *New York Times*, 23 April: 1.

Weber, A. 1991, 'Reputation and credibility in the European Monetary System', *Economic Policy: A European Forum*, 6(1): 57–103.

Weber M. 1976 [1896], *The Protestant Ethic and the Spirit of Capitalism*, London: George Allen & Unwin.

Weber, M. 1978, *Economy and Society*, eds G. Roth & C. Wittich, Berkeley CA: University of California Press.

Weber, M. 2000 [1924], 'Commerce on the Stock and Commodity Exchanges', transl. S. Lestition, *Theory and Society*, 29(3): 339–71.

Weiner, B. 1986, *An Attributional Theory of Motivation and Emotion*, New York: Springer-Verlag.

Weitz, E., & Y. Shenhav 2000, 'A longitudinal analysis of technical and organizational uncertainty in management', *Organization Studies*, 21(1): 243–65.

Wennerlind, C. 2001, 'Money Talks, but What Is It Saying? Semiotics of Money and Social Control', *Journal of Economic Issues*, 35(3): 557–74.

Williams, R. 1989, *The Politics of Modernism*, London: Verso.

Williamson, O. E. 1991a, 'Introduction'. In O. E. Williamson & S. G. Winter (eds), *The Nature of the Firm*, New York: Oxford University Press.

Williamson, O. E. 1991b, 'The Logic of Economic Organization'. In Williamson & Winter, *The Nature of the Firm*.

Williamson, O. E. 1993, 'Calculativeness, Trust and Economic Organization', *Journal of Law & Economics*, 36, April: 453–86.

Woodward, B. 2000, *Maestro: Greenspan's Fed and the American Boom*, New York: Simon & Schuster.

Wray, L. R. 1990, *Money and Credit in Capitalist Economies*, Aldershot: Edward Elgar.

Wray, L. R. 1996, 'Money in the Circular Flow'. In G. Deleplace & E. Nell (eds), *Money in Motion*, London, Macmillan.

Young, J. J. 2003, 'Constructing, persuading and silencing', *Accounting, Organizations and Society*, 28(6): 621–38. <http://www.sciencedirect.com/science?_ob=ArticleURL&udi_B6VCK-45BCR0D-1&_user=37161&_handla=W-WA-A-A-Z_MsSAYWW-UUA-AUCYZDVAU on 18.07.2003>

Zucker, L. 1986, 'Production of Trust: Institutional sources of Economic Structure, 1840–1920', *Research in Organizational Behavior*, 8: 53–111.

Zuckerman, E. W. 1999, 'The Categorical Imperative: Securities Analysts and the Illegitimacy Discount', *American Journal of Sociology*, 104(5): 1398–438.

Index